Getting Started with Angular

Create and Deploy Angular Applications

Victor Hugo Garcia

Getting Started with Angular: Create and Deploy Angular Applications

Victor Hugo Garcia
Santiago Del Estero, Santiago del Estero, Argentina

ISBN-13 (pbk): 978-1-4842-9208-2   ISBN-13 (electronic): 978-1-4842-9206-8
https://doi.org/10.1007/978-1-4842-9206-8

Managing Director, Apress Media LLC: Welmoed Spahr
Acquisitions Editor: Divya Modi
Development Editor: Laura Berendson
Coordinating Editor: Divya Modi

Cover designed by eStudioCalamar

Cover image designed by Freepik (www.freepik.com)

Distributed to the book trade worldwide by Springer Science+Business Media New York, 1 New York Plaza, Suite 4600, New York, NY 10004-1562, USA. Phone 1-800-SPRINGER, fax (201) 348-4505, e-mail orders-ny@ springer-sbm.com, or visit www.springeronline.com. Apress Media, LLC is a California LLC and the sole member (owner) is Springer Science + Business Media Finance Inc (SSBM Finance Inc). SSBM Finance Inc is a **Delaware** corporation.

For information on translations, please e-mail booktranslations@springernature.com; for reprint, paperback, or audio rights, please e-mail bookpermissions@springernature.com.

Apress titles may be purchased in bulk for academic, corporate, or promotional use. eBook versions and licenses are also available for most titles. For more information, reference our Print and eBook Bulk Sales web page at http://www.apress.com/bulk-sales.

Any source code or other supplementary material referenced by the author in this book is available to readers on GitHub via the book's product page, located at https://github.com/Apress/The-Beginning-Angular-by-Victor-Hugo-Garcia. For more detailed information, please visit http://www.apress.com/source-code.

Printed on acid-free paper

To my wife, my parents, and to all those who have taught me something, by example or word.

Table of Contents

About the Author

Victor Hugo Garcia has a Master's degree in Computer Science, and more than 12 years of experience as a full-stack developer, using different frameworks such as Angular, Laravel, Yii, Zend, Cake, and Vue. He has developed multiple web and mobile applications for various organizations. He has also developed various courses on web development for Udemy. He loves teaching, reading, and writing technical and fantasy books.

About the Technical Reviewer

 **Sourabh Mishra** is an entrepreneur, developer, speaker, author, corporate trainer, and animator. He is a Microsoft guy; he is very passionate about Microsoft technologies and a true .NET warrior. Sourabh started his career when he was just 15 years old. He's loved computers from childhood. His programming experience includes C/C++, ASP.NET, C#, VB.NET, WCF, SQL Server, Entity Framework, MVC, Web API, Azure, jQuery, Highcharts, and Angular. Sourabh has been awarded a Most Valuable Professional (MVP) status. He has the zeal to learn new technologies and shares his knowledge on several online community forums.

He is the author of *Practical Highcharts with Angular* by Apress, which talks about how you can develop stunning and interactive dashboards using Highcharts with Angular. He is the founder of "IECE Digital" and "Sourabh Mishra Notes," an online knowledge-sharing platform where one can learn new technologies very easily and comfortably.

He can be reached via the following:

- YouTube: sourabhmishranotes

- Twitter: sourabh_mishra1

- Facebook: facebook.com/sourabhmishranotes

- Instagram: sourabhmishranotes

- Email: sourabh_mishra1@hotmail.com

You can read his books on www.amazon.com/stores/author/B084DMG1WG.

Introduction

Web developers are in an all-time demand. Frontend developers, those in charge of building the parts of the applications that interact directly with the end user, are a crucial part of software companies, providing a navigation experience that is in no short measure responsible for the success of a project.

Frontend developers use different programming languages, such as JavaScript, HTML, and CSS. However, in the current state of affairs, they also need to get a firm grasp of libraries and frameworks.

Angular is a very powerful, enterprise-grade framework that lets you build apps of any size that are scalable and maintainable. It has a vibrant community and is continually updated with new features to improve productivity.

This book aims to form you as a competent Angular developer who can easily work in a company or as a freelancer, making the process enjoyable.

Who Should Read This Book

This book is intended for those with a basic knowledge of JavaScript, HTML, and CSS who want to become frontend developers or incorporate a new set of skills. You will learn the fundamentals of TypeScript, the superset of JavaScript used to define the classes of our applications, and then start learning about Angular by practice. By the end of the book, you will have completed a series of projects including

- An app that performs CRUD operations against an API

- An app that performs authentication and authorization using a service provider

- A blog that communicates with a Node server and consumes data from a MongoDB database

All this should give you a very firm start in your career.

How to Read This Book

Chapter 1 deals with configuring our development environment. Usually, this is the most tedious part. Chapter 2 introduces TypeScript. The following chapters develop the applications. I recommend you to read all the chapters in order.

CHAPTER 1

Introduction to Angular Framework

The purpose of this chapter is to give a brief introduction of Angular and then proceed with the setup of our development environment. There are a few mandatory installations; the rest, although not required, are convenient. A good IDE is a tremendous help, and having the right packages can significantly boost our productivity.

If you are reading this book, you have probably already heard about Angular. It is even likely that you have followed some tutorials and even developed applications. However, my goal is to start without making assumptions about the level from which you start.

We will start from the basics, to build increasingly complex examples that allow you to acquire the necessary skills to work with Angular in real projects.

About Angular

On its website `https://angular.io/`, Angular is defined as a platform for developing web applications. This brief definition, however, hides the power of this framework, which can be used to build web, mobile, and even desktop applications.

The name Angular was originally known as AngularJS. This was a framework that reached a lot of popularity, with interesting features but with limitations. So, Angular 2 arrived. However, this name can lead to confusion, since in fact Angular 2 was not a simple update, but a completely different framework. In fact, migrating an application made with AngularJS to Angular 2 is a process that is not at all simple and that should be considered with extreme care.

We quickly saw how Angular 2 became 3, 4, and so on. At the time of writing these words, Angular is in version 15.

© Victor Hugo Garcia 2023
V. H. Garcia, *Getting Started with Angular*, https://doi.org/10.1007/978-1-4842-9206-8_1

But I want to make clear the following: in the book, we will simply refer to the platform as Angular. Each time updates are made that involve substantial changes, the sections will be updated accordingly, so that this book will continue to be useful for many years.

Therefore, it seems necessary to explain the way in which Angular handles its versions.

Semantic Versioning

Angular works using what is known as semantic versioning. That is to say, Angular versions are always presented in the **major.minor.patch** form, for example, **5.2.7**.

Then from right to left, we have

- **7.** A version that increases the number of a patch and refers to an update that includes bug fixes, maintaining compatibility at all times with minor versions.

- **2.** A minor version increase means that functionality is added while maintaining compatibility. Usually, it will not be necessary to make modifications to the applications, but it can be done if you wish to use these new capacities where it is convenient.

- **5.** A new major version that implies changes in the API, requiring a careful analysis in order to perform the migration of applications.

It could be considered tedious to have to deal with these version changes at an accelerated rate, and even this could discourage us from doing our learning. But I want to assure you that it is in fact something positive. A framework that does not launch new releases is a framework that does not adapt and eventually dies.

Frequency of Releases

A new major version is usually expected every six months. Before each major update, it is expected to have one to three minor updates. The patches are launched practically every week.

It is useful to have a release calendar on hand. This can be found in angular.io. Of course, these dates are not written in stone and can be modified, but they provide a general guide.

We are ready to start now. Let's do it!

Installations Needed

NodeJS

https://nodejs.org/en/

What we are interested in from Node is npm (node package manager), a powerful package manager that comes with Node and that allows us to install libraries using just a line of code. It's essential. To verify that everything went correctly, we can type node --version in the command line as shown in Figure 1-1.

```
Victor@DESKTOP-OQOHJ2Q MINGW64 ~
$ node --version
v16.17.1
```

Figure 1-1. *Node version*

If you have a version equal to or greater than this, we can continue without problems.

Google Chrome

www.google.es/chrome/browser/desktop/

While the examples we will use will work in any modern browser, it is advisable to use Chrome for the valuable developer tools that it has.

TypeScript

www.typescriptlang.org/

TypeScript is a superset of JavaScript, which has very interesting features such as being strongly typed and the introduction of proper classes. We will make intensive use of TypeScript to define our Angular components, but do not worry, in this book there is a whole section dedicated to this language where everything needed to work with confidence is explained and shown by examples. Those of you who already have experience with TypeScript can simply skip the section without problems.

We'll be installing TypeScript globally, so we can use the tsc command anywhere in our terminal. We can verify the installation typing the command tsc --version as shown in Figure 1-2.

```
Victor@DESKTOP-OQOHJ2Q MINGW64 ~
$ tsc --version
Version 4.8.3
```

Figure 1-2. *TypeScript version*

Angular CLI

angular.io

angular-cli (`https://github.com/angular/angular-cli`)

The Angular CLI is Angular's command line and allows us to automatically generate the skeleton of our components, pipes, services, and others. Here, the command that interests us is `ng version`, which should give us an output similar to the one in Figure 1-3.

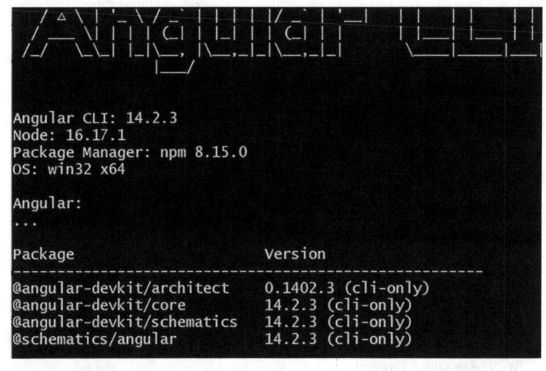

Figure 1-3. *Angular CLI version*

Ionic

Ionic is a framework for the development of hybrid mobile applications, which allows deploying these apps on devices with Android, iOS, and Windows from a single code base.

This framework deserves a book by itself, but from its beginnings, it had a great integration with Angular. A section is included in this book where a complete Ionic application is developed, in order to illustrate concepts that we will need in the following Angular applications that are presented, such as impure pipes.

IDE

If you already have an IDE or text editor of your choice, you can probably work with it without any problem. However, the examples in this book are made using the IDE Visual Studio Code (`https://code.visualstudio.com/`). It is a free and open source application, and it really is excellent.

If you decide to install VS Code – again I recommend it – then I ask you to install the following packages:

- Angular 2 TypeScript Emmet
- Angular 5 Snippets – TypeScript, HTML, Angular Material, etc.
- Angular Language Service
- Angular v5 Snippets
- Angular2-inline
- Bootstrap 4 and Font Awesome snippets
- HTML CSS Support
- JavaScript (ES6) code snippets
- JS-CSS-HTML Formatter
- JSHint
- Material Icon Theme
- Prettier – Code Formatter
- Terminal

- TSLint

- TypeScript Hero

- TypeScript Importer

Not required, but they will make the development much simpler.

1. To install a package in VS Code, we must click the icon shown in Figure 1-4.

Figure 1-4. *Install packages in VS Code*

2. Then we will access the next screen where we simply type the name of the package to be installed, select it, and install it, as shown in Figure 1-5.

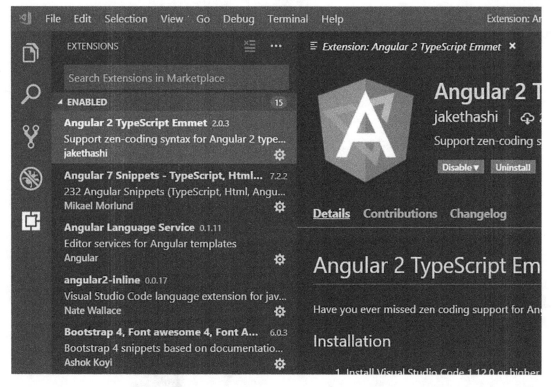

Figure 1-5. *Install packages in VS Code*

Another excellent option to work with is Atom (`https://atom.io/`). On its website, it is presented as a text editor, but that name does not do it justice. It has a number of features that make it extremely useful and powerful.

If you decide to work with Atom or have already done so, these are the packages I recommend installing:

- Angular 2 TypeScript Snippets

- Atom Bootstrap3

- Atom TypeScript

- File Icons

- PlatformIO Terminal IDE

- V Bootstrap4

To install a package in Atom, we proceed as shown in Figure 1-6.

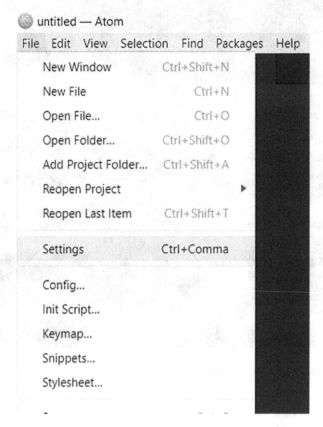

Figure 1-6. *Install packages in Atom*

1.   From File ➤ Settings, we access the screen shown in Figure 1-7.

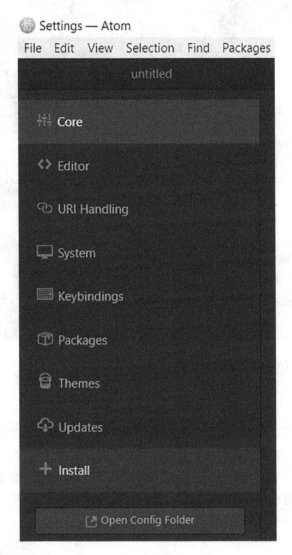

Figure 1-7. *Install packages in Atom*

2.   From the Install option, we will access a new screen where we can type the name of the packages that interest us, choosing those we want to install (Figure 1-8).

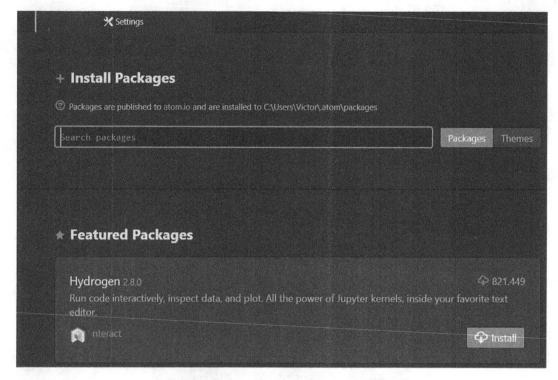

Figure 1-8. *Install packages in Atom*

Note   The installations of TypeScript, the Angular CLI, and Ionic can present problems or not work as expected, especially if you have previous versions. Remember that it is very possible that Google is the answer. The ability to investigate and find solutions is invaluable for a developer.

Postman

Postman (www.getpostman.com/) is an API development environment. When we work with services, we will be using APIs from both third parties and their own. This tool allows us to test these APIs, sending GET, POST, PUT, and patch requests, authentication tokens, and many other things. The functionality of this tool goes much more than what will be touched in this book, and I recommend that you investigate it as thoroughly as possible.

Errors

Each line of code included in the book has been carefully reviewed. However, errors can occur, and in that case, I would greatly appreciate being contacted and informed of any problem in order to be able to correct it immediately. Everyone will benefit from it.

On the other hand, where the code of the example exceeds a few lines of code, in addition to presenting it in the book, I will be providing the link to the code snippet in the official book repo, so that you can refer to that link and copy the code more comfortably if you wish.

Writing the code on your own, following the examples presented, would be an excellent way to gain confidence and get used to the syntax, but you will always have the complete code of the applications to be able to use it.

Summary

This chapter started with a brief introduction of Angular and then dealt with the setup of our development environment. Other than Node, TypeScript, and angular-cli, the rest of the installations are not mandatory, but they are convenient. A good IDE is a tremendous help, and having the right packages can significantly boost our productivity.

Learning any new framework can be a bit intimidating at the beginning, especially one as powerful as Angular. But continue and be patient; let's address it one step at a time. Learning it will be easy for some people, while others will have to work harder to achieve it. But what I can guarantee is that as we move forward, the development of applications will become a pleasant and exciting experience. The time and effort we dedicate will be highly rewarded. Let's get started!

CHAPTER 2

Introduction to TypeScript and ES6

In this chapter, we will touch on the bases of TypeScript: data types, let and const, functions, arrow functions, classes, and interfaces. Although not extensive, this guide is complete enough to understand every bit of code we will be building and to understand pieces of code from other sources when you need to look for something later on your journey as a developer.

Getting Started

We are ready to start working. First, we will create a folder called Angular, where we will save the code of all the applications that we will build throughout the book.

You can place this directory anywhere you wish. Inside this folder, we will create a new one called typescript.

Now let's open this folder with our IDE or text editor; we should see something similar to Figure 2-1.

© Victor Hugo Garcia 2023
V. H. Garcia, *Getting Started with Angular*, https://doi.org/10.1007/978-1-4842-9206-8_2

Figure 2-1. *TypeScript*

With this folder in place, we are ready to start learning about the main characteristics of TypeScript. We'll start learning how to declare variables and constants and when to use one or the other.

let and const

As we said in the previous chapter, TypeScript is a JavaScript superset. As such, all JavaScript functionality will be available in TypeScript, as well as new possibilities that simplify the writing of the code.

First File

1. Inside the IDE, let's create a new file called 01-let-const.ts with the following code:

```
var i = 1;

for (var i = 1; i <= 5; i ++ ) {
```

```
    // do something
}

console.log( i );
```

2. Now create a file named index.html with the following content:

```
<html lang="en">

<head>
    <meta charset="UTF-8">
    <meta name="viewport" content="width = device-width,
    initial-scale = 1.0">
    <meta http-equiv="X-UA-Compatible" content="ie = edge">
    <title>var let and const</title>
</head>

<body>
    <script src="01-let-const.js"> </script>
</body>

</html>
```

For those who are working with VS Code, you will probably have installed by default (otherwise, it would be convenient to install it) a package called HTML Snippets. If so, you can see that simply by typing "doc" and pressing enter, you will get a simple page skeleton (Figure 2-2).

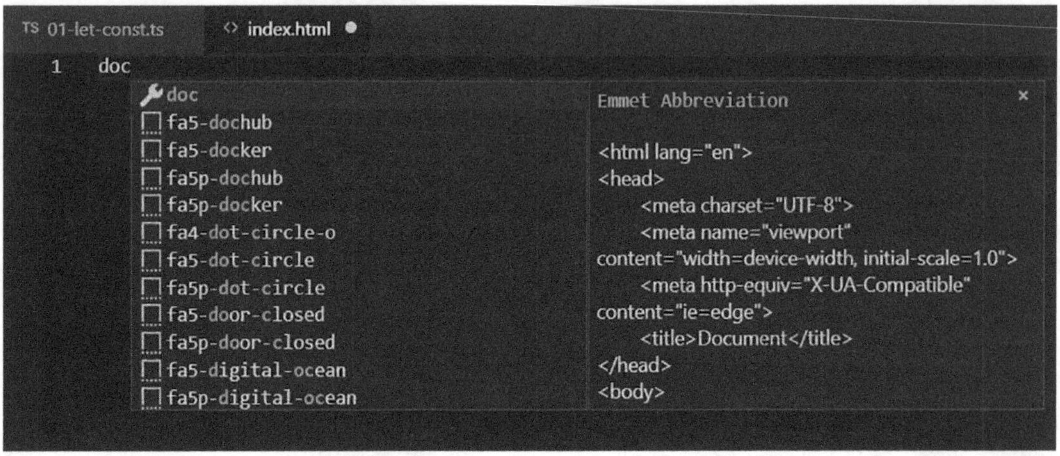

Figure 2-2. *Snippets*

3. Now we open the index.html file in the browser to get a blank
    page. Probably some of you already detected what happens, but
    we will take advantage of the Chrome developer tools (Figure 2-3).

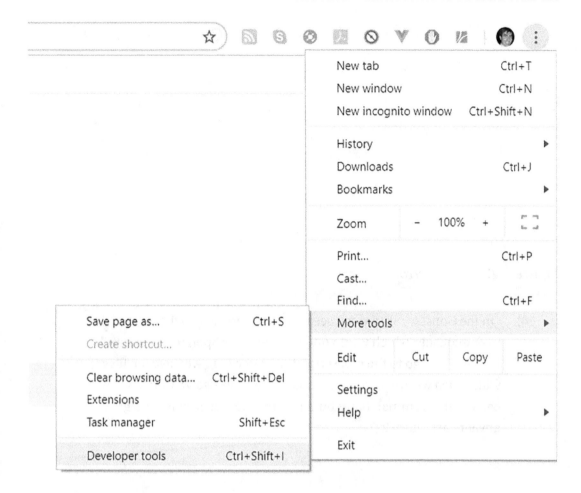

Figure 2-3. *Chrome tools*

The developer tools will appear by default to the right of the browser, although we can change this location according to our convenience (Figure 2-4).

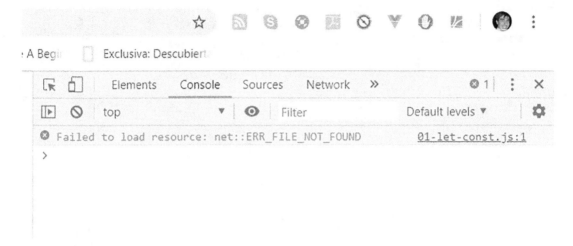

Figure 2-4. *Console error*

4. On the Console tab, we can see that it is referring to a file called
    01-let-const.js, which we do not have yet. Let's open the command
    line now and go to the typescript directory where we have the files
    with which we are working. Alternatively, if we use VS Code, we
    can use the terminal that is built into the interface, which is a great
    advantage (Figure 2-5).

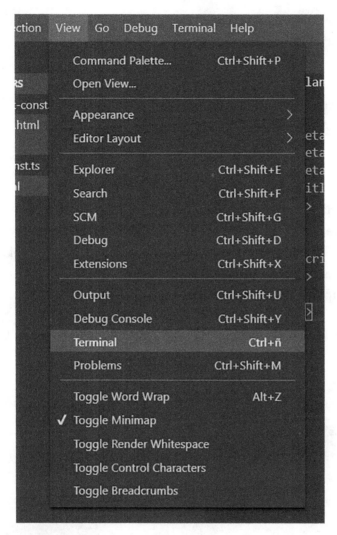

Figure 2-5. *VS Code terminal*

5. From the terminal, type the following command:

    `tsc 01-let-const`

    and press enter.

    With this command, we are calling the typescript compiler, passing as a parameter the name of a file – in this case, 01-let-const.ts – from which it will generate the corresponding js file. Note how it is not necessary to indicate the .ts extension, although it can be done without problems if desired.

Now if we refresh the browser, the error will have disappeared. But let's not do it yet. Let's analyze the code again:

```
var i = 1;

for (var i = 1; i <= 5; i ++ ) {
    // do something
}

console.log( i );
```

We declare a variable i and initialize it with a value of 1. Then we have a loop where the variable is redeclared, and finally we show the value in the console. What do you think the value of the variable i will be? Let's see. Refresh the browser; you should see the output shown in Figure 2-6.

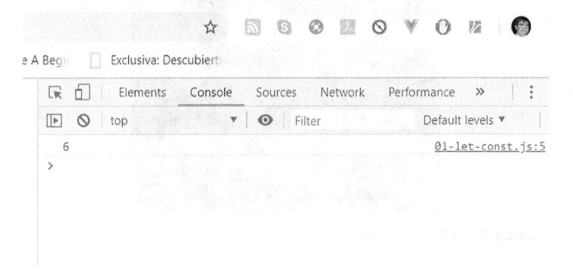

Figure 2-6. *Console output*

The output is 6. Now let's make some small changes to the code:

```
let i = 1;
for (let i = 1; i <= 5; i ++ ) {
    // do something
}

console.log( i );
```

The only changes are that we have replaced var with let. Now, what do you think the output will be? If you went ahead, you will see that it continues to be 6. But what happens is that we have not recompiled the file 01-let-const.ts.

If we open the file 01-let-const.js, we will see that the content is the following:

```
var i = 1;
for (var i = 1; i <= 5; i++) {
    // do something
}
console.log(i);
```

6. Recompile the file by typing again `tsc 01-let-const`. If we now refresh the browser, we will obtain the output shown in Figure 2-7.

Figure 2-7. *Console output*

The result is 1. To obtain more clues about this behavior, open the generated 01-let-const.js file again:

```
var i = 1;
for (var i_1 = 1; i_1 <= 5; i_1++) {
    // do something
}
console.log(i);
```

Can you tell the difference? Now in the loop, no reference is made to the same variable i, but the tsc has created a new variable i_1. And that is the difference between var and let. Let allows us to declare variables with the same name, as long as their scopes are different. And what is the scope of a variable? We can define it as the fragment of code in which a variable lives.

Returning to the 01-let-const file, if before the `console.log(i)` `statement` we add `let i = 2`, our editor will show us the code in Figure 2-8.

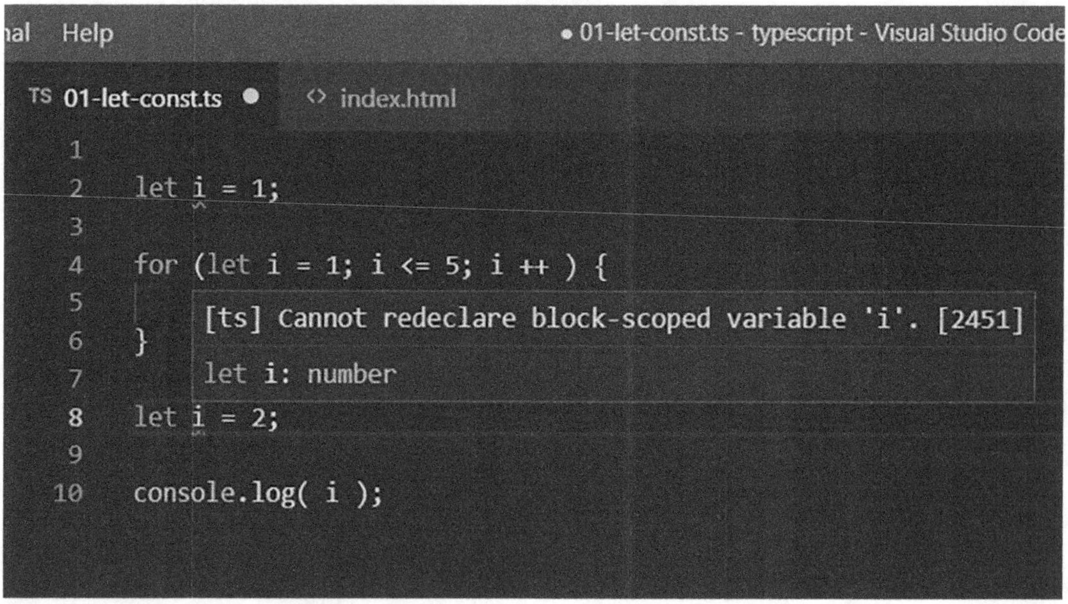

```
ial   Help                                                  • 01-let-const.ts - typescript - Visual Studio Code

TS 01-let-const.ts  ●        <> index.html

 1
 2     let i = 1;
 3
 4     for (let i = 1; i <= 5; i ++ ) {
 5
           [ts] Cannot redeclare block-scoped variable 'i'. [2451]
 6     }
           let i: number
 7
 8     let i = 2;
 9
10     console.log( i );
```

Figure 2-8. *Redeclaring a variable*

And it is natural that this is so because the two sentences let i = 1 and let i = 2 live in the same scope, while the loop determines a different scope. Let's eliminate this problematic sentence and leave the file as before.

Something you may have noticed is that when we made changes to the ts file, we had to recompile it to produce the js file again and that the output is reflected in the browser. If you think there should be a way to automate the process, you are right.

7. Open the console and this time type the following command:

```
tsc 01-let-const -w
```

The only difference is the w flag, which tells the tsc to be aware of any changes that occur in the file. For example, the VS Code terminal produces the output before that command (Figure 2-9).

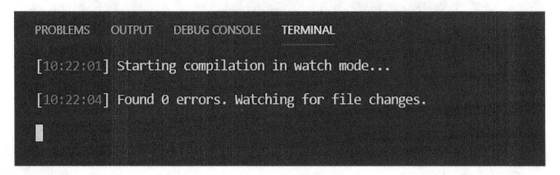

Figure 2-9. *VS Code terminal*

Let's test it. Add the following lines to the ts file:

```
const START = 10;

console.log(START);
```

8. If we now simply refresh the browser, we will see the output shown in Figure 2-10.

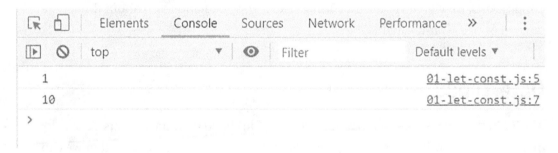

Figure 2-10. *Console output*

We did not have to recompile the file, because the tsc is monitoring the changes and generating the js file automatically. Fantastic.

What happens if we now add the following line after the last call to the console?

```
START = 20;
```

Well, we will get the error shown in Figure 2-11.

```
const START = 10;

  [ts] Cannot assign to 'START' because it is a constant. [2588]

  const START: 10

START = 20;
```

Figure 2-11. *Assignment error*

This is logical considering that a constant – which we declare with const – will have a value that is not expected to change.

This is the same reason why we cannot just write:

```
const START;
```

Any constant must be initialized at the time of its declaration.

Meanwhile, the tsc continues to monitor the changes. How do we make this stop? Simply with the combination Ctrl+C in our terminal.

And these are the differences between var, let, and const. When we work on our applications, we will never use var. Now we can go ahead and learn about the different data types of the language.

Data Types

Always in the typescript directory, let's create a file called 02-data-types.ts. As we mentioned earlier, TypeScript is a JavaScript typed superset. This means that we can define the type of variables that we declare. This fact allows us to detect errors before our programs are executed, which is a great advantage.

Boolean

A Boolean type variable can contain the value true or false. In our new file, add the following line of code:

```
let taskCompleted: boolean = false;
```

Since we have declared the taskCompleted variable as Boolean, if we try to assign it another type of data, we will get the error shown in Figure 2-12.

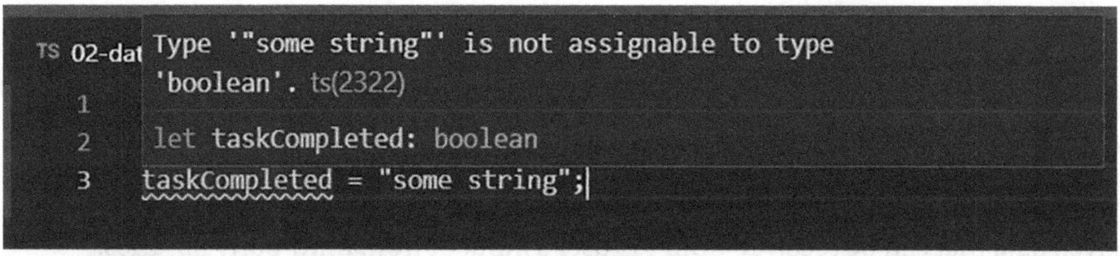

```
TS 02-da  Type '"some string"' is not assignable to type
          'boolean'. ts(2322)
   1
   2      let taskCompleted: boolean
   3      taskCompleted = "some string";
```

Figure 2-12. *Assignment error*

Number

As in JavaScript, all numbers in TypeScript are floating-point numbers. Add the following statements:

```
let decimal: number = 6;
let hex: number = 0xf00d;
let binary: number = 0b1010;
let octal: number = 0o744;
```

String

A string is basically a chain of characters. Normally, you can use it to display messages or any kind of information to the user. Almost every language has tools to manipulate strings, and TypeScript is no exception.

```
let plan: string = "basic";
```

Array

An array is a set of elements. Every element in the array is identified with a position called index. In TypeScript, arrays start at 0 (zero). We have two ways to write them. The first is

```
let statuses: number[] = [0, 10 20, 30];
```

and also

```
let statuses2: Array<number> = [0, 10 20, 30];
```

Any

Variables of type any can contain a data of any type. Although apparently a contradiction, these types of variables are useful when you are not sure of the type of a given data that can be received from the user's input or from third-party libraries.

```
let list: any[] = [decimal, plan, taskCompleted];
```

There are other types of data, but we will see them as the applications we develop require it. As a precaution, here is the content of the complete file:

```
let taskCompleted: boolean = false;

let decimal: number = 6;
let hex: number = 0xf00d;
let binary: number = 0b1010;
let octal: number = 0o744;

let plan: string = "basic";

let statuses: number[] = [0, 10 20, 30];

let statuses2: Array<number> = [0, 10 20, 30];

let list: any[] = [decimal, plan, taskCompleted];
```

Let's now create a new directory within the typescript folder, called template-strings.

Template Strings

Manipulating Strings

1. Now we create a file called app.ts. Think about the following situation. We have the declaration of some variables, which we want to concatenate producing a text string:

```
let firstName = 'Peter';
let lastName = 'Parker';
let age = 18;

let text = firstName + '\n' + lastName + '\n' + age;
```

Then we sent it to the console:

```
console.log( text );
```

2. Now, we will generate an index.html file to test what we have written:

```
<html lang="en">

<head>
   <meta charset="UTF-8">
   <meta name="viewport" content="width = device-width, initial-
   scale = 1.0">
   <meta http-equiv="X-UA-Compatible" content="ie = edge">
   <title>Template String</title>
</head>

<body>
   <script src="app.js"></script>
</body>

</html>
```

We already know that if we open this file in the browser and access the console, we'll get an error because the file app.js doesn't exist yet.

Of course, we can generate the app.js file with the command

```
tsc app
```

Also, we know that if we want to not have to repeat this command every time we make a change to app.ts, we can use the w flag:

```
tsc app -w
```

A question that may have arisen is what happens if there is more than one ts file. In fact, there could be dozens of them. Do we have to manually compile each of them? Fortunately not.

3. Execute the following command from the terminal, always located within the template-strings directory:

```
tsc -init
```

This command must have generated a tsconfig.json file (Figure 2-13), which indicates that our directory is a typescript project and defines the configuration options of the compiler.

Figure 2-13. *tsconfig.json*

The content of this file is long, although most of the lines are commented, but let's see one of them in particular:

```
" target ": "es5",
```

This indicates to what standard the file will be compiled, in this case ECMAScript 5, which is the most supported by the different browsers.

4. Now, from the terminal, we simply type:

```
tsc -w
```

5. If we open the index.html file in the browser, we will see the output in the console (Figure 2-14).

Figure 2-14. *Exit by console*

The output is as expected. However, there is a neater and better way, using the `` `` `` backtick characters.

Let's talk about the line where the string is concatenated, and then write the following:

```
let text = `${ firstName}
${ lastName}
${ age }`;
```

6. Save the changes and refresh the browser. The output is exactly the same.

Everything between ${} will be evaluated as an expression, which can be variables, operations, or function calls.

7. Through the template string, we can not only present ordinary text but also HTML tags. Let's add the following lines:

```
let hi = `<h1>Hello</h1>
    <p>World</p>`;

document.write( hi );
```

8. Let's refresh the browser, and we'll get the output shown in Figure 2-15.

Hello

World

Figure 2-15. *Exit by console*

9. There are other things we can do with the templates. Modify the file by adding the following lines:

```
let message = `The square root of 2000 is ${ Math.sqrt( 2000 )}`;

console.log( message );
```

As you can see, we have included a call to a function between ${}. In fact, everything that is enclosed by these symbols will be evaluated as an expression. The output is shown in Figure 2-16.

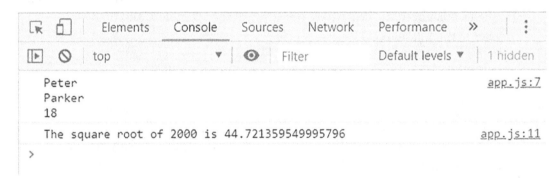

Figure 2-16. *Output via console*

Knowing about the different data types is a big step, but we need a way to call a set of statements without code repetition. It's time to learn about functions.

Functions

Functions are a fundamental component of any programming language. In the case of JavaScript, the functions have a predominant importance, since they are used not only to describe procedures but, for example, to imitate classes.

In the case of TypeScript, we have proper classes, but even so within a class, a method is nothing but a function so its importance is still huge.

1. Create a new directory called functions, at the same level as the template-strings directory. Initialize the directory as a typescript project. Recall that the command is

```
tsc -init
```

2. Now let's create a file called functions.ts. Let's define a function that calculates a discounted price:

```
function calculateDiscount(price) {
    return price * 0.50;
}
```

3. Let's test the function in the console:

```
console.log( calculateDiscount( 25 ) );
```

4. We must add the corresponding index file:

```
<html lang="en">

<head>
    <meta charset="UTF-8">
    <meta name="viewport" content="width = device-width, initial-
    scale = 1.0">
    <meta http-equiv="X-UA-Compatible" content="ie = edge">
    <title>Functions</title>
</head>

<body>
    <script src="functions.js"></script>
</body>

</html>
```

5. And, as we know, we need to compile the file:

```
tsc -w
```

The console output is as we expected (Figure 2-17).

Figure 2-17. *Functions*

However, our function can be improved a lot. Observe the message in our IDE (Figure 2-18).

```ts
function calculateDiscount(price) {
    return price * 0.50;
}
console.log( calculateDiscount( 25 ) );
```

Parameter 'price' implicitly has an 'any' type. ts(7006)

(parameter) price: any

Figure 2-18. *Functions*

We have not defined a type for the price parameter, and therefore it has an implicit type of **any**.

6. Let's start by restricting the type to a numerical value:

```ts
function calculateDiscount( price: number ) {
    return price * 0.50;
}
```

This is not simply an aesthetic detail, since it prevents errors. If now we modify the call to the function in the following way:

```ts
console.log( calculateDiscount( "somevalue" ) );
```

we will get a clear message from the compiler (Figure 2-19).

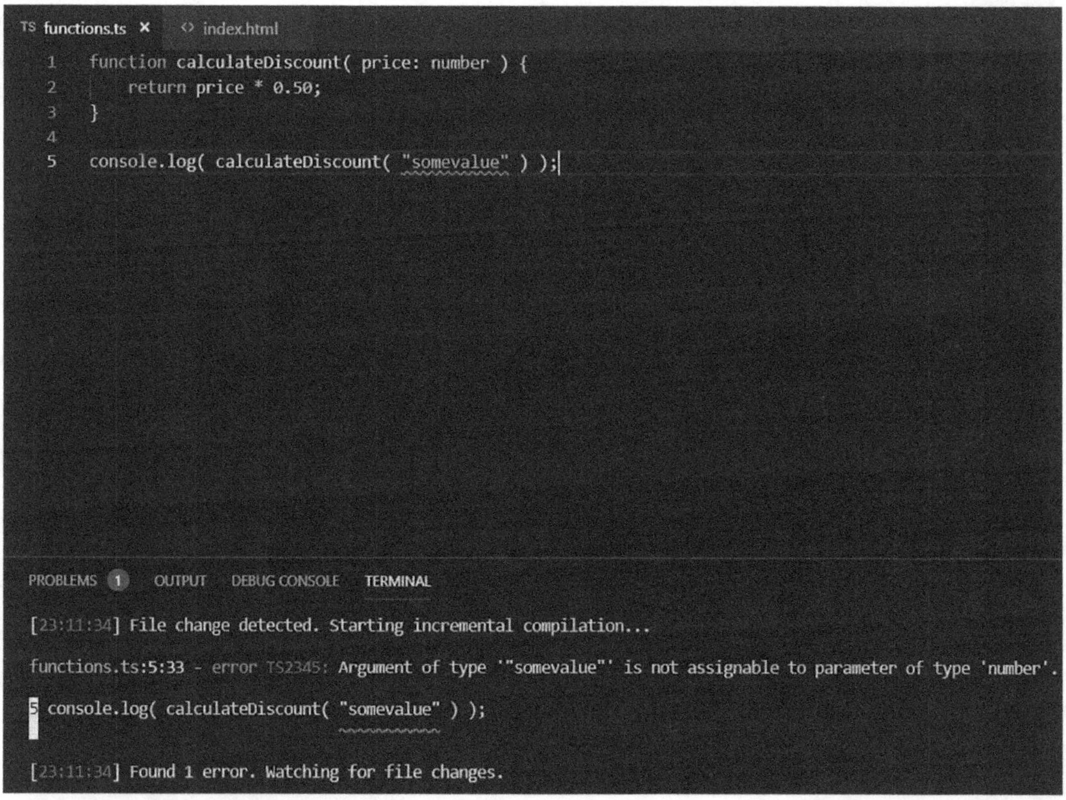

```
TS functions.ts  ✕      <> index.html
1     function calculateDiscount( price: number ) {
2         return price * 0.50;
3     }
4
5     console.log( calculateDiscount( "somevalue" ) );
```

```
PROBLEMS  1     OUTPUT    DEBUG CONSOLE    TERMINAL

[23:11:34] File change detected. Starting incremental compilation...

functions.ts:5:33 - error TS2345: Argument of type '"somevalue"' is not assignable to parameter of type 'number'.

5 console.log( calculateDiscount( "somevalue" ) );

[23:11:34] Found 1 error. Watching for file changes.
```

Figure 2-19. *Assignment error*

Let's leave the line as it was before.

7. In addition to defining the type of parameters, we can define what type of data the function is expected to return. In our case, it is again a number:

```
function calculateDiscount( price: number ): number {
    return price * 0.50;
}
```

8. Much better, but we still have a problem that surely several of you will have noticed. We are setting the discount at 50%. Would it not be better if the discount to apply were received as another parameter? Let's do just that:

```
function calculateDiscount( price: number, discount: number
): number {
    return price * discount;
}
```

Perfect, but now we have an error in the call to the function
(Figure 2-20).

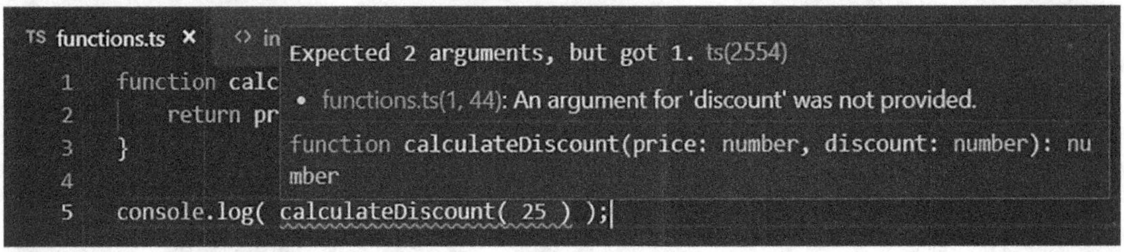

```
TS functions.ts  ✕    <> in    Expected 2 arguments, but got 1. ts(2554)
  1    function calc
  2        return pr    • functions.ts(1, 44): An argument for 'discount' was not provided.
  3    }                function calculateDiscount(price: number, discount: number): nu
  4                     mber
  5    console.log( calculateDiscount( 25 ) );|
```

Figure 2-20. *Functions*

9. It would probably be a good idea to define a default discount. Let's
   do just that:

   ```
   function calculateDiscount( price: number, discount:
   number = 0.50 ): number {
       return price * discount;
   }
   ```

   Now the error will be gone. Let's try adding a new call to the function
   and sending it to the console:

   ```
   console.log( calculateDiscount( 25, 0.30 ) );
   ```

10. If we refresh the browser, we will see that the function works as
    expected (Figure 2-21).

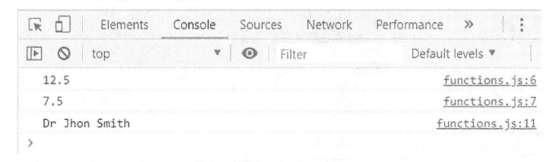

Figure 2-21. *Functions*

11. In addition to parameters with default values, we can define optional parameters. Define a new function:

```
function displayName( firstName: string, lastName: string,
prefix?: string) {
 return (prefix) ? `${prefix } ${firstName} ${lastName}` :
`${firstName} ${lastName}`
}
```

12. And show in the console the following:

```
console.log( displayName("Jhon", "Smith", "Dr") );
```

13. Refreshing the browser, we obtain the output in Figure 2-22.

⬚ 🔲	Elements	Console	Sources	Network	Performance	»	⋮
▶ ⊘	top	▼	◉	Filter		Default levels ▼	
12.5						functions.js:6	
7.5						functions.js:7	
Dr Jhon Smith						functions.js:11	
>							

Figure 2-22. *Functions*

14. And the next call will omit the prefix:

```
console.log( displayName("Jhon", "Smith") );
```

Arrow Functions

To understand arrow functions, let's analyze some previous concepts.

JavaScript has first-class functions. That is, functions can be passed as any other parameter.

For example:

```
setTimeout(function() {
    console.log("Hi");
}, 3000);
```

We have a function that is passed as a parameter to the setTimeout function. This function, which has no proper name, is known as an anonymous function.

The ES6 standard introduces a new way to define anonymous functions:

```
setTimeout(() => {
    console.log("Hi");
}, 3000);
```

This can be further shortened by taking into account that the body of the anonymous function contains a single line:

```
setTimeout(() => console.log("Hi"), 3000);
```

Let's see more examples. Let's add a new directory called arrow-functions and an arrow-functions.ts file inside it. Also, add the corresponding index.html file.

Define a simple function and assign it to a variable:

```
let add = function( a: number, b: number ) {
    return to + b;
}
```

We can write the arrow function version:

```
let addF = ( a: number, b: number ) => a + b;
```

We see that since it is a single line of code, the curly braces and the reserved word **return** can be ignored.

We have exemplified the first advantage of arrow functions.

They allow a more compact notation.

But there is an even more important use of arrow functions.

Suppose we have the following lines:

```
let speed = 100;

let car = {
    speed: 10
    Accelerate: function() {
        this.speed + = 10;
        console.log( this.speed );
    }
}

car.accelerate();
```

When compiling the file and viewing the output in the browser, we get the output shown in Figure 2-23.

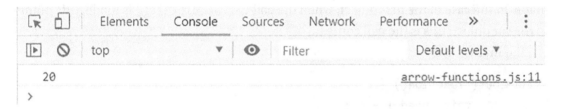

Figure 2-23. *Arrow functions*

That is correct, but let's define a new object:

```
let car2 = {
    speed: 10
    Accelerate: function() {
        setTimeout( function() {
            this.speed + = 10;
            console.log( this.speed );
        }, 3000)
    }
}
```

And make the new call:

```
car2.accelerate();
```

What is the output now? If we refresh the browser and wait for the three seconds of the timeout, we will see the output in Figure 2-24.

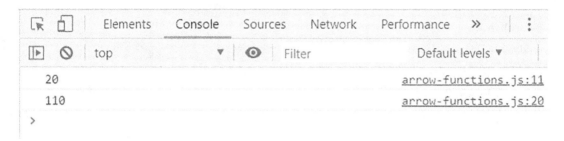

Figure 2-24. *Arrow functions*

The output in this case is 110, which is incorrect. What has happened? Well, the difference in the output has to do with the context.

What happens is that the value of **this** in a function depends on the way the call is made. In the case of the first object, when the call `car.accelerate()` is made, **this** points to the car object; this is the call context.

But in this case:

```
setTimeout( function() {
        this.speed + = 10;
        console.log( this.speed );
    }, 3000)
```

the call context is not the object car2, but the global object where we previously defined the variable speed with `let speed = 100`, and therefore the output is 100.

We can solve this by using an arrow function:

```
let car3 = {
   speed: 10
   Accelerate: function() {
       setTimeout( () => {
           this.speed + = 10;
           console.log( this.speed );
       }, 3000)
   }
}
```

If we then call accelerate of car3:

```
car3.accelerate();
```

the output will be as shown in Figure 2-25.

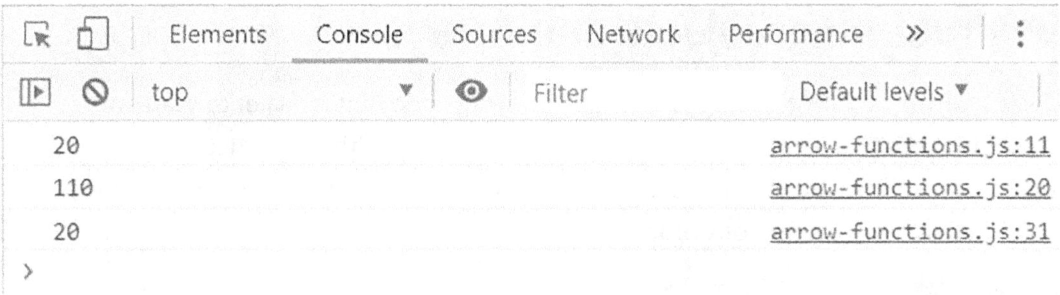

Figure 2-25. *Arrow functions*

We see that the value obtained is correct. And this brings us to the second advantage of the arrow functions. **The arrow functions correctly capture the context of this.**

In case you are wondering, yes, we could have solved the problem without resorting to an arrow function, in the following way:

```
let car4 = {
    speed: 10
    Accelerate: function() {
        let _this = this;
        setTimeout( function() {
            _this.speed + = 10;
            console.log( _this.speed );
        }, 3000)
    }
}
```

```
car4.accelerate();
```

The key is in the following line:

```
let _this = this;
```

It was necessary to capture the reference to **this** before calling the anonymous function. Arrow functions make this unnecessary.

Another powerful feature of the language is the ability to assign object properties and array elements to variables. This process is called destructuring, and we'll learn about it in the next section.

Destructuring Objects and Arrays

Destructuring objects and arrays allows us to write code that is easier to read and maintain. Let's add a new directory called destructuring with a destructuring.ts file. We already know how to create the index.html file with which we will obtain the output.

Define an object with four properties:

```
let rect = {
    x: 5,
    y: 10,
    width: 20,
    height: 25
};
```

We can access the values of the properties of the object and assign them to variables, in a single statement as follows:

```
let {x, Y, width, height} = rect;
```

Now we can use the obtained variables:

```
console.log(x, Y, width, height);
```

We can see the result in the browser (Figure 2-26).

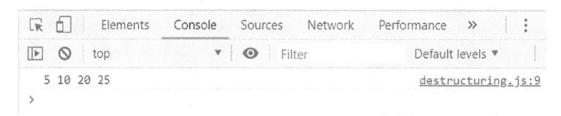

Figure 2-26. *Destructuring*

Note that the name of the variables corresponds to the name of the properties of the object. If you want to rename some variables, this can be done in the following way.

First, let's comment out the lines:

```
/* let {x, y, width, height} = rect;

console.log (x, y, width, height); */
```

And now let's add the following lines:

```
let {x, Y, width: w, height: h} = rect;

console.log( x, Y, w, h );
```

The output is exactly the same.
Perfect, but what happens if we want to ignore some values?
Now let's comment out the following lines:

```
/* let {x, y, width: w, height: h} = rect;

console.log (x, y, w, h); */

let { x, Y, ...remaining } = rect;

console.log( x, Y );
console.log( remaining );
```

The output is now as shown in Figure 2-27.

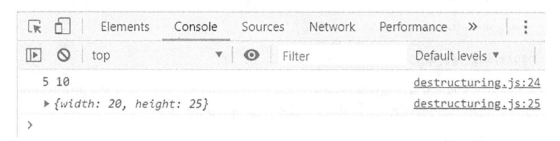

Figure 2-27. *Destructuring*

Destructuring can also be used when parameters are received:

```
let person = {
    firstName: "George",
    lastName: "Martin",
```

```
    prefix: "Dr"
}

function sayHi({ firstName, lastName, prefix }) {
    return `${prefix} ${firstName} ${lastName}`;
}

console.log( sayHi(person) );
```

We will see the output shown in Figure 2-28.

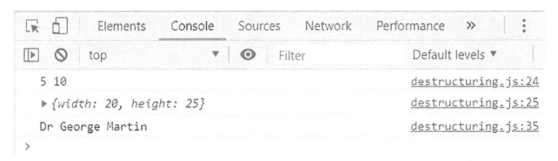

Figure 2-28. *Destructuration*

Destructuring can also be used with arrays. Add the following line:

```
let [p, q] = [ 3, 4 ];
```

Let's show the values in the console:

```
console.log( p, q );
```

An application of arrangement destructuring, for example, is to solve the problem of exchanging the values of two variables, without using a third one:

```
[p, q] = [q, p];
```

If we send again p and q to the console, we will check that their values have been exchanged, as shown in Figure 2-29.

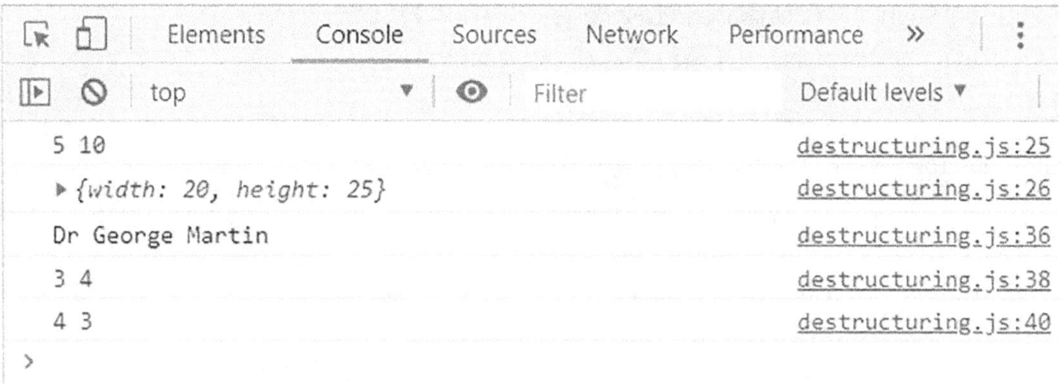

```
⌞⌟  ⌂    Elements    Console    Sources    Network    Performance    »    ⋮

▷  ⊘  | top              ▾ |  ◉  | Filter              Default levels ▾

   5 10                                              destructuring.js:25
   ▷ {width: 20, height: 25}                         destructuring.js:26
   Dr George Martin                                  destructuring.js:36
   3 4                                               destructuring.js:38
   4 3                                               destructuring.js:40

 >
```

Figure 2-29. *Destructuration*

To finish this section, I provide you with the complete code of the file:

```
let rect = {
   x: 5,
   and: 10,
   width: 20,
   height: 25
};
/* let {x, y, width, height} = rect;

console.log (x, y, width, height); */

/* let {x, y, width: w, height: h} = rect;

console.log (x, y, w, h); */

let { x, Y, ...remaining } = rect;

console.log( x, Y );
console.log( remaining );

let person = {
   firstName: "George",
   lastName: "Martin",
   prefix: "Dr"
}
```

```
function sayHi({ firstName, lastName, prefix }) {
    return `$ {prefix} $ {firstName} $ {lastName}`;
}

console.log( sayHi(person) );

let [p, q] = [ 3, 4 ];

console.log( p, q );

[p, q] = [q, p];

console.log( p, q );
```

It's time to move to a concept that can have a significant impact on the quality of the product, especially in complex applications where many developers are involved. This concept is known as interfaces.

Interfaces

Interfaces play a very important role not only in TypeScript but in many programming languages. A useful way to think about an interface is like a contract. This contract allows us to define a type of data and give it a name. All the variables that are declared as belonging to that type must implement the interface, that is, they must present the structure that has been defined in the interface.

Let's see an example. Our new directory will be called interfaces. In it, we will have the file interfaces.ts and the file index.html.

Define the following interface:

```
interface employee {
    firstName: string,
    lastName: string,
    birthDate: Date
}
```

That is our contract. Any variable of type employee must provide values for firstName, lastName, and birthDate.

Next, we define a simple function:

```
function displayFullName( emp: employee ) {
    return `$ { emp.firstName } $ { emp.lastName }`;
}
```

Something very interesting is that by defining the parameter emp as employee type, we will have the help of our IDE (Figure 2-30).

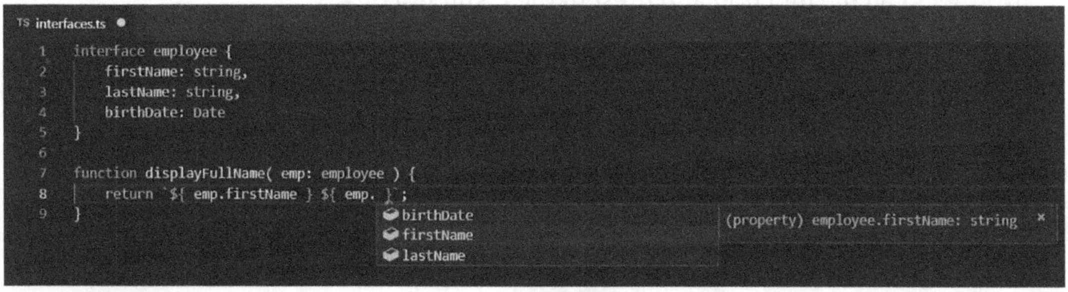

Figure 2-30. *Interfaces*

If we now try to declare an employee variable that does not have any of the properties of the interface, an error will occur as shown in Figure 2-31.

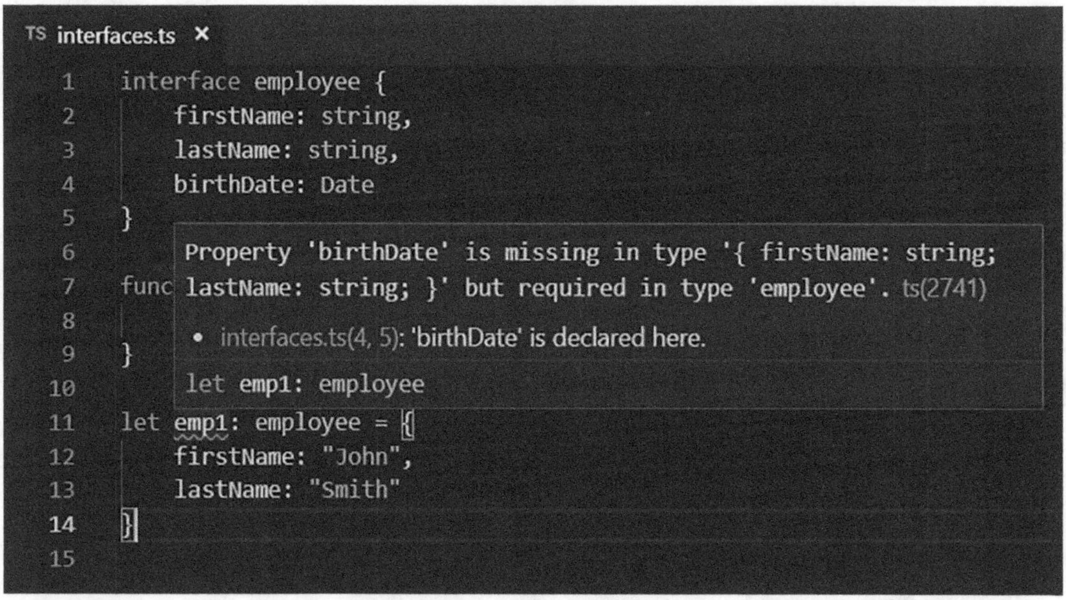

Figure 2-31. *Interfaces*

Correct that:

```
let emp1: employee = {
    firstName: "John",
    lastName: "Smith",
    birthDate: new Date('1975-08-21')
}
```

Now let's call the function and present the result by console:

```
console.log( displayFullName( emp1 ) );
```

As always, let's compile the project and observe the result in the browser (Figure 2-32).

Figure 2-32. *Interfaces*

Object-oriented programming is a paradigm that is present in the vast majority of projects. It deals with objects that model a problem in the real world. Object definitions are called classes and are the subject of the next section.

Classes

TypeScript is an object-oriented language. For those of you who have worked on object-oriented programming (OOP), the concepts you will see here will be absolutely natural and easy to understand.

If you have not worked in OOP before, you will need a little more work. But don't worry, we will go step by step.

What Is a Class?

We can think of a class as a plane for the construction of an object. The class contains the description of all the properties and behaviors that an object must possess to be considered as belonging to the class.

For example, let's think of a Person class. A person, in general terms, will have a name, a surname, and a certain age. We are talking about the attributes of people in general. The objects created from this description will have specific values for those attributes. A person, in addition, can have a behavior that is to say hello.

In the OOP language, we call attributes **properties** and behaviors **methods**.

But let's go directly to the code.

First, our new directory will be called classes. We initialize it as a project of typescript and create a file classes.ts and the index.html that will invoke the compiled file.

In our file classes.ts, we dump the following content:

```
class Person {
    firstName: string;
    lastName: string;
    birthDate: Date;

    constructor(firstName: string, lastName: string, birthDate: Date) {
        this.firstName = firstName;
        this.lastName = lastName;
        this.birthDate = birthDate;
    }
}
```

Our class is called Person. It is a convention that the first letter of the name of a class is capitalized.

Then, we have the list of attributes that a person must possess:

```
firstName: string;
lastName: string;
birthDate: Date;
```

Two of them are of type string, and one of them is of type date. We have simply specified the name of the properties and their type, but we have not explicitly defined the type of access they allow. The type of access, both for properties and methods, can be defined as public, private, or protected.

Having not specified the access type of the preceding properties, they are implicitly considered to be of type public.

But what do these types of access mean? Soon we will see it.

Now let's move on to our first method:

```
constructor(firstName: string, lastName: string, birthDate: Date) {
        this.firstName = firstName;
        this.lastName = lastName;
        this.birthDate = birthDate;
    }
```

This method has a special name. It is the constructor of the class, a method that is invoked at the moment of creation of an object of the Person type. Creating an object is known as instantiate.

As we can see, it is a function like the ones we have seen in the corresponding section; therefore, it can have mandatory parameters, with default values, and optional ones. The only difference is that this function is defined in the context of a class.

Consider the line:

```
this.firstName = firstName;
```

In this line, we are assigning the value of the firstName parameter to the firstName property.

The word **this** will point to the instance of the object that is obtained during its creation. That is, if we create an object called person1 of type Person, this will be a synonym of person1.

Let's instantiate our first object:

```
let person1 = new Person("George", "Martin", new Date("2019-08-03"));
```

Now, we have an object named person1. It does not really do much, but it will allow us to experiment a bit. Let's send an output to the console:

```
console.log( person1.firstName );
```

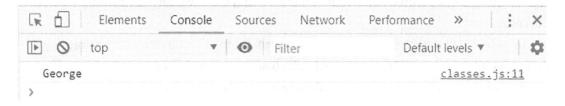

Figure 2-33. *Classes*

Good. We can perfectly access the value of the firstName property of the person1 object from outside the class, since as we mentioned previously, the access type of this and the other properties is of type public.

But this can have unintended consequences. Let's add the following two lines:

```
person1.firstName = "Brandon";

console.log( person1.firstName );
```

If we refresh the browser, we get the output in Figure 2-34.

Figure 2-34. *Classes*

We have been able to change the value of a property of the object from outside it. Why is this a bad idea? Because it violates the principles of encapsulation and information hiding.

Without going into too many details, the principle of information hiding tells us that the user of a class must have access only to what he needs. You should not know details of how an object belonging to that class structures its data and implements its methods. You should only know which methods to invoke to obtain a certain behavior.

By hiding details of its implementation, the integrity of the objects is guaranteed. This is of fundamental importance. Let's suppose we have a class named account, representing the account of a client in a bank. In that class, we have a property named balance.

In order to change the balance of an account, there must be procedures that guarantee that said modification is authorized and is carried out correctly. It would be unthinkable to allow the value of said property to be modified simply by doing something like `account1.balance = ....`

We are going to make the following modification to the definition of the properties:

```
private firstName: string;
private lastName: string;
private birthDate: Date;
```

Now we have a series of errors in our IDE (Figure 2-35).

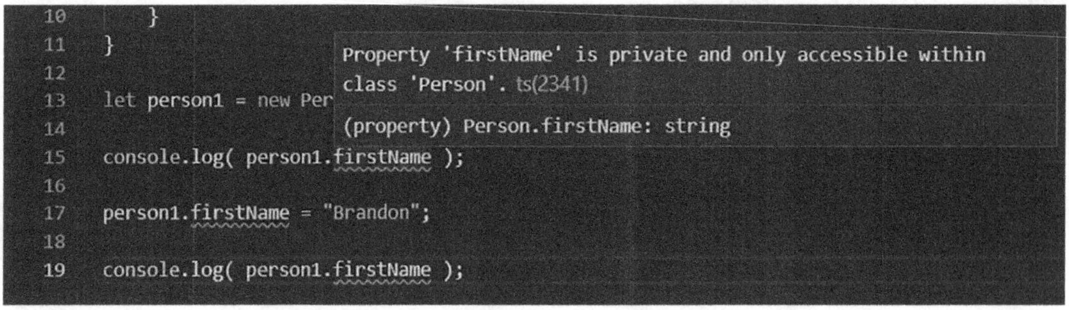

```
10          }
11    }                          Property 'firstName' is private and only accessible within
12                               class 'Person'. ts(2341)
13    let person1 = new Per
14                               (property) Person.firstName: string
15    console.log( person1.firstName );
16
17    person1.firstName = "Brandon";
18
19    console.log( person1.firstName );
```

Figure 2-35. *Visibility error*

And if we use the integrated console (Figure 2-36).

```
PROBLEMS  3   OUTPUT   DEBUG CONSOLE   TERMINAL

classes.ts:15:22 - error TS2341: Property 'firstName' is private and only accessible within class 'Person'.

15  console.log( person1.firstName );

classes.ts:17:9 - error TS2341: Property 'firstName' is private and only accessible within class 'Person'.

17  person1.firstName = "Brandon";

classes.ts:19:22 - error TS2341: Property 'firstName' is private and only accessible within class 'Person'.

19  console.log( person1.firstName );

[11:18:09] Found 3 errors. Watching for file changes.
```

Figure 2-36. *Console error*

Now that the properties are private, we cannot read or change their value directly. Then, how do we do it? Well, through special methods called accessors.

```
getFirstName(): string {
    return this.firstName;
}

getLastName(): string {
    return this.lastName;
}

getBirthDate(): Date {
    return this.birthDate;
}
```

We have three methods that allow us to read the values of the properties. It seems too much effort for something so simple, but think that the logic of such methods could be much more complex, for example, only returning a value when an authorized user requests it.

Now we can replace the line:

```
console.log( person1.firstName );
```

by

```
console.log( person1.getFirstName() );
```

However, although not very common, there may be cases in which the first and last names change, so we are going to add two methods that allow us to do exactly that:

```
setFirstName( firstName: string ) {
    this.firstName = firstName;
}

setLastName( lastName: string ) {
    this.lastName = lastName;
}
```

Now we can replace the line:

```
person1.firstName = "Brandon";
```

by

```
person1.setFirstName("Brandon");
```

Of course, the last line must also be modified to be:

```
console.log( person1.getFirstName() );
```

Now all the errors have disappeared. Again, the logic of these new methods could be much more complex, with checks being carried out before modifying the values.

Just to be sure, here is the complete code of our file so far:

```
class Person {
    private firstName: string;
    private lastName: string;
    private birthDate: Date;

    constructor(firstName: string, lastName: string, birthDate: Date) {
        this.firstName = firstName;
        this.lastName = lastName;
        this.birthDate = birthDate;
    }

    getFirstName(): string {
        return this.firstName;
    }
```

```typescript
    getLastName(): string {
        return this.lastName;
    }

    getBirthDate(): Date {
        return this.birthDate;
    }

    setFirstName( firstName: string ) {
        this.firstName = firstName;
    }

    setLastName( lastName: string ) {
        this.lastName = lastName;
    }
}

let person1 = new Person("George", "Martin", new Date("2019-08-03"));

console.log( person1.getFirstName() );

person1.setFirstName("Brandon");

console.log( person1.getFirstName() );
```

You can find the code in this file of the GitHub repo:

Class Person

```
https://github.com/Apress/The-Beginning-Angular-by-Victor-Hugo-Garcia/
blob/main/Chapter-02/01-classes-01.ts
```

Inheritance

As in most object-oriented languages, we can define classes that inherit from others. For example, think of an Employee class that inherits from the Person class. To express this relationship, we use the keyword extends:

```typescript
class Employee extends Person {

}
```

These few lines have allowed us to define an Employee class that extends the Person class. Therefore, it inherits all its methods and properties, including the constructor. We can therefore write:

```
let emp1 = new Employee( "Mary Jane", "Watson", new Date("1965-06-01") );
```

But the idea of declaring a class that inherits from another is precisely to extend the functionality. And we have not done any of that yet. Let's modify the definition of our class in the following way:

```
class Employee extends Person {
    private department: string = "";

    setDepartment( department: string ) {
        this.department = department;
    }

    getDepartment(): string {
        return this.department;
    }
}
```

We have a new property of type string to store the employee's department. We are initializing this variable with an empty string. We see that in the definition of our class the constructor is absent. This is because, as we mentioned, the new class inherits the properties and methods of the parent class.

But it would be perfectly possible to overwrite some or all of the methods of the parent class, for example, the constructor:

```
constructor(
        firstName: string,
        lastName: string,
        birthDate: Date,
        department: string ) {

            super(firstName, lastName, birthDate);
            this.department = department;
    }
```

The constructor receives the three parameters expected by the parent class, plus a new one corresponding to the department. On the line:

```
super(firstName, lastName, birthDate);
```

the constructor of the parent class (Person) is invoked. Then we have the line where the value is assigned to the department:

```
this.department = department;
```

But now, we have an error as shown in Figure 2-37.

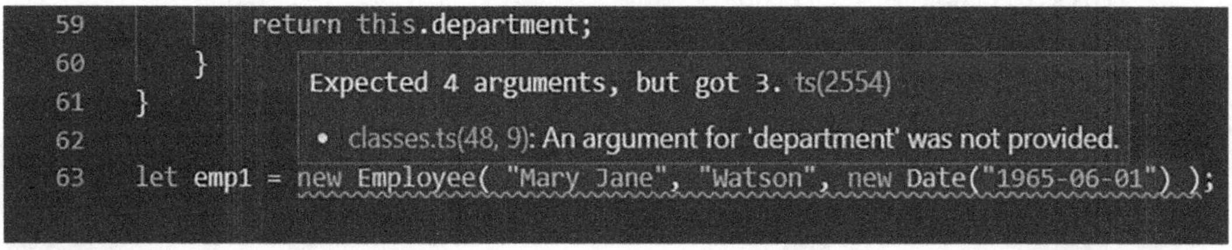

```
59                  return this.department;
60          }
                    Expected 4 arguments, but got 3. ts(2554)
61      }
62                  • classes.ts(48, 9): An argument for 'department' was not provided.
63      let emp1 = new Employee( "Mary Jane", "Watson", new Date("1965-06-01") );
```

Figure 2-37. *Argument error*

This is because the constructor expects a fourth parameter, department, that we are not assigning.

But suppose that we have a situation in which we want to model an employee can enter without having yet a department assigned. To reflect this situation, we can define this fourth parameter as optional. We have already seen how to do that, using a question sign next to the parameter name. Our modified constructor will be as follows:

```
constructor(
        firstName: string,
        lastName: string,
        birthDate: Date,
        department?: string ) {

            super(firstName, lastName, birthDate);

            if ( department ) this.department = department;
    }
```

It is a simple and clean code. For security, here is the complete code of our file:

```typescript
class Person {
    private firstName: string;
    private lastName: string;
    private birthDate: Date;

    constructor(firstName: string, lastName: string, birthDate: Date) {
        this.firstName = firstName;
        this.lastName = lastName;
        this.birthDate = birthDate;
    }

    getFirstName(): string {
        return this.firstName;
    }

    getLastName(): string {
        return this.lastName;
    }

    getBirthDate(): Date {
        return this.birthDate;
    }

    setFirstName( firstName: string ) {
        this.firstName = firstName;
    }

    setLastName( lastName: string ) {
        this.lastName = lastName;
    }
}

let person1 = new Person("George", "Martin", new Date("2019-08-03"));

console.log( person1.getFirstName() );

person1.setFirstName("Brandon");

console.log( person1.getFirstName() );
```

```typescript
class Employee extends Person {
    private department: string = "";

    constructor(
        firstName: string,
        lastName: string,
        birthDate: Date,
        department?: string ) {

            super(firstName, lastName, birthDate);

            if ( department ) this.department = department;
    }

    setDepartment( department: string ) {
        this.department = department;
    }

    getDepartment(): string {
        return this.department;
    }
}

let emp1 = new Employee( "Mary Jane", "Watson", new Date("1965-06-01") );
```

And here is the corresponding file:

Class Person

https://github.com/Apress/The-Beginning-Angular-by-Victor-Hugo-Garcia/blob/main/Chapter-02/02-classes-02.ts

One last thing, we exemplify a consequence of having defined the properties firstName, lastName, and birthDate as private in the Person class. Let's add the following method within the child class Employee:

```typescript
sayFullName() {
    return `${ this.firstName } ${ this.lastName }`;
}
```

Nothing bad happens to the naked eye. However, our IDE will reveal the errors shown in Figure 2-38.

```
59        getDepartment(): string {
60            return this.depa   Property 'firstName' is private and only accessible within
61        }                      class 'Person'. ts(2341)
62
63        sayFullName() {        (property) Person.firstName: string
64            return `${ this.firstName } ${ this.lastName }`;
65        }
66    }
67
68    let emp1 = new Employee( "Mary Jane", "Watson", new Date("1965-06-01") );
```

Figure 2-38. *Visibility error*

Private properties can only be accessed by methods of the class itself. If we wanted to rewrite the method correctly, it would be like this:

```
sayFullName() {
    return `${ this.getFirstName() } ${ this.getLastName() }`;
}
```

An alternative is the use of properties declared as protected.

Unlike the public ones, which can be accessed from any program, and the private ones, which can only be accessed by instances of the class in which they are defined, the protected properties can be accessed by methods of the instances of the class and by all those objects of derived classes.

We see an example.

We are going to create a new file called classes2.ts. In this file we will define the following class:

```
class Vehicle {
    protected brand: string = "";
    protected color: string;
    protected wheels: number;

    constructor( wheels: number, color: string ) {
        this.colour = color;
        this.wheels = wheels;
    }

    setColor( color: string ) {
        this.colour = color;
    }
```

```
getColor(): string {
    return this.color;
}
}
```

The brand property has a default value; therefore, it is not mandatory to assign a value to it in the constructor. All properties are protected.

Now let's define a class that extends from it:

```
class Automobil extends Vehicle {
    constructor( color: string, brand: string) {
        super( 4, color );
        this.brand = brand;
    }
}
```

Since the brand property is protected, we can assign it a value in the constructor. But let's change the type of brand from protected to private now, and we'll get the error shown in Figure 2-39.

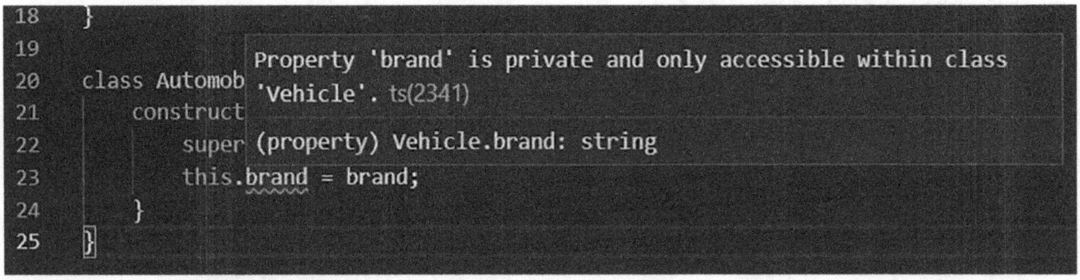

Figure 2-39. *Visibility error*

Alright, let's change the brand property from private to protected again to get rid of the error.

With our classes defined, we can perfectly create instances of both:

```
let v1 = new Vehicle( 2, "white");
let a1 = new Automobil( "red", "porsche" );
```

However, we can question whether it is really logical to be able to instantiate, that is, to create objects of the generic Vehicle class. Sometimes, it is convenient or necessary to be able to define classes that can be extended, but not instantiated directly. We thus arrive at the concept of abstract classes.

Abstract Classes

So far, the full content of classes2.ts is as follows:

```
class Vehicle {
    protected brand: string = "";
    protected color: string;
    protected wheels: number;

    constructor( wheels: number, color: string ) {
        this.colour = color;
        this.wheels = wheels;
    }

    setColor( color: string ) {
        this.colour = color;
    }

    getColor(): string {
        return this.color;
    }
}

class Automobil extends Vehicle {
    constructor( color: string, brand: string) {
        super( 4, color );
        this.brand = brand;
    }
}

let v1 = new Vehicle( 2, "white");
let a1 = new Automobil( "red", "porsche" );
```

And to be doubly sure, here is the file:

Classes

https://github.com/Apress/The-Beginning-Angular-by-Victor-Hugo-Garcia/
blob/main/Chapter-02/03-classes-03.ts

We are going to modify the definition of the base class in the following way:

```
abstract class Vehicle {...
```

We confirm that now it is not possible to instantiate objects of the Vehicle class
(Figure 2-40). Let's eliminate the conflicting line.

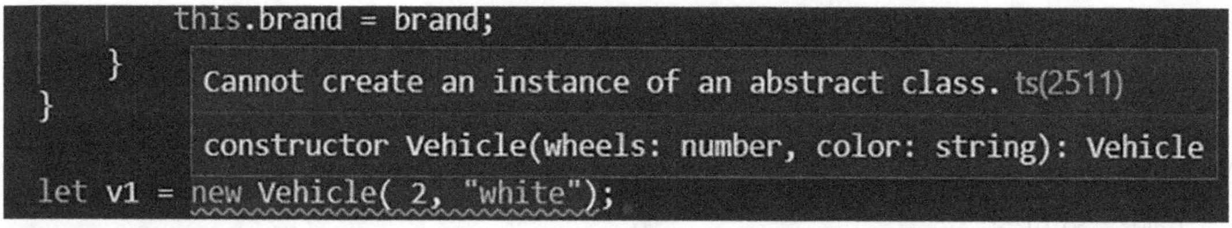

Figure 2-40. *Abstract classes*

Classes and Interfaces

Previously, we introduced the interfaces. We define interfaces as contracts that
guarantee that certain rules are respected. For example, at the time we defined the
following interface:

```
interface employee {
    firstName: string,
    lastName: string,
    birthDate: Date
}
```

At that time, we used the interfaces as a type in the definition of a variable, for
example:

```
let emp1: employee = {
    firstName: "John",
    lastName: "Smith",
    birthDate: new Date('1975-08-21')
}
```

But interfaces can do much more.

When complex software architectures are being created, it is extremely useful to define interfaces that are implemented by classes, thus achieving a consistent design, especially when working as a team. But let's see an example.

Let's create a new file called classes3.ts with the following content:

```
interface Animal {
    name: string;
    family: string;
}
```

It is an extremely simple interface with two unique properties. But in addition to properties, we can have method statements:

```
interface Animal {
    name: string;
    family: string;

    makeSound(): string;
}
```

Pay attention to the following: we have the name of the method, makeSound, followed by the type of return value, then a semicolon. The method has no body. And that is a difference with an abstract class. The interfaces can only declare methods, but not implementations of them.

Now we declare a class that implements this interface. The interfaces are implemented, they are not extended:

```
class Dog implements Animal {

}
```

However, our class will give us the error, as shown in Figure 2-41.

```
 1    interface Animal {
 2        name: string;
 3        fa  Class 'Dog' incorrectly implements interface 'Animal'.
 4              Type 'Dog' is missing the following properties from type
 5        ma  'Animal': name, family, makeSound ts(2420)
 6    }
 7            class Dog
 8    class Dog implements Animal {
 9
10    }
11
```

Figure 2-41. *Implementation error*

This is so because as we said an interface is a contract, and if the Dog class wants to implement the Animal interface, it must comply with the contract. Let's fix that:

```
class Dog implements Animal {
    name: string;
    family: string = "canidae";

    constructor( name: string ) {
        this.yam = name;
    }

    makeSound(): string {
        return 'Woof';
    }
}
```

Now the Dog class correctly implements the interface. We can begin to understand the power of interfaces. A programmer can define the interfaces, and in this way, it will be guaranteed that the classes that implement it will be consistent.

In many applications, we'll have to wait for a server response. That means that we have to deal with asynchronous processes without degrading the user experience. Fortunately, promises come to our rescue and are the subject of our next section.

Promises

Promises were introduced to deal with asynchronous processes. But to understand its usefulness, let's first see another way of handling asynchronous processes: callbacks.

1. Let's create a new directory called promises and inside the promises.ts file. As always, initialize the project and create the corresponding index.html. An asynchronous process is a nondeterministic process. That is, we cannot know exactly when it will end. Let's think, for example, that we are accessing an API that should return data.

2. We need to operate when that data is returned, but at the same time, we cannot freeze the user interface while we wait. Let's see a small initial example. Let's add the following content:

```
function asyncTask(callback: any) {
    setTimeout(() => {
        console.log("Async Task Calling Callback");
        callback();
    }, 3000);
}

asyncTask(() => console.log("Callback Called"));
```

We have a function called asyncTask in the first place. This function simulates an asynchronous process, in this case using the setTimeout function. The asyncTask function receives a parameter. This parameter is the function that we want to execute when the asynchronous process ends.

3. Opening the index.html file in the browser, after three seconds we will obtain the output shown in Figure 2-42.

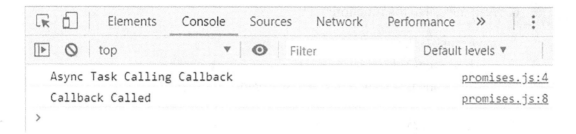

Figure 2-42. *Asynchronous call*

So far, so good. But we must bear in mind that asynchronous processes can find all sorts of errors in real contexts.

If an error occurs in the asynchronous process, then the callback will never be called.

4. The simplest form of a promise is the following:

```
let asyncTask2 = new Promise( ( resolve, reject) => {

})
```

The two arguments, resolve and reject, can be called as desired, but it is a convention to call them that.

resolve and reject are in fact two functions. When the asynchronous process finishes, it will be called resolve(). If an error occurs, reject will be called.

5. Let's see the full version of the promise:

```
let asyncTask2 = new Promise( ( resolve, reject) => {
    setTimeout( ()=>{
        console.log("Resolving Promise");

        // All good
        resolve();

        // Something went wrong
        // reject();
    }, 3000 )
})
```

6. And the call to the function:

```
asyncTask2.then(
    function() {
        console.log("Promise resolved");
    },
    function() {
        console.error("Something went wrong");
    }
)
```

The output is now shown in Figure 2-43.

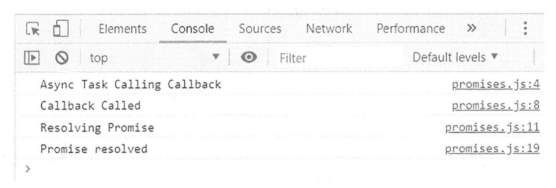

Figure 2-43. *Promises*

7. If we comment out the line resolve() and uncomment the line
    reject(), we will see the output in Figure 2-44.

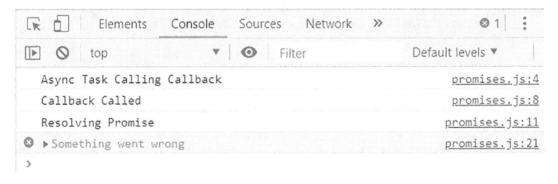

Figure 2-44. *Promise error*

So far, it may not be too clear what the advantage of the promises on callbacks is. One of them is that promises can be chained. Suppose we have three asynchronous methods. The second method must be called when the first one has finished, and the third when the second one has done it. Let's see how we can solve this by using chaining of promises.

8. Let's create a new file named promises2.ts with the following code:

```
let firstMethod = function() {
    let promise = new Promise(function(resolve, reject){
        setTimeout(function() {
            console.log('first method completed');
            resolve({data: '123'});
        }, 2000);
    });
    return promise;
};

let secondMethod = function(someStuff) {
    let promise = new Promise(function(resolve, reject){
        setTimeout(function() {
            console.log('second method completed');
            resolve({newData: someStuff.data + ' some more data'});
        }, 2000);
    });
    return promise;
};
 let thirdMethod = function(someStuff) {
    let promise = new Promise(function(resolve, reject){
        setTimeout(function() {
            console.log('third method completed');
            resolve({result: someStuff.newData + ' and even more
            data'});
        }, 3000);
```

```
        });
        return promise;
    };
      firstMethod()
        .then(secondMethod)
        .then(thirdMethod)
        .then(
            (res: any) => console.log( res )
        )
```

Here is the file:

https://github.com/Apress/The-Beginning-Angular-by-Victor-Hugo-Garcia/blob/main/Chapter-02/04-promises2.ts

If we told the compiler to monitor the changes with tsc -w, having initialized the project with tsc -init, a promises2.js file should be created automatically. We just need to change the reference in the index.html to include that file.

Let's analyze the content.

Each method returns a promise. This promise will contain a future result that will be available when executing resolve when the asynchronous process ends. Let's analyze the chain calls:

```
firstMethod()
    .then(secondMethod)
    .then(thirdMethod)
    .then(
        (res: any) => console.log( res )
    )
```

By calling firstMethod.then, we are subscribing to the promise that returns this method. At that point, we could have simply used the result returned by the promise, like this:

```
firstMethod()
    .then(
        (res: any) => console.log( res )
    )
```

In this case, we would have obtained the output shown in Figure 2-45.

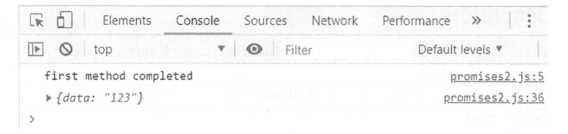

Figure 2-45. Chained calls

However, instead, the received output is sent directly to the second method:

```
firstMethod()
    .then(secondMethod)
```

Then again we subscribe to the promise using then. This output is sent in turn to the third method, and we subscribe again.

When the third exit has been obtained, we can finally use it. Run the file index.html in the browser and see how each method is completed until the last, where we can have the complete data (Figure 2-46).

Figure 2-46. Chained methods

As we will see when we start defining our classes in Angular, those classes make extensive use of a kind of annotation called decorators. We'll learn about it in the next section.

Decorators

Decorators are annotations that can be added to a class, method, interface, property, or parameter declaration.

The decorators' purpose is to add functionality to existing code without having to modify the code itself.

We see an example.

Our new directory will have the name decorators and inside it a decorators.ts file.

Let's write the following code:

```
function log( constructor: Function ) {
    console.log( "Constructor log" );
}

@log
class Test {
    constructor() {}
}
```

The compiler will give us the error shown in Figure 2-47.

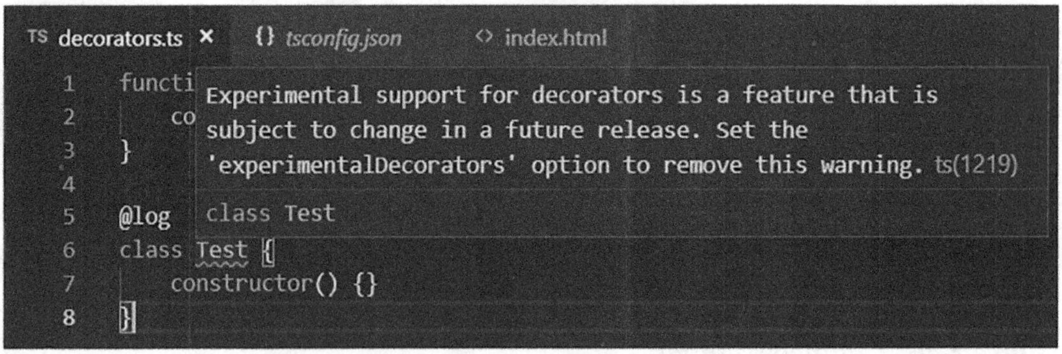

Figure 2-47. *Decorators*

To fix it, we must uncomment the following line in tsconfig.json:

```
,"experimentalDecorators": true,
```

Once this is done, we can compile the project.

In the console, we can observe the output shown in Figure 2-48.

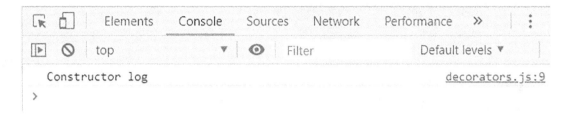

Figure 2-48. *Class decorators*

In addition to class decorators, we can have decorators of methods. Modify the file as follows:

```
function log( constructor: Function ) {
    console.log( "Constructor log" );
}

function authorize(target: Object,
    propertyKey: string,
    descriptor: TypedPropertyDescriptor<any>): any {

    console.log('target:', target);
    console.log('propertyKey:', propertyKey);
    console.log('descriptor:', descriptor);

    // save a reference to the original method
    let originalMethod = descriptor.value;

    descriptor.value = function (...args: any[]) {
        // pre
        console.log('New method..');
        console.log('The method args are: ' + JSON.stringify(args));

        // run and store the result
        let result = originalMethod.apply(this, args);

        // post
        console.log('The return value is: ' + result);

        // return the result of the original method
        return result;
    };
```

```
    return descriptor;
}

@log
class Test {
    constructor() {}

    @authorize
    hello( name: string ): string {
        return "Hello " + name;
    }
}

let t = new Test();
t.hello("Victor");
```

@authorize is a more complex decorator. As we said previously, the decorators' goal is to assign new properties and behaviors. In this case, we are adding functionality to the hello method. But what could be the use of decorators? Think, for example, of checking and validation tasks. The decorators will usually be in separate files that can be imported where they are required. Thus, the modifications to the functionality that are necessary to the functionality will be made in those files and will be reflected wherever the decorators are used.

Summary

This chapter may have been a bit extensive, but I hope it was entertaining and useful. We have seen the bases of TypeScript: data types, let and const, functions, arrow functions, classes, and interfaces. Although to be honest we have only touched the surface, what we have seen is more than enough to develop the applications of the book.

If you have been able to perform the exercises, then you can proceed with the next chapter. New and exciting sections are coming. Cheer up!

Questions and Answers

Questions

1. What is the command to install TypeScript globally?

2. What are the basic data types of TypeScript?

3. How is an interface defined?

4. How is a class defined?

5. How is the constructor of the parent class called from a child class?

6. What is the basic form of a promise?

7. What are decorators?

Answers

1. npm install -g typescript

2. number, string, boolean, null, undefined

3. interface x { }

4. class X { }

5. super

6. let prom = New Promise((resolve, reject) => { })

7. Annotations that can be added to a class, method, interface, property, or parameter declaration to add functionality

CHAPTER 3

RestApp Part 1

In this chapter, we'll learn how to generate a new project using angular-cli. We'll create new components and a service to communicate with a rest API. As for the purely aesthetic aspect, we'll include bootstrap in our application through CDNs.

Creating a New Project

Whether you have directly arrived at this chapter or have previously gone through the previous one, this is the time to make our first application with Angular.

This application will allow us to lay the foundations for all the following applications, which will lead us to have a deep understanding of how to build projects.

Without further delay, open the terminal and, located inside the Angular folder, type the command to create our first application:

```
ng new rest
```

The process may take a few minutes depending on our connection, giving us the output shown in Figure 3-1.

© Victor Hugo Garcia 2023
V. H. Garcia, *Getting Started with Angular*, https://doi.org/10.1007/978-1-4842-9206-8_3

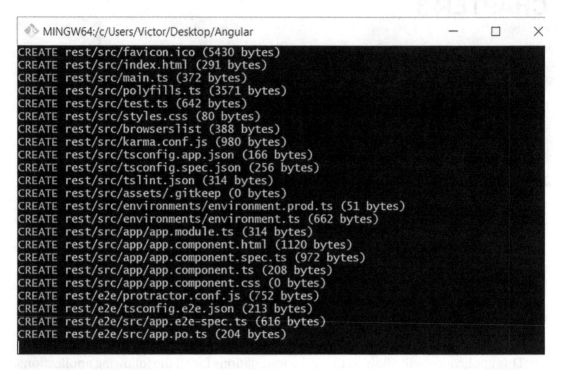

Figure 3-1. *New project*

When the process has finished, we will have a new directory called rest. Let's open it with our IDE (Figure 3-2).

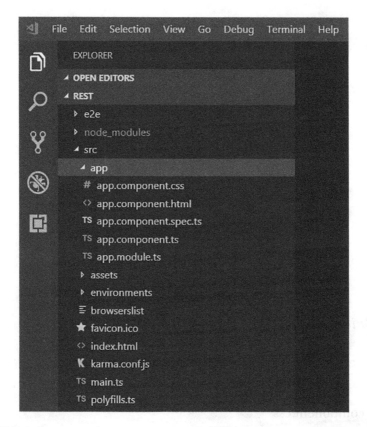

Figure 3-2. *Directory structure*

The number of directories can seem overwhelming, but our work will be limited mostly to the src directory.

But let's take a look at the structure that angular-cli has given us. In the terminal, go to the rest directory and type the following:

```
ng serve -o
```

ng serve boots the embedded server of Angular, making our application available at http://localhost:4200, but if we use the flag -o, our browser by default will open this address in a new tab (Figure 3-3).

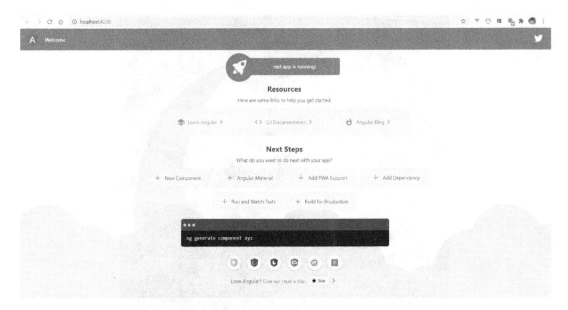

Figure 3-3. *Initial screen*

A simple interface, but it gives us everything necessary to start our work.

Let's go back to the code of our application. We can notice the presence of five files:

app.component.css

app.component.html

app.component.spec.ts

app.component.ts

app.module.ts

We can see the files in Figure 3-4.

Figure 3-4. *App files*

For now, let's ignore the app.component.spec.ts file.

Let's see the content of the app.component.ts file:

```
import { Component } from '@angular/core';

@Component({
 selector: 'app-root',
 templateUrl: './app.component.html',
 styleUrls: ['./app.component.css']
})
export class AppComponent {
 title = 'rest';
}
```

This file defines the structure of a basic component. At Angular, we structure our applications using components. Think of components as reusable blocks that define a part of our user interface: for example, a navigation bar with the main menu, a sidebar, etc.

The components are responsible for defining both their own internal logic and their appearance.

But at its root, the components are not something that we have not seen before. Classes:

```
export class AppComponent {
 title = 'rest';
}
```

We have an AppComponent class, in which a title property is defined. Although the type of the variable has not been specified, when assigning a text string, the compiler infers that it is a property of type string.

What may be curious is the word `export` before the word `class`. By adding the export modifier, we are making our class available for use from another file through an import statement.

As it happens, for example, in the first line of our file:

```
import { Component } from '@angular/core';
```

an import of the Component class that is defined in the module @angular/core is being done here.

Then we have the following code section:

```
@Component({
  selector: 'app-root',
  templateUrl: './app.component.html',
  styleUrls: ['./app.component.css']
})
```

If you think it looks like a decorator, you're right. @Component is a decorator that marks a class as an Angular component, providing configuration metadata that determines how the component should be processed, instantiated, and used.

Three configuration options are included:

selector: The selector defines a new HTML tag that will tell Angular where to insert the component. That is, in any sector of a page where the tags `<app-root> </app-root>` are placed, the AppComponent component will be rendered.

We can see this if we open the file index.html:

```
<body>
  <app-root> </app-root>
</body>
```

There is a label that indicates rendering our component.

> templateUrl: This indicates the path of a file where the HTML code that is used to render the component is contained. If the HTML code were a small fragment, you could use the option `template` that accepts templated strings like the ones we saw in the previous chapter.

> styleUrls: This indicates the path of a CSS file where specific styles are defined for the component.

Now let's go to the app.component.html file. We are going to replace all the HTML code that is there by the following:

```
<h1>{{title}}</h1>
```

That's it. If we remember in our AppComponent class, a title property is defined. Everything that is between double braces will be evaluated as an expression by Angular, and therefore the value of the title property will be displayed.

app.module.ts

Every Angular application is structured in modules. When we generate a new Angular project, a root module is created by us, which is in charge of launching our application. While this module can be called in any way, it is a convention to call it AppModule. Let's analyze it for a moment:

```
import { BrowserModule } from '@angular/platform-browser';
import { NgModule } from '@angular/core';

import { AppComponent } from './app.component';

@NgModule({
  declarations: [
    AppComponent
  ],
  imports: [
    BrowserModule
  ],
  providers: [],
  bootstrap: [AppComponent]
})
export class AppModule {}
```

In the declarations array, we have all the components that belong to the module. That is why the components we create should be included in this section.

The imports array contains the modules that are necessary for the application. When we generate a new module that depends directly on the AppModule, we must add it here.

What We Will Be Building

The final result is shown in Figure 3-5.

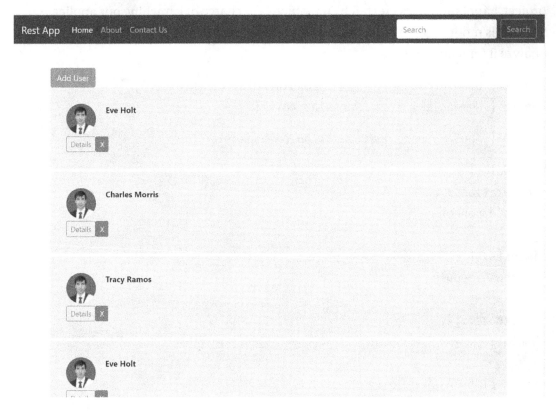

Figure 3-5. *Final result*

We have an application with user information (I'm using my own picture to avoid copyright issues). The user data comes from a rest API, so we will use a service to communicate with this API.

When clicking the details of a user, we will obtain a new screen with the information shown in Figure 3-6.

Lorem ipsum pain sit amet, consectetur adipiscing elit. Maecenas convallis sed elit ac sagittis. Integer facilisis scelerisque erat quis finibus. Nunc euismod molesie eros, id semper lacus euismod tempus. Nulla at just id felis venenatis varius. Morbi eu rutrum nibh, at tempor quam. Aenean interdum eu sapien ac sodales. Aenean ut gravida eros, id tincidunt massa. Vivamus accumsan pain nec malaise sagittis. Sed lobortis sit amet Ligula eu molestie. Nulla facilisi. Nam elit dui, rutrum nec massa nec, volutpat gravida ante. Nulla tempus hate et interdum tincidunt. Aliquam lacinia ulcers pretium. Phasellus convallis consequat lacus sed suscipit. Fusce annoy lobortis lorem nec convallis.

User List

Charles

Name: Charles

Save

Figure 3-6. *User details*

Bootstrap 4

Before starting to work fully on the code, let's give a little style to our application.

Bootstrap is a library of frontend components, beautifully stylized, that allow us to build applications that will be perfectly visualized from any device. It is not the only one, of course, and in the future I will include sections to work with Material Design, for example.

We will go to the Bootstrap (`https://getbootstrap.com/`) page and then to the Download section (Figure 3-7).

Bootstrap

Build responsive, mobile-first projects on the web with the world's most popular front-end component library.

Bootstrap is an open source toolkit for developing with HTML, CSS, and JS. Quickly prototype your ideas or build your entire app with our Sass variables and mixins, responsive grid system, extensive prebuilt components, and powerful plugins built on jQuery.

Get started   Download

Figure 3-7. *Bootstrap download*

In the Download section, we have different ways to include bootstrap. Let's start with the simplest, then we will see a cleaner and tidier way (Figure 3-8).

BootstrapCDN

Skip the download with BootstrapCDN to deliver cached version of Bootstrap's compiled CSS and JS to your project.

```
                                                                    Copy
<link rel="stylesheet" href="https://stackpath.bootstrapcdn.com/bootstrap/4.3.1/css/bootstrap.min.css" integrity="sha
<script src="https://stackpath.bootstrapcdn.com/bootstrap/4.3.1/js/bootstrap.min.js" integrity="sha384-JjSmVgyd0p3pXB
```

If you're using our compiled JavaScript, don't forget to include CDN versions of jQuery and Popper.js before it.

```
                                                                    Copy
<script src="https://code.jquery.com/jquery-3.3.1.slim.min.js" integrity="sha384-q8i/X+965DzO0rT7abK41JStQIAqVgRVzpbz
<script src="https://cdnjs.cloudflare.com/ajax/libs/popper.js/1.14.7/umd/popper.min.js" integrity="sha384-UO2eT0CpHqd
```

Figure 3-8. *Bootstrap CDN*

In this section, we find the way to include bootstrap through a CDN.

First, we will include the style sheet, just before the closing tag </head> of our index.html:

```
<link rel="stylesheet"
href="https://stackpath.bootstrapcdn.com/bootstrap/4.5.2/css/bootstrap.
min.css"
integrity="sha384-JcKb8q3iqJ61gNV9KGb8thSsNjpSLOn8PARn9HuZOnIxNOhoP+VmmDGMN
5t9UJ0Z"
crossorigin="anonymous">
```

Next, we will include the jQuery, popper, and bootstrap libraries first, in that order:

```
<script src="https://code.jquery.com/jquery-3.5.1.slim.min.js"
integrity="sha384-DfXdz2htPHOlsSSs5nCTpuj/zy4C+OGpamoFVy38MVBnE+IbbVYUew+
OrCXaRkfj"
crossorigin="anonymous"></script>
<script src="https://cdn.jsdelivr.net/npm/popper.js@1.16.1/dist/umd/
popper.min.js"
integrity="sha384-9/reFTGAW83EW2RDu2S0VKaIzap3H66lZH81PoYlFhbGU+6BZp6G7n
iu735Sk7lN"
```

```
crossorigin="anonymous"></script>
<script src="https://stackpath.bootstrapcdn.com/bootstrap/4.5.2/js/
bootstrap.min.js"
integrity="sha384-B4gt1jrGC7Jh4AgTPSdUt0BvfO8shuf57BaghqFfPlYxofvL8/
KUEfYiJOMMV+rV"
crossorigin="anonymous"></script>
```

To be sure, the index file should be at this point as follows:

index.html (https://github.com/Apress/The-Beginning-Angular-by-Victor-Hugo-Garcia/blob/main/Chapter-03/01-index.html)

Perfect. We already have bootstrap in our project.

Components of Our Application

We will have to create four new components, called navbar, about, contact, and home.

To create a component, we must write the following command, which we can execute from the terminal included in VS Code:

```
ng g c components/navbar
```

This will give us the output in Figure 3-9.

```
PS C:\Users\Victor\Desktop\Angular\rest> ng g c components/navbar
CREATE src/app/components/navbar/navbar.component.html (25 bytes)
CREATE src/app/components/navbar/navbar.component.spec.ts (628 bytes)
CREATE src/app/components/navbar/navbar.component.ts (269 bytes)
CREATE src/app/components/navbar/navbar.component.css (0 bytes)
UPDATE src/app/app.module.ts (407 bytes)
PS C:\Users\Victor\Desktop\Angular\rest> []
```

Figure 3-9. *NavbarComponent*

Since the components directory does not exist, angular-cli will create it for us.

The navbar.component.html code is extremely simple:

```
<p>
 navbar works!
</p>
```

Let's replace the app.component.html code with:

```
<app-navbar> </app-navbar>
```

And we'll see the one shown in Figure 3-10 in the browser.

navbar works!

Figure 3-10. *NavbarComponent*

Although its usefulness is limited, our component is working.

Navbar Component

Very good. On the bootstrap site, let's go to the documentation section and look for the Navbar component (Figure 3-11).

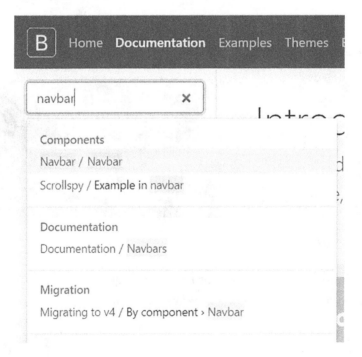

Figure 3-11. *NavbarComponent*

Let's copy the example code and paste it into navbar.component.html:

```
<nav class="navbar navbar-expand-lg navbar-light bg-light">
    <a class="navbar-brand" href="#">Navbar</a>
    <button class="navbar-toggler" type="button" data-toggle="collapse"
data-target="#navbarSupportedContent" aria-
controls="navbarSupportedContent"
aria-expanded="false" aria-label="Toggle navigation">
        <span class="navbar-toggler-icon"> </span>
    </button>

    <div class="collapse navbar-collapse" id="navbarSupportedContent">
        <ul class="navbar-nav mr-auto">
            <li class="nav-item active">
                <a class="nav-link" href="#">
                  Home
                  <span class="sr-only">
                    (current)
                  </span>
                </a>
            </li>
            <li class="nav-item">
                <a class="nav-link" href="#">Link</a>
            </li>
            <li class="nav-item dropdown">
                <a class="nav-link dropdown-toggle" href="#"
                id="navbarDropdown"
role="button" data-toggle="dropdown" aria-haspopup="true" aria-
expanded="false">
            Dropdown
        </a>
                <div class="dropdown-menu">
                    <a class="dropdown-item" href="#">Action</a>
                    <a class="dropdown-item" href="#">Another action</a>
                    <div class="dropdown-divider"> </div>
                    <a class="dropdown-item" href="#">Something else here</a>
```

```
              </div>
          </li>
          <li class="nav-item">
              <a class="nav-link disabled" href="#" tabindex="-1"
              aria-disabled="true">Disabled</a>
          </li>
        </ul>
        <form class="form-inline my-2 my-lg-0">
            <input class="form-control mr-sm-2" type="search"
            placeholder="Search"
aria-label="Search">
            <button class="btn btn-outline-success my-2 my-sm-0"
            type="submit">
              Search
            </button>
        </form>
    </div>
</nav>
```

The output of our browser is shown in Figure 3-12.

Navbar   Home   Link   Dropdown ▼   Disabled

Figure 3-12. *Navbar links*

We are going to make several changes. First, let's replace the following line:

```
<nav class="navbar navbar-expand-lg navbar-light bg-light">
```

with

```
<nav class="navbar navbar-expand-lg navbar-dark bg-dark">
```

This will give us a nice dark color in our navigation bar (Figure 3-13).

Figure 3-13. *Dark navbar*

Now we are going to eliminate the following lines:

```
<li class="nav-item dropdown">
  <a class="nav-link dropdown-toggle" href="#" id="navbarDropdown"
  role="button"
data-toggle="dropdown" aria-haspopup="true"
aria-expanded="false">
          Dropdown
  </a>
  <div class="dropdown-menu" aria-=labelledby"navbarDropdown">
    <a class="dropdown-item" href="#">Action</a>
    <a class="dropdown-item" href="#">Another action</a>
     <div class="dropdown-divider"> </div>
      <a class="dropdown-item" href="#">Something else here</a>
  </div>
</li>
        <li class="nav-item">
            <a class="nav-link disabled" href="#" tabindex="-1"
aria-disabled="true">Disabled</a>
        </li>
```

We are getting rid of the dropdown and the disabled link. Then we must add another two. Here is the complete code of the file up to this point:

```
<nav class="navbar navbar-expand-lg navbar-dark bg-dark">
   <a class="navbar-brand" href="#">Rest App</a>
   <button class="navbar-toggler" type="button" data-toggle="collapse"

data-target="#navbarSupportedContent" aria-controls="navbarSupportedContent"
aria-expanded="false" aria-label="Toggle navigation">
```

```
    <span class="navbar-toggler-icon"> </span>
  </button>

  <div class="collapse navbar-collapse" id="navbarSupportedContent">
      <ul class="navbar-nav mr-auto">
          <li class="nav-item active">
              <a class="nav-link" href="#">
                Home
                <span class="sr-only">
                  (current)
                </span>
              </a>
          </li>
          <li class="nav-item">
              <a class="nav-link" href="#">About</a>
          </li>
          <li class="nav-item">
              <a class="nav-link" href="#">Contact Us</a>
          </li>
      </ul>
      <form class="form-inline my-2 my-lg-0">
          <input class="form-control mr-sm-2" type="search"
placeholder="Search"
aria-label="Search">
          <button class="btn btn-outline-success my-2 my-sm-0" type="submit">
            Search
          </button>
      </form>
  </div>
</nav>
```

And the corresponding file for convenience:
navbar.component.html
https://github.com/Apress/The-Beginning-Angular-by-Victor-Hugo-Garcia/
blob/main/Chapter-03/02-navbar.component-v1.html

It's enough for now. We will use the terminal to create three new components: about, contact, and home.

We could have created the components manually, but the advantage of doing so using the angular-cli is that the tool will be responsible for making the corresponding import in our app.module.ts file. If we open it, you will see that the following lines have been added:

```
import { AboutComponent } from './components/about/about.component';
import { ContactComponent } from './components/contact/contact.component';
import { HomeComponent } from './components/home/home.component';
```

And in the declarations section, the necessary lines will have been added:

```
declarations: [
    AppComponent,
    NavbarComponent,
    AboutComponent,
    ContactComponent,
    HomeComponent
],
```

Routing

To move forward, let's now establish the navigation of our application. To do this, we will create a new file called app.routes.ts, at the same level as the app.module.ts file.

If we are working with VS Code, and we have installed the corresponding packages, we can take advantage of the Angular 10 Snippets package, and simply by starting to type **ng-**, we will be shown a series of suggestions (Figure 3-14).

Figure 3-14. *Router*

The option that we are interested in is ng-router-appmodule, which will give us the following skeleton. It is important to note that this skeleton would include references to two components, FeatureComponent and PageNotFoundComponent, that we don't have. We will not use these components, and we'll be changing the paths accordingly:

```
import { NgModule } from '@angular/core';
import { RouterModule, Routes } from '@angular/router';

const routes: Routes = [
    { path: '', component: HomeComponent },
    { path: 'path', component: FeatureComponent },
    { path: '**', component: PageNotFoundComponent },
];

@NgModule({
    imports: [RouterModule.forRoot(routes)],
    exports: [RouterModule]
})
export class AppRoutingModule {}
```

This is a module that will handle the routes of our application.

Let's focus on the following fragment:

```
const routes: Routes = [
    { path: '', component: HomeComponent },
    { path: 'path', component: FeatureComponent },
    { path: '**', component: PageNotFoundComponent },
];
```

The constant routes is an array of routes that basically have two elements: a path and the component that will respond to that path.

We need to make a small change. Simply by convention, we change the constant routes by uppercase:

```
const ROUTES: Routes = [
    { path: '', component: HomeComponent },
    { path: 'path', component: FeatureComponent },
    { path: '**', component: PageNotFoundComponent },
];
```

And we must also do it here:

```
imports: [RouterModule.forRoot(ROUTES)],
```

We have a path that directs to the HomeComponent. Define two paths that lead us to about and contact:

```
const ROUTES: Routes = [
    { path: '', component: HomeComponent },
    { path: 'about', component: AboutComponent },
    { path: 'contact', component: ContactComponent },
    { path: '**', component: PageNotFoundComponent },
];
```

Let's make sure we have the corresponding imports:

```
import { HomeComponent } from './components/home/home.component';
import { AboutComponent } from './components/about/about.component';
import { ContactComponent } from './components/contact/contact.component';
```

The last route of our array has the path: **. This path is used when a certain route has not been found. Let's change the component that will be addressed by our HomeComponent:

```
const ROUTES: Routes = [
    { path: '', component: HomeComponent },
    { path: 'about', component: AboutComponent },
    { path: 'contact', component: ContactComponent },
    { path: '**', component: HomeComponent },
];
```

The complete file must have this content:

```
import { NgModule } from '@angular/core';
import { RouterModule, Routes } from '@angular/router';
import { HomeComponent } from './components/home/home.component';
import { AboutComponent } from './components/about/about.component';
import { ContactComponent } from './components/contact/contact.component';

export const ROUTES: Routes = [
    { path: '', component: HomeComponent },
    { path: 'about', component: AboutComponent },
    { path: 'contact', component: ContactComponent },
    { path: '**', component: HomeComponent },
];

@NgModule({
    imports: [RouterModule.forRoot(ROUTES)],
    exports: [RouterModule]
})
export class AppRoutingModule {}
```

And here is the corresponding file just in case:

app.routes.ts

https://github.com/Apress/The-Beginning-Angular-by-Victor-Hugo-Garcia/blob/main/Chapter-03/03-app.routes.ts

We need to address the AppModule to add our new module to the imports array:

```
imports: [
  BrowserModule,
  AppRoutingModule
 ],
```

Of course, for this to work, the corresponding import must be present:

```
import { AppRoutingModule } from './app.routes';
```

With this, we have defined the routes of our application.

Let's return now to the file navbar.component.html.

Let's go to the following fragment:

```
<li class="nav-item active">
  <a class="nav-link" href="#">Home <span class="sr-only">(current)</
span> </a>
</li>
```

And replace it with the following:

```
<li class="nav-item" routerLinkActive="active">
<a class="nav-link" [routerLink]="['/home']">
  Home <span class="sr-only">(current)</span>
</a>
</li>
```

The most important is that we have removed the href and replaced it with:

```
[routerLink]="['/home']"
```

We are just passing a route, "home," but we could also pass parameters as follows:

```
[routerLink]="['/path', routeParam]"
```

where routeParam should be replaced with the actual parameter to be sent.

We can also notice that the "active" class of the element has been removed. This class is responsible for highlighting an element of the menu when we are on that page. routerLinkActive works in conjunction with routerLink and assigns it to the element in which the class passed as a parameter is located, in this case "active," when the selected route corresponds to the one assigned to routerLink.

We must proceed in the same way for the rest of the menu items.

Again, here is the complete navbar code up to this point:

```
<nav class="navbar navbar-expand-lg navbar-dark bg-dark">
  <a class="navbar-brand" href="#">Rest App</a>
  <button class="navbar-toggler" type="button" data-toggle="collapse"
data-target="#navbarSupportedContent"
aria-controls="navbarSupportedContent"
aria-expanded="false" aria-label="Toggle navigation">
    <span class="navbar-toggler-icon"> </span>
  </button>

  <div class="collapse navbar-collapse" id="navbarSupportedContent">
    <ul class="navbar-nav mr-auto">
      <li class="nav-item" routerLinkActive="active">
        <a class="nav-link" [routerLink]="['/home']">
          Home
            <span class="sr-only">(current)</span>
        </a>
      </li>
      <li class="nav-item" routerLinkActive="active">
        <a class="nav-link" [routerLink]="['/about']">About</a>
      </li>
      <li class="nav-item" routerLinkActive="active">
        <a class="nav-link" [routerLink]="['/contact']">Contact Us</a>
      </li>
    </ul>
    <form class="form-inline my-2 my-lg-0">
      <input class="form-control mr-sm-2" type="search"
      placeholder="Search"
aria-label="Search">
        <button class="btn btn-outline-success my-2 my-sm-0" type="submit">
          Search
        </button>
```

```
        </form>
    </div>
</nav>
```

And here is the corresponding file:

`navbar.component.html`

https://github.com/Apress/The-Beginning-Angular-by-Victor-Hugo-Garcia/ blob/main/Chapter-03/04-navbar.component-v2.html

We have now defined the routes of our application and the links of the menu. If you click any of them, you'll see that the class "active" is properly applied, but the template of the components is not being displayed. Let's fix it.

Right now, the content of app.component.html is this only line:

```
<app-navbar></app-navbar>
```

After that line, we need to add the following:

```
<router-outlet></router-outlet>
```

This line represents a placeholder that Angular dynamically fills with the output of the component being called.

Now the links should work as expected.

Services

A service is responsible for communicating with endpoints that provide data. Our services will be responsible for sending get, post, put, or patch requests to an API endpoint.

Processes that involve communication with an API are inherently asynchronous. Therefore, we must have means to notify us of the moment when the data is available.

We can create a new service with the following command:

```
ng g s services/reqres
```

Since the services folder does not exist, angular-cli will create it for us. Let's execute the command.

A service folder has been created, and in it we have a file named reqres.service.ts:

```
import { Injectable } from '@angular/core';

@Injectable({
 providedIn: 'root'
})
export class ReqresService {

 constructor() {}
}
```

That is the basic structure of a service. Now, unlike what happens with the components, angular-cli does not add the necessary imports or declarations in app. module.ts so we must do it ourselves.

In app.module.ts, we have the following array:

```
imports: [
   BrowserModule,
   AppRoutingModule
 ],
```

We must add the module HttpClientModule to the imports section:

```
imports: [
   BrowserModule,
   AppRoutingModule,
   HttpClientModule
 ],
```

If we are using an IDE as VS Code, the necessary import statement will have been automatically added. If this were not the case, we must add it:

```
import { HttpClientModule } from '@angular/common/http';
```

An Interface for Users

To facilitate the control of types as well as the exchange of data between our application and the endpoint from which we obtain them, we will use a resource that we have used previously, that is, an interface.

Inside the app directory, let's create a file called user.ts with the following content:

```
export interface User {
    id: number;
    first_name: string;
    last_name: string;
    avatar: string;
}
```

API

In order to have data to work with, we need someone to provide it. In a real scenario, this function would be fulfilled by an external API. However, for our purposes, we will simulate a communication with an external server using the in-memory Web API module, which is a third-party module. Here (https://github.com/angular/angular/tree/main/packages/misc/angular-in-memory-web-api) you can find the repo.

The function of this module is to intercept requests made using the HttpClient, effectively simulating communication with a server.

To install this module, we use the command:

```
npm install angular-in-memory-web-api@0.14.0 --save
```

Important   The part with the @ points to a particular version of the package which, at the time of this writing, is compatible with the version of Angular. The version of the package you need to use could be different.

After the installation is complete, we will do two imports in the AppModule. The newly installed module and a class that we will create in a few moments:

```
import { HttpClientInMemoryWebApiModule } from 'angular-in-memory-web-api';
import { InMemoryDataService } from './services/in-memory-data.service';
```

Important   We are importing a service we have not yet defined, so the compiler should throw an error. We'll fix it later.

Then we'll add the following to the Imports array of the AppModule:

```
HttpClientInMemoryWebApiModule.forRoot(
  InMemoryDataService, { dataEncapsulation: false }
)
```

Again, we will see a compile error because the service is not defined.

Just to be safe, here is the full Imports array:

```
imports: [
    BrowserModule,
    AppRoutingModule,
    HttpClientModule,
    HttpClientInMemoryWebApiModule.forRoot(
      InMemoryDataService, { dataEncapsulation: false }
    )
  ]
```

After adding the InMemoryDataService, you may get a compiler error because we haven't defined the class yet. This error will go away.

Our next step is to define the InMemoryDataService class. For this, we will use the following command:

```
ng g s services/InMemoryData
```

Let's replace the content of the file with the following:

```
import { Injectable } from '@angular/core';
import { InMemoryDbService } from 'angular-in-memory-web-api';
import { User } from '../user';

@Injectable({
  providedIn: 'root',
})
export class InMemoryDataService implements InMemoryDbService {
```

```
  createDb() {
    const users = [
      { id: 11, first_name: 'Eve', last_name: 'Holt',
avatar: 'assets/img/user.jpg' },
      { id: 12, first_name: 'Charles', last_name: 'Morris',
avatar: 'assets/img/user.jpg' },
      { id: 13, first_name: 'Tracy', last_name: 'Ramos',
avatar: 'assets/img/user.jpg' },
      { id: 14, first_name: 'Eve', last_name: 'Holt',
avatar: 'assets/img/user.jpg' },
      { id: 15, first_name: 'Charles', last_name: 'Morris',
avatar: 'assets/img/user.jpg' },
      { id: 16, first_name: 'Tracy', last_name: 'Ramos',
avatar: 'assets/img/user.jpg' },
      { id: 17, first_name: 'Eve', last_name: 'Holt',
avatar: 'assets/img/user.jpg' },
      { id: 18, first_name: 'Charles', last_name: 'Morris',
avatar: 'assets/img/user.jpg' },
      { id: 19, first_name: 'Tracy', last_name: 'Ramos',
avatar: 'assets/img/user.jpg' },
      { id: 20, first_name: 'Eve', last_name: 'Holt',
avatar: 'assets/img/user.jpg' }
    ];
    return {users};
  }

  genId(users: User[]): number {
    return users.length > 0 ? Math.max(...users.map(user => user.id))
    + 1 : 11;
  }
}
```

As you can see, we are using an image stored in our local system in order for this to work. We need to create an img folder inside the assets folder and put inside this new folder an image called user.jpg. You can use any image you like, or you can download my profile picture from here (https://github.com/Apress/The-Beginning-Angular-by-Victor-Hugo-Garcia/blob/main/images/user.jpg).

Just to make sure, here is the corresponding file (https://github.com/Apress/The-Beginning-Angular-by-Victor-Hugo-Garcia/blob/main/Chapter-03/05-in-memory-data.service.ts).

We are going to start working on our service to make a request to an API endpoint. Remember, this is the ReqRes service that we created before.

As a first measure, we must inject in our constructor a variable of type HttpClient that will allow us to carry out the requests:

```
constructor( private http: HttpClient ) { }
```

We must have the corresponding import:

```
import { HttpClient } from '@angular/common/http';
```

A detail to keep in mind regarding properties declarations. What we did earlier in the constructor is equivalent to the following:

```
private http: HttpClient;
```

```
constructor(  ) { }
```

Let's add a variable that points to the base of our endpoints:

```
private url = 'api/users';
```

We are now going to define a very rudimentary function that returns a list of users:

```
getUsers(): Observable<User[]> {
    return this.http.get<User[]>(this.url);
}
```

For this to work, you must have the following imports:

```
import { Observable } from 'rxjs';
import { User } from '../user';
```

The body of the function contains a single line of code. The http variable makes a get request to the API endpoint to obtain data that contains a list of users.

All HttpClient methods return an Observable.

An observable is a method of communication through messages, between a sender, known as a publisher, and a receiver, known as a subscriber. Observables are fancy ways to handle asynchronous communication.

By defining a function that returns an observable, we are declaring a function that publishes data, but doesn't run until someone subscribes to the observable.

The advantage of using an observable is that it will be monitoring changes in the data flow, and these changes will be informed to all subscribers. It will become clearer soon.

Also, note that it is expected to receive an array of User type elements, with which we are already making our interface useful.

The code of reqres.service.ts at this point should look as follows:

```
import { HttpClient } from '@angular/common/http';
import { Injectable } from '@angular/core';
import { Observable } from 'rxjs';
import { User } from '../user';

@Injectable({
  providedIn: 'root'
})
export class ReqresService {
  private url = 'api/users';

  constructor( private http: HttpClient ) { }

  getUsers(): Observable<User[]> {
    return this.http.get<User[]>(this.url);
  }

  getUser( id: number ): Observable<User> {
    const url = `${this.url}/${id}`;

    return this.http.get<User>(url);
  }
}
```

Let's put our service to the test from HomeComponent.

First, let's inject the service into the constructor:

```
constructor( private reqresService: ReqresService ) { }
```

Now, let's add a method that gets a list of users using the service:

```
getUsers() {
    this.reqresService.getUsers().subscribe(
      (res: User[]) => {
        console.log(res);
      },
      (err) => {
        console.error(err);
      }
    );
  }
```

We must add the import of our interface:

```
import { User } from '../../user';
```

Within the function, we subscribe to the service with subscribe. This method takes two parameters, both arrow functions.

The first is the one that will be executed when the service has published data (in this case, represented by the variable res, although it could be called in any way), while the second will be executed when a problem has occurred.

At this time, the function is not being called. Let's modify the constructor as follows:

```
constructor( private reqresService: ReqresService ) {
    this.getUsers();
 }
```

If we use the developer tools, we can see the output in the console (Figure 3-15).

Figure 3-15. Service output

We are going to define a variable that will help us to contain our users:

```
users: User[] = [];
```

Now we can rewrite the getUser function of the HomeComponent as follows:

```
getUsers() {
    this.reqresService.getUsers().subscribe(
      (res: User[]) => {
        this.users = res;
      },
      (err) => {
```

```
      console.error(err);
    }
  );
}
```

Now we are going to modify the content of home.component.html to have a quick output:

```
<ul>
  <li *ngFor="let user of users">
    <h1>{{ user.first_name}} {{ user.last_name }}</h1>
  </li>
</ul>
```

We have a for loop in our li element. Therefore, this element will be repeated for every element in the loop. In this cycle, we define a user variable that will take the value of each element of the users property for each cycle of the loop.

Then we simply generate an h1 tag showing the user's first and last name. The output in the browser is shown in Figure 3-16.

. George Bluth

. Janet Weaver

. Emma Wong

Figure 3-16. *User list*

It looks pretty bad, but at least we know that the data is being received correctly.

Now let's give it a little flair. Let's copy the following into the home.component. css file:

```
ul {
  list-style-type: none;
  margin: 0;
  padding: 0;
}
```

```css
ul li {
    background: rgb(238, 238, 238);
    padding: 2em;
    border-radius: 4px;
    margin-bottom: 7px;
    display: grid;
    grid-template-columns: 60px auto;
}

ul li p {
    font-weight: bold;
    margin-left: 20px;
}

ul li img {
    border-radius: 50%;
    width: 100%;
}
```

An important aspect to note is that when working in the style sheet that is associated with the home component, the styles that we include will only affect the elements found in the template of our component.

Therefore, any unordered list that we define outside the component will not be affected by the styles determined here.

If we want to define global styles, we must do it in the styles.css file.

Now let's add the users image to our list at home.component.html:

```html
<ul>
    <li *ngFor="let user of users">
        <img [src]="user.avatar">
        <p>{{ user.first_name }} {{ user.last_name }}</p>
    </li>
</ul>
```

The browser output is now shown in Figure 3-17.

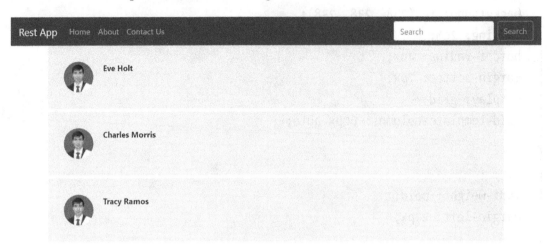

Figure 3-17. *User list*

Better. We have our list of users in a nice list. We now need a way to view the details of an individual user. Let's do it with a button:

```
<ul>
    <li *ngFor="let user of users">
        <img [src]="user.avatar">
        <p>{{ user.first_name }} {{ user.last_name }}</p>
        <div style="padding-top: 5px; width: 18rem;">
            <button class="btn btn-outline-primary"
            (click)="userDetails(user.id)">
                Details
            </button>
        </div>
    </li>
</ul>
```

Let's pay attention to the following code snippet:

```
(click)="userDetails(user.id)"
```

What we do here is tell Angular that it must be aware of the click event on the button element, and in response to this event, it must call a userDetails function that receives the user's id as a parameter. However, this function is not yet defined, so if we click the button, we will get an error. Let's now add this function to home.component.ts:

```
userDetails( id: number ) {
   console.log( 'User id: ', id );
 }
```

We will simply send the value of the received id to the console. Let's see the result (Figure 3-18).

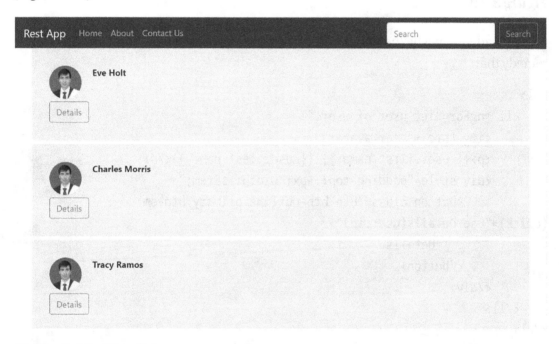

Figure 3-18. *User list*

If we now click the button, we'll see that the function is called, and it shows the user id (Figure 3-19).

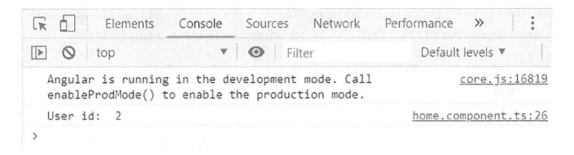

Figure 3-19. *User id*

Not bad, but maybe the buttons are too big in relation to the photos. Let's remedy that:

```
<ul>
    <li *ngFor="let user of users">
        <img [src]="user.avatar">
        <p>{{ user.first_name }} {{ user.last_name }}</p>
        <div style="padding-top: 5px; width: 18rem;">
            <button class="btn btn-outline-primary btn-sm"
(click)="userDetails(user.id)">
                Details
            </button>
        </div>
    </li>
</ul>
```

What we have done is add the btn-sm class to the button (Figure 3-20).

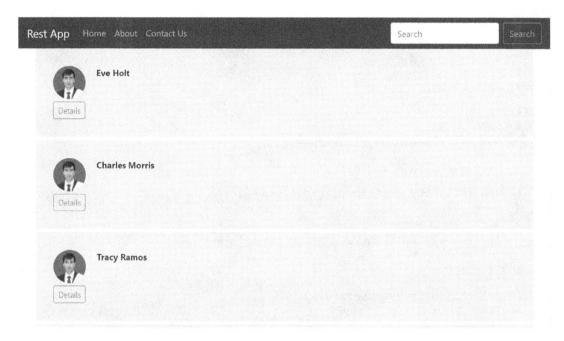

Figure 3-20. *Smaller buttons*

I think it looks a lot better.

Let's add in our service the function that will be in charge of making the request to obtain information from a user based on their id:

```
getUser( id: number ): Observable<User> {
    const url = `${this.url}/${id}`;

    return this.http.get<User>(url);
  }
```

It receives as a parameter an id, which will always be of the numeric type, and it will make the corresponding request, which in this case is also of the get type.

Let's take a little pause here to consider a bit of refactoring. The two functions present in our service are currently seen as follows:

At this point, I include for security the complete code of our service:

```
import { HttpClient } from '@angular/common/http';
import { Injectable } from '@angular/core';
import { Observable } from 'rxjs';
import { User } from '../user';
```

```
@Injectable({
  providedIn: 'root'
})
export class ReqresService {
  private url = 'api/users';

  constructor( private http: HttpClient ) { }

  getUsers(): Observable<User[]> {
    return this.http.get<User[]>(this.url);
  }

  getUser( id: number ): Observable<User> {
    const url = `${this.url}/${id}`;

    return this.http.get<User>(url);
  }
}
```

and its corresponding file (https://github.com/Apress/The-Beginning-Angular
-by-Victor-Hugo-Garcia/blob/main/Chapter-03/06-reqres.service.ts):

Next, we will create a new component that will be in charge of displaying the details
of a selected user. But this time we are going to proceed slightly differently. Let's first
create, inside the components directory, a new folder called user. Then we execute the
following command:

```
ng g c components/user/user-detail --flat
```

The --flat flag tells angular-cli that we don't want to create a new directory. The
reason for proceeding here is that we will group all the components related to a user in
this user directory.

The result will be as shown in Figure 3-21.

Figure 3-21. *UserDetailComponent*

Our UserDetail component will be where the information of an individual user will be displayed.

This is a new route for our application, and therefore we must make modifications to our app.routes.ts file. So far, the path arrangement is as follows:

```
const ROUTES: Routes = [
    { path: '', component: HomeComponent },
    { path: 'about', component: AboutComponent },
    { path: 'contact', component: ContactComponent },
    { path: '**', component: HomeComponent },
];
```

We need a new route that takes us to the details of the user, and this route will receive the user's id as a parameter:

```
const ROUTES: Routes = [
    { path: '', component: HomeComponent },
    { path: 'about', component: AboutComponent },
    { path: 'contact', component: ContactComponent },
    { path: 'user/:id', component: UserDetailComponent },
    { path: '**', component: HomeComponent },
];
```

Note the form of the path, 'user/:id'. We have a ':id' that works as a placeholder that will later be replaced by a value.

If our IDE has not done it for us, we must import the corresponding component:

```
import { UserDetailComponent } from './components/user/user-detail.
component';
```

Now it is time to put our attention precisely on the UserDetail component. There we need access to the id parameter. For that, we need to inject a variable of the type ActivatedRoute. We'll also inject the service:

```
constructor( private activatedRoute: ActivatedRoute,
private reqresService: ReqresService ) {}
```

Perfect. We also need a variable that contains the user that the service will return:

```
user: User = {
    id: 0,
    first_name: '',
    last_name: '',
    avatar: ''
};
```

And we need the corresponding import:

```
import { User } from '../../user';
```

We need to initialize the property, either upon declaration or in the constructor.
And now let's rewrite the constructor:

```
constructor(
    private activatedRoute: ActivatedRoute,
    private reqresService: ReqresService
) {
    this.activatedRoute.params.subscribe((params) => {
      reqresService.getUser(params ['id'])
        .subscribe((res: User) => this.user = res);
    });
}
```

ActivatedRoute is an interface that contains information on a route associated with a component. The "params" property is an Observable, and as such we can subscribe to it.

The observable, if executed successfully, will return a function whose argument is an array of all received parameters.

Then, it is a matter of using our service to obtain the information of the selected user, remembering at all times that our service will always return an Observable because it is executed asynchronously.

Of course, we must verify that we have the necessary imports:

```
import { ActivatedRoute } from '@angular/router';
import { ReqresService } from '../../services/reqres.service';
```

We have defined a route that expects a parameter and the logic that processes said parameter. But now we need to program the logic that leads from our HomeComponent to UserDetailComponent. At the moment, we have a userDetails function defined as follows:

```
userDetails( id: number ) {
    console.log( 'User id: ', id );
 }
```

To navigate to a new page – and its associated component – we need as a first measure to inject a variable of type Router. In home.component.ts, rewrite the constructor as follows:

```
constructor( private reqresService: ReqresService, private router:
Router ) {
    this.getUsers();
 }
```

and the import:

```
import { Router } from '@angular/router';
```

We are able to modify the userDetails function:

```
userDetails( id: number ) {
    this.router.navigate( ['user', id] );
 }
```

Now we can work on the component template. To do this, we are going to use a nice Bootstrap component called Card (Figure 3-22).

Figure 3-22. *Card*

Let's copy the first example that appears in the Bootstrap documentation:

```
<div class="card" style="width: 18rem;">
    <img src="..." class="card-img-top" alt="...">
    <div class="card-body">
        <h5 class="card-title">Card title</h5>
        <p class="card-text">Some quick example text to build on the card
        title and make up the bulk of the card's content.</p>
        <a href="#" class="btn btn-primary">Go somewhere</a>
    </div>
</div>
```

Let's modify this code to serve our purposes:

```
<div class="card" style="width: 18rem;">
    <img [src]="user.avatar" class="card-img-top img-thumb" [alt]="user.
    first_name">
    <div class="card-body">
```

```
        <h5 class="card-title">{{user.first_name}}</h5>
        <p class="card-text">Some quick example text to build on the card
        title and make up the bulk of the card's content.</p>
        <a href="#" class="btn btn-primary">User List</a>
    </div>
</div>
```

If we now click the Details button, we will see something like Figure 3-23.

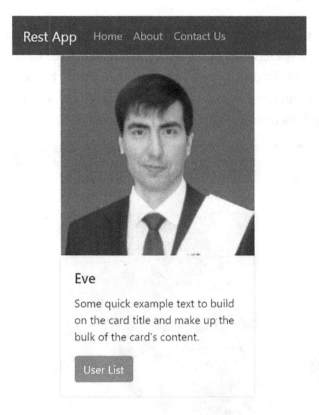

Figure 3-23. *User detail*

It works, but it looks too close to the edges. Let's fix that:

```
<div class="container" style="margin-top: 40px;">
    <div class="card" style="width: 18rem;">
        <img [src]="user.avatar"
class="card-img-top img-thumb"
[alt]="user.first_name">
```

```
    <div class="card-body">
        <h5 class="card-title">{{user.first_name}}</h5>
        <p class="card-text">Some quick example text to build on the
        card title and make up the bulk of the card's content.</p>
        <a href="#" class="btn btn-primary">User List</a>
    </div>
  </div>
</div>
```

We put all the content inside a div with the container and m-5 classes. In bootstrap, containers are the basic elements of the layout and can be fixed or fluid. When using the container class, we will obtain an element with a fixed width, but whose value for the max-width property will change with each breakpoint. Then we add a margin at the top to make everything look neater (Figure 3-24).

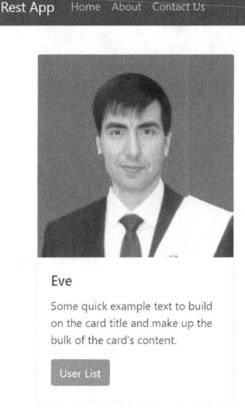

Figure 3-24. *User detail*

Let's now work on some details.

First, we are going to replace the text below the user's name with some text that acts as a filler representing a bio.

It is common to find dummy text known as lorem ipsum on websites that are under development.

This Latin text is used for the client to whom the design is being presented to concentrate on the layout without being distracted by readable pieces of text (unless, of course, they understand Latin). This brings us to the following website:

`www.lipsum.com/`

We can find the lorem ipsum generator in Figure 3-25.

humour, or randomised words which don't look even slightly believable. If you are going to use a passage of Lorem Ipsum, you need to be sure there isn't anything embarrassing hidden in the middle of text. All the Lorem Ipsum generators on the Internet tend to repeat predefined chunks as necessary, making this the first true generator on the Internet. It uses a dictionary of over 200 Latin words, combined with a handful of model sentence structures, to generate Lorem Ipsum which looks reasonable. The generated Lorem Ipsum is therefore always free from repetition, injected humour, or non-characteristic words etc.

- paragraphs
- words   5
- bytes
- lists

☑ Start with 'Lorem ipsum dolor sit amet...'

Generate Lorem Ipsum

Figure 3-25. *Lorem ipsum generator*

Let's generate a one-paragraph text and use it in our card, as shown in Figure 3-26.

Figure 3-26. *User detail*

We already have a piece of text that looks more real, but now the problem is that the design is very vertical.

Let's change the layout of our user details page:

```
<div class="container" style="margin-top: 40px;">
    <div class="card" style="width: 100%;">
        <div class="card-body">
            <div class="row">
                <div class="col-4" style="text-align: center;">
                    <img [src]="user.avatar" class="card-img-top img-thumb"
[alt]="user.first_name">
                    <h5 class="card-title">{{user.first_name}}</h5>
            </div>
```

```
            <div class="col-8">
                <p class="card-text">Lorem ipsum pain sit amet,
                consectetur
adipiscing elit. Maecenas convallis sed elit ac sagittis. Integer facilisis
scelerisque erat quis finibus. Nunc euismod molesie eros, id semper
lacus euismod
tempus. Nulla at just id felis venenatis varius. Morbi eu rutrum nibh,
at tempor
quam.
Aenean interdum eu sapien ac sodales. Aenean ut gravida eros, id
tincidunt massa.
Vivamus accumsan pain nec malaise sagittis. Sed lobortis sit amet Ligula eu
molestie.
                            Nulla facilisi. Nam elit dui, rutrum nec massa nec,
volutpat gravida ante. Nulla tempus hate et interdum tincidunt.
Aliquam lacinia
ulcers pretium. Phasellus convallis consequat lacus sed suscipit.
Fusce annoy
lobortis lorem nec convallis.</p>
                <a href="#" class="btn btn-primary">User List</a>
            </div>
        </div>
      </div>
    </div>
</div>
```

The main change is that inside the card-body, we have added a row and inside it two columns. This way:

```
<div class="row">
    <div class="col-4">
        ...
    </div>
    <div class="col-8">
        ...
    </div>
</div>
```

Bootstrap uses a 12-column grid system, of which we are distributing 4 to the left and 8 to the right. The result should be as shown in Figure 3-27.

Figure 3-27. User detail

Better. If we now click the User List button, we will return home, but that happens simply because it points to a nonexistent route, #, which activates the default route of our router:

```
{ path: '**', component: HomeComponent },
```

So we have to modify the link so that it has the desired behavior:

```
<a [routerLink]="['/home']" class="btn btn-primary">User List</a>
```

Now yes, it works as it should. However, there is another problem that we must take care of. If we now click any user to see their info, and depending on the connection, it may be that in the console we see something like Figure 3-28.

Figure 3-28. Null error

The problem lies in the availability of the user's image. Later, we will use a custom pipe to deal with situations where the user's image is missing, among others. But for the moment, let's modify the line where the image is shown as follows:

```
<img *ngIf="user.avatar" [src]="user.avatar" class="card-img-top img-thumb" [alt]="user.first_name">
```

We have added:

```
*ngIf="user.avatar"
```

The ngIf directive allows us to display a DOM element only when the expression passed to it evaluates to true – in this case, when the user's image exists.

For a similar reason, we will add a condition that will show the entire div only if we have a user:

```
<div *ngIf="user" class="container" style="margin-top: 40px;">
```

We are going to end this section with the file that has the complete code for our user screen:

user-detail.component.html (https://github.com/Apress/The-Beginning-Angular-by-Victor-Hugo-Garcia/blob/main/Chapter-03/07-user-detail.component.html)

and the code of the class of our component:

user-detail.component.ts (https://github.com/Apress/The-Beginning-Angular-by-Victor-Hugo-Garcia/blob/main/Chapter-03/08-user-detail.component.ts)

Summary

In this chapter, we learned how to generate a new project using angular-cli. We created new components and a service to communicate with a rest API. As for the purely aesthetic aspect, we saw how to include bootstrap in our application, although to tell the truth we did it in a way that may not be suitable for all cases, such as through CDNs. In the next chapter, we will learn how to include bootstrap using npm, the node package manager, and we will continue to add functionality to our application.

CHAPTER 4

RestApp Part 2

In the previous chapter, we included the fantastic Bootstrap framework in our application, in the fastest way possible, that is, using CDNs. However, we have an alternative, and it is to use the node package manager to install bootstrap. In this chapter, we'll learn how to use npm to install bootstrap. We'll also build a simple contact form, the logic to perform CRUD operations on our users, a loading component to improve the user experience, and a pipe to handle the case of missing user profile images. Then you can decide which of these two alternatives is the most convenient.

Let's start.

Bootstrap

Currently, our index.html looks like this:

```
<!doctype html>
<html lang="en">

<head>
    <meta charset="utf-8">
    <title>Rest</title>
    <base href="/">

    <meta name="viewport" content="width=device-width, initial-scale=1">
    <link rel="icon" type="image/x-icon" href="favicon.ico">

    <link rel="stylesheet"
    href="https://stackpath.bootstrapcdn.com/bootstrap/4.3.1/css/bootstrap.
    min.css"
    integrity="sha384-ggOyR0iXCbMQv3Xipma34MD+dH/1fQ784/j6cY/
    iJTQUOhcWr7x9JvoRxT2MZw1T"
```

© Victor Hugo Garcia 2023
V. H. Garcia, *Getting Started with Angular*, https://doi.org/10.1007/978-1-4842-9206-8_4

```
crossorigin="anonymous">
</head>

<body>
    <script src="https://code.jquery.com/jquery-3.3.1.slim.min.js"
    integrity="sha384-q8i/X+965DzO0rT7abK41JStQIAqVgRVzpbzo5smXKp4YfRvH+8abt
    TE1Pi6jizo"
crossorigin="anonymous"></script>
    <script
    src="https://cdnjs.cloudflare.com/ajax/libs/popper.js/1.14.7/umd/
    popper.min.js"
    integrity="sha384-UO2eT0CpHqdSJQ6hJty5KVphtPhzWj9WO1clHTMGa3JDZwrnQq4sF8
    6dIHNDzOW1"
    crossorigin="anonymous"></script>
    <script
    src="https://stackpath.bootstrapcdn.com/bootstrap/4.3.1/js/
    bootstrap.min.js"
    integrity="sha384-JjSmVgyd0p3pXB1rRibZUAYoIIy6OrQ6VrjIEaFf/
    nJGzIxFDsf4xOxIM+B07jRM"
    crossorigin="anonymous"></script>

    <app-root></app-root>
</body>

</html>
```

Let's remove the references to bootstrap, popper, and jQuery:

```
<!doctype html>
<html lang="en">

<head>
    <meta charset="utf-8">
    <title>Rest</title>
    <base href="/">

    <meta name="viewport" content="width = device-width, initial-scale = 1">
    <link rel="icon" type="image/x-icon" href="favicon.ico">
</head>
```

```
<body>
    <app-root> </app-root>
</body>

</html>
```

Our application will now look like Figure 4-1.

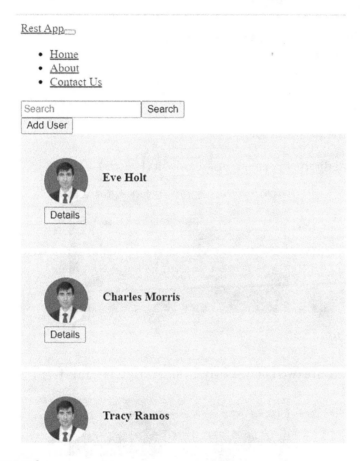

Figure 4-1. *No styles*

Now open a new instance of your terminal, or use the terminal of your IDE, and type the following command:

```
npm install bootstrap@4.6.0 --save
```

This will give us the output shown in Figure 4-2.

Figure 4-2. *Installing Bootstrap*

After installing bootstrap, it's jQuery's turn:

```
npm install jquery --save
```

and finally popper:

```
npm install popper.js --save
```

We must now edit the file called angular.json (Figure 4-3).

{} tslint.json
⚙ .editorconfig
◆ .gitignore
{} angular.json
{} package-lock.json
{} package.json

Figure 4-3. *angular.json*

In this file, there are two changes, styles and scripts (Figure 4-4).

```
"styles": [
  "src/styles.css"
],
"scripts": [],
```

Figure 4-4. *Styles and scripts*

Let's modify these two arrays:

```
"styles": [
        "src/styles.css",
        "node_modules/bootstrap/dist/css/bootstrap.min.css"
      ],
```

128

```
"scripts": [
              "node_modules/popper.js/dist/umd/popper.min.js",
              "node_modules/jquery/dist/jquery.slim.min.js",
              "node_modules/bootstrap/dist/js/bootstrap.min.js"
        ],
```

Now, we probably do not notice any changes in the way our application is viewed yet. We must stop the Angular development server from the terminal where it is running with Ctrl+C and then restart it with ng serve. At this time, we will have recovered the styles of our application.

AboutComponent

For our About page, we simply use the lorem ipsum generator to give us two paragraphs of text. In addition, we enclose these paragraphs with a container. In about.component. html, add:

```
<div class="container">
   <p>Lorem ipsum pain sit amet, consectetur adipiscing elit. Nulla
   mollis metus
vel velit cursus porta. Ut id enim mollis orci tempus euismod. Praesent
tristique
augue sit amet pain ullamcorper auctor. Pellentesque at nulla ut
nulla dapibus
dignissim
       nec non nisi. Curabitur bibendum velit a erat iaculis, blandit
       congue sapien
ornare. In thirsty fritilla elit. Sed quis aliquet orci. Mauris
massa augue,
consectetur ut cursus sit amet, dictum in eros. Nam mauris hate,
condimentum vel
pulvinar nec, egestas tincidunt nulla. Quisque a massa facilisis,
lacinia purus et, dapibus ante.</p>

   <p>Aliquam erat volutpat. Cras cursus accumsan mauris, eget lacinia
   ex iaculis
```

```
id. Sed sodales nisl ac venenatis porta. Nullam posuere quis quam in
porta. Nunc
unfortunate pulvinar urn, vitae lobortis ex annoying non. Nullam
vestibulum,
lectus in
luctus
        fringilla, dui neque pretium diam, vel ullamcorper lectus
        felis vitae
magna. Fusce vitae ligula faucibus, mattis erat eleifend, pretium
felis. In hac
habitasse
platea dictumst. Cras vitae sapien faucibus, posuere erat sed, congue
erat. Aliquam
        ornare ullamcorper just eget mollis. Aliquam eu bibendum enim, vel
        faucibus
diam. Maecenas felis nibh, tempus pretium est in, suscipit semper neque.
Fusce felis
arcu, venenatis ac mauris sed, vehicula egestas tortor. Aenean eu enim
ulcorcorper,
        condimentum lectus sit amet, lobortis erat. Vestibulum rhoncus
        magna mi,
vel posuere orci vehicula sit amet.</p>
</div>
```

It will give us a very simple page (Figure 4-5).

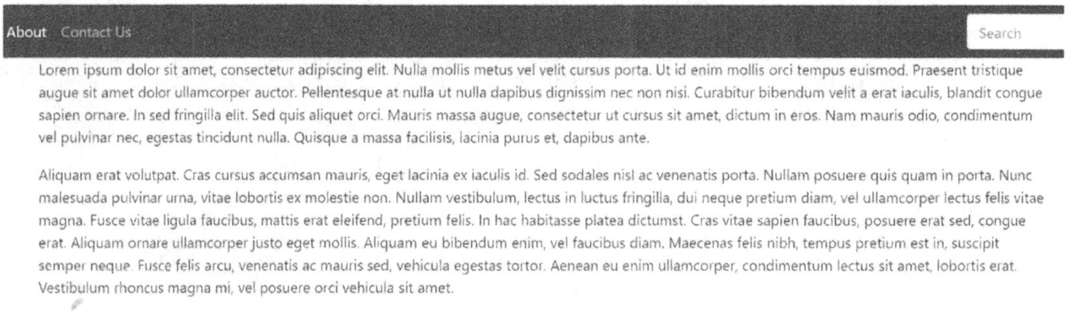

Figure 4-5. *AboutComponent*

Forms: ContactComponent

As the first media, in app.module.ts add the following import:

```
import { ReactiveFormsModule, FormsModule } from '@angular/forms';
```

These modules will allow us to easily build forms. But to be able to use them, we must add them in the imports array:

```
imports: [
    BrowserModule,
    AppRoutingModule,
    HttpClientModule,
    HttpClientInMemoryWebApiModule.forRoot(
      InMemoryDataService, { dataEncapsulation: false, delay: 1500 }
    ),
    ReactiveFormsModule,
    FormsModule
],
```

Let's continue with contact.component.ts. At this moment, it has the following content:

```
import { Component, OnInit } from '@angular/core';

@Component({
 selector: 'app-contact',
 templateUrl: './contact.component.html',
 styleUrls: ['./contact.component.css']
})
export class ContactComponent implements OnInit {

 constructor() {}

 ngOnInit() {
 }

}
```

Let's add the following imports:

```
import { FormBuilder, FormGroup, Validators } from '@angular/forms';
```

We now need to add three properties:

```
messageForm: FormGroup;
submitted = false;
success = false;
```

The first one will represent our entire form, and the following ones will serve to indicate if the form has been sent and if the validation has been successful.

Then we must inject a variable of type FormBuilder in the constructor:

```
constructor( private formBuilder: FormBuilder ) {}
```

We will use this property to define the properties of our form:

```
constructor( private formBuilder: FormBuilder ) {
  this.messageForm = this.formBuilder.group({
    name: ['', Validators.required],
    message: ['', Validators.required]
  });
}
```

Finally, we need a method that will be executed when the form is sent:

```
onSubmit() {
  this.submitted = true;

  if (this.messageForm.invalid) {
      return;
  }

  this.success = true;
}
```

For now, our function simply changes the value of the property submitted to true. Then, if the validation is not successful, the method returns; otherwise, the success variable takes the value true.

Now let's define our form. In contact.component.html, add:

```
<div class="container" style="margin-top: 40px;">
```

```
<form [formGroup]="messageForm" (ngSubmit)="onSubmit()">

    <h5 *ngIf="success">Your form is valid!</h5>

    <div class="form-group">
        <label for="name">Name:</label>
        <input type="text" formControlName="name" class="form-control">
        <div *ngIf="submitted && messageForm.controls['name'].errors"
        class="error">
            <div *ngIf="messageForm.controls['name'].
            errors['required']">
                Your name is required
            </div>
        </div>

    </div>

    <div class="form-group">
        <label for="message">Message:</label>
        <textarea formControlName="message" class="form-control">
        </textarea>
        <div *ngIf="submitted && messageForm.controls
        ['message'].errors"
        class="error">
            <div *ngIf="messageForm.controls['message'].errors
            ['required']">
                A message is required
            </div>
        </div>

    </div>

    <button type="submit" class="btn btn-primary">Send message</button>
</form>

<div *ngIf="submitted" class="results">
    <p> <strong>Name: </strong>
        <span>{{messageForm.controls['name'].value}}</span> </p>
```

```
    <p> <strong>Message: </strong>
        <span>{{messageForm.controls['message'].value}}</span> </p>
  </div>
</div>
```

Finally, let's add the following styles in contact.component.css:

```
.error {
  margin-top: -10px;
  color: network;
  padding: .5em;
  display: inline-block;
  font-size: .9em;
  margin-bottom: 10px;
}
```

This will give us the output shown in Figure 4-6.

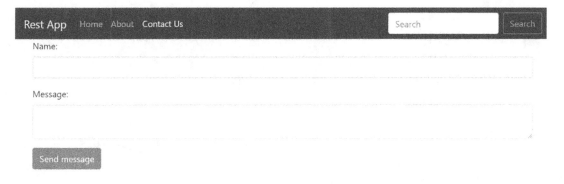

Figure 4-6. *Form*

If we try to send the form without completing the required fields, we will obtain the errors shown in Figure 4-7.

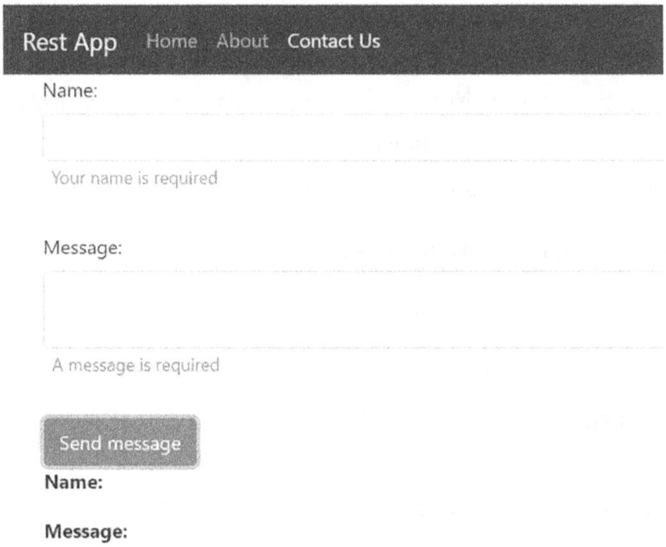

Figure 4-7. *Form errors*

Let's make a small aesthetic change. Let's add a small margin to the container:

```
<div class="container" style="margin-top: 40px;">
```

With this, we have finished most of the aesthetics, so now we can concentrate on improving the app reliability.

Error Handling

So far, we have been quite optimistic when it comes to the availability of our data. But when we are working with a remote server, there is a possibility that the data does not arrive for different reasons. Since our ReqRes service is in charge of communicating with the server, that is where we should include error handling.

Our method of getting all users currently looks like this:

```
getUsers(): Observable<User[]> {
    return this.http.get<User[]>(this.url);
  }
```

It returns an Observable, that is, a data stream that will be activated when someone has subscribed to it. There is a library, RxJs, that provides a series of very useful operators to manipulate the flow of data from an Observable before it is sent to subscribers. One of them is the **pipe** operator, which allows us to pass the data through different operators that are chained together to manipulate the output. Another operator is **catchError**, which fires when the output of an Observable fails.

Let's add the following amount to our service:

```
import { catchError, map } from 'rxjs/operators';
```

Now let's rewrite the getUsers method as follows:

```
getUsers(): Observable<User[]> {
    return this.http.get<User[]>(this.url)
      .pipe(
        catchError(this.handleError<User[]>('getUsers', []))
      );
  }
```

We are using the pipe operator to chain the output through other operators, in this case catchError. When the Observable fails, catchError will catch that failure and send the error to the function we define within the operator – in this case, a handleError function that we have not defined yet, but we will do it next. Before we have to change the import:

```
import { Observable } from 'rxjs';
```

by

```
import { Observable, of } from 'rxjs';
```

and now our function:

```
private handleError<T>(operation = 'operation', result?: T): any {
    return (error: any): Observable<T> => {

      // TODO: send the error to remote logging infrastructure
      console.error(error); // log to console instead

      // Let the app keep running by returning an empty result.
      return of(result as T);
    };
  }
```

This method receives two parameters, the operation that failed and optionally a result that will be returned instead of the expected output.

The operation has not been affected, but working with remote data, our service will be ready to deal with the problems that may arise.

Now let's rewrite the method that a user gets from its id:

```
getUser( id: number ): Observable<User> {
    const url = `${this.url}/${id}`;

    return this.http.get<User>(url)
      .pipe(
        catchError(this.handleError<User>(`getUser id=${id}`))
      );
  }
```

Update a User

One of the advantages of using the in-memory Web API module is that we can simulate CRUD operations on the data collections that we define. We are going to test this by adding the functionality to edit a user's name.

Just to be sure, at this point, our user-detail.component.ts should look like this:

```
import { Component, OnInit } from '@angular/core';
import { ActivatedRoute } from '@angular/router';
import { ReqresService } from '../../services/reqres.service';
import { User } from '../../user';

@Component({
  selector: 'app-user-detail',
  templateUrl: './user-detail.component.html',
  styleUrls: ['./user-detail.component.css']
})
export class UserDetailComponent implements OnInit {
  user: User = {
    id: 0,
    first_name: '',
    last_name: '',
```

```
    avatar: ''
  };

  constructor(
    private activatedRoute: ActivatedRoute,
    private reqresService: ReqresService
  ) {
    this.activatedRoute.params.subscribe((params) => {
      reqresService.getUser(params ['id'])
        .subscribe((res: User) => this.user = res);
    });
  }

  ngOnInit() {
  }

}
```

Now let's modify the view of the user detail (user-detail.component.html) as follows:

```html
<div *ngIf="user" class="container" style="margin-top: 40px;">
    <div class="card" style="width: 100%;">
        <div class="card-body">
            <div class="row">
                <div class="col-4" style="text-align: center;">
                    <img *ngIf="user.avatar" [src]="user.avatar"
                    class="card-img-top img-thumb" [alt]="user.first_name">
                    <h5 class="card-title">{{user.first_name}}</h5>
                    <div class="form-inline">
                        <label for="user-name">Name: </label>
                        <input id="user-name" [(ngModel)]="user.first_name"
                        placeholder="name" class="form-control">
                        <button (click)="save()" class="btn btn-success">
                        Save</button>
                    </div>
                </div>
                <div class="col-8">
```

```
                <p class="card-text">Lorem ipsum pain sit amet,
consectetur
adipiscing elit. Maecenas convallis sed elit ac sagittis.
Integer facilisis scelerisque erat quis finibus. Nunc euismod molesie eros,
id semper lacus euismod tempus.
Nulla at just id felis venenatis
                    varius. Morbi eu rutrum nibh, at tempor
quam. Aenean
interdum eu sapien ac sodales. Aenean ut gravida eros, id tincidunt massa.
Vivamus accumsan pain nec malaise sagittis. Sed lobortis sit amet Ligula eu
molestie. Nulla
facilisi.
                    Nam elit dui, rutrum nec massa nec, volutpat
gravida ante. Nulla tempus hate et interdum tincidunt. Aliquam lacinia
ulcers pretium.
Phasellus convallis consequat lacus sed suscipit. Fusce annoy lobortis
lorem nec convallis.</p>
                <a [routerLink]="['/home']" class="btn btn-
                primary">User List</a>
            </div>
        </div>
      </div>
    </div>
</div>
```

And here is the file:

https://github.com/Apress/The-Beginning-Angular-by-Victor-Hugo-Garcia/blob/
main/Chapter-04/01-user-detail.component.html

The view should look like Figure 4-8.

Lorem ipsum pain sit amet, consectetur adipiscing elit. Maecenas convallis sed elit ac sagittis. Integer facilisis scelerisque erat quis finibus. Nunc euismod molesie eros, id semper lacus euismod tempus. Nulla at just id felis venenatis varius. Morbi eu rutrum nibh, at tempor quam. Aenean interdum eu sapien ac sodales. Aenean ut gravida eros, id tincidunt massa. Vivamus accumsan pain nec malaise sagittis. Sed lobortis sit amet Ligula eu molestie. Nulla facilisi. Nam elit dui, rutrum nec massa nec, volutpat gravida ante. Nulla tempus hate et interdum tincidunt. Aliquam lacinia ulcers pretium. Phasellus convallis consequat lacus sed suscipit. Fusce annoy lobortis lorem nec convallis.

User List

Name: Charles   Save

Figure 4-8. *User update*

We have the possibility to modify the name of the user. The Save button for the moment calls a nonexistent method in our component. Now we will write it:

```
save(): void {
    this.reqresService.updateUser(this.user)
      .subscribe(() => this.router.navigate( ['users'] ));
  }
```

We need to inject a router variable in the constructor of UserDetailComponent:

```
private router: Router
```

And if our IDE has not done it for us, add the corresponding import:

```
import { ActivatedRoute, Router } from '@angular/router';
```

Now let's go back to our service. In reqres.service.ts, first change the import:

```
import { HttpClient } from '@angular/common/http';
```

to

```
import { HttpClient, HttpHeaders } from '@angular/common/http';
```

And now add the following property:

```
httpOptions = {
    headers: new HttpHeaders({ 'Content-Type': 'application/json' })
  };
```

We can now add the updateUser method:

```
updateUser(user: User): any {
    return this.http.put(this.url, user, this.httpOptions)
      .pipe(
        catchError(this.handleError<User>('updateUser'))
      );
  }
```

We define the httpOptions variable as follows:

```
httpOptions = {
    headers: new HttpHeaders({ 'Content-Type': 'application/json' })
  };
```

If we now modify the user's name and click Save, we will see how the data is updated (Figures 4-9 and 4-10), and the application returns to the list of users.

Figure 4-9. *User update*

Figure 4-10. *User updated*

Adding a New User

Let's now deal with the logic for adding a new user. First, we will add a button in the list of users that leads to a form in which we will enter the data of the new user.

Let's rewrite the home component view as follows:

```
<div class="btn-toolbar" role="toolbar">
    <div class="btn-group">
        <button class="btn btn-success" (click)="addUser()">Add
        User</button>
    </div>
</div>
<ul>
    <li *ngFor="let user of users">
        <img [src]="user.avatar">
        <p>{{ user.first_name }} {{ user.last_name }}</p>
        <div style="padding-top: 5px; width: 18rem;">
            <button class="btn btn-outline-primary btn-sm"
            (click)="userDetails(user.id)">
                Details
            </button>
        </div>
    </li>
</ul>
```

This will give us the button at the top. Notice that we are referencing an addUser method that does not exist yet. We will define it now:

```
addUser(): void {
    this.router.navigate( ['add'] );
  }
```

Both the route and the component that will be activated when that route is invoked do not yet exist. Let's start first by creating the new component:

```
ng g c components/user/user-add --flat
```

We must add the new route in app.routes.ts:

```
{ path: 'add', component: UserAddComponent },
```

without forgetting the corresponding import:

```
import { UserAddComponent } from './components/user/user-add.component';
```

In the section where we designed the contact page, we saw how to define a form, so we will not comment too much and just copy the code that will replace the content of our user-add.component.html:

```
<div class="container" style="margin-top: 40px;">
    <form [formGroup]="userForm" (ngSubmit)="onSubmit()">

        <div class="form-group">
            <label for="first_name">First Name:</label>
            <input type="text" formControlName="first_name" class="form-
            control">
            <div *ngIf="submitted && userForm.controls['first_
            name'].errors"
class="error">
                <div *ngIf="userForm.controls['first_name'].
                errors['required']">
                    Your first name is required
                </div>
            </div>
        </div>

    </div>
```

```
<div class="form-group">
    <label for="last_name">Last Name:</label>
    <input type="text" formControlName="last_name" class="form-
    control">
    <div *ngIf="submitted && userForm.controls['last_name'].errors"
    class="error">
        <div *ngIf="userForm.controls['last_name'].
        errors['required']">
            Your last name is required
        </div>
    </div>

</div>

    <button type="submit" class="btn btn-primary">Save</button>
</form>
</div>
```

And here is the file:

https://github.com/Apress/The-Beginning-Angular-by-Victor-Hugo-Garcia/blob/
main/Chapter-04/02-user-add.component.html

We have a simple form with two inputs. Submitting the form invokes an onSubmit method that of course we haven't created yet.

We will now start with the code for our class. First, let's add the necessary imports:

```
import { FormBuilder, FormGroup, Validators } from '@angular/forms';
import { Router } from '@angular/router';
import { ReqresService } from '../../services/reqres.service';
import { User } from '../../user';
```

Then we add a couple of properties:

```
userForm: FormGroup;
submitted = false;
```

And we reformulate our constructor:

```
constructor(
    private formBuilder: FormBuilder,
```

```
      private reqresService: ReqresService,
      private router: Router
) {
    this.userForm = this.formBuilder.group({
      first_name: ['', Validators.required],
      last_name: ['', Validators.required]
    });
  }
```

Then add a small method to access the controls of the form in a shortened way:

```
get f(): any { return this.userForm.controls; }
```

And finally add our onSubmit method:

```
onSubmit(): void {
    this.submitted = true;

    if (this.userForm.invalid) {
        return;
    }

    const avatar = 'assets/img/user.jpg';

    const first_name: string = this.f.first_name.value;

    const last_name: string = this.f.last_name.value;

    this.reqresService.addUser( { first_name, last_name, avatar } as User )
      .subscribe(() => this.router.navigate( ['users'] ));
  }
```

We verify that the form is valid, and if so, we proceed to call the addUser method of our service, which of course does not exist yet.

Let's go to our service and write the method, which at this point will be very familiar to us:

```
addUser( user: User ): Observable<User> {
    return this.http.post<User>(this.url, user, this.httpOptions)
```

```
    .pipe(
      catchError(this.handleError<User>('addUser'))
    );
}
```

If everything went well, we can add a new user (Figures 4-11 and 4-12) and see it in the list.

First Name:

Daniel

Last Name:

Goodman

Save

Figure 4-11. *Adding a user*

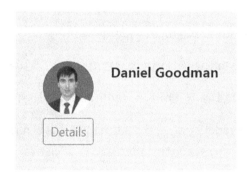

Figure 4-12. *Adding a user*

We have not included the functionality to upload an image, since we are simulating data from a server in memory, so we simply encode the avatar.

Deleting a User

First, we will add a button in our home component that allows us to delete a user. We will do it under the button that calls the detail view:

```
<button class="btn btn-danger btn-sm" title="Delete user"
(click)="deleteUser(user)">X</button>
```

This will look like Figure 4-13.

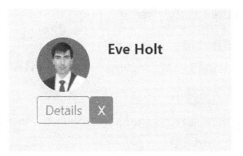

Figure 4-13. *Delete a user*

It is the turn now to add the deleteUser method in the HomeComponent:

```
deleteUser(user: any) {
    this.users = this.users.filter( u => u !== user );
    this.reqresService.deleteUser(user).subscribe();
  }
```

What we should note here is that although we are calling a deleteUser method of our service that will be in charge of the deletion, it is the responsibility of the component to update its own list of users.

Now in our ReqresService, let's add the method in charge of the elimination:

```
deleteUser( user: User ): Observable<User> {
    const url = `${this.url}/${user.id}`;

    return this.http.delete<User>(url, this.httpOptions)
      .pipe(
        catchError(this.handleError<User>('deleteUser id=${user.id}'))
      );
  }
```

Now we can select any of the users and delete it.

Loading

By default, our API returns the data with a delay of 500 ms to simulate latency, but in a real case, this time could be much longer. Let's simulate a slower response by altering the settings in our AppModule as follows:

```
HttpClientInMemoryWebApiModule.forRoot(
    InMemoryDataService, { dataEncapsulation: false, delay: 1500 }
  ),
```

We have introduced a delay of a second and a half, so it is very likely that we will end up with a blank screen (Figure 4-14).

Figure 4-14. *White screen*

From an interface point of view, it is not a good idea to display an idle screen when a process is in progress. It would be convenient to show a load indicator, to give feedback to our user.

We are going to do just that, for which we will use a great icon set such as Font Awesome.

Let's open the console and write the following command:

```
npm install --save-dev @fortawesome/fontawesome-free
```

We are using npm to install the package, just like we did with Bootstrap.

As you remember, we must modify the angular.json file, adding the following line:

```
"node_modules/@fortawesome/fontawesome-free/css/all.css"
```

after this one:

```
"node_modules/bootstrap/dist/css/bootstrap.min.css",
```

We will need to stop the angular-cli live server, pressing Ctrl+C, and restart it for the changes to be registered.

To verify that Font Awesome has been installed successfully, let's modify the home. component.html as follows:

```
<div class="row text-center">
    <div class="col">
        <i class="fa fa-sync fa-spin fa-5x" aria-hidden="true"> </i>
    </div>
</div>
<div class="btn-toolbar" role="toolbar">
    <div class="btn-group">
        <button class="btn btn-success" (click)="addUser()">Add
        User</button>
    </div>
</div>
<ul>
    <li *ngFor="let user of users">
        <img [src]="user.avatar">
        <p>{{ user.first_name }} {{ user.last_name }}</p>
        <div style="padding-top: 5px; width: 18rem;">
            <button class="btn btn-outline-primary btn-sm"
            (click)="userDetails(user.id)">
                Details
            </button>
            <button class="btn btn-danger btn-sm" title="Delete user"
            (click)="deleteUser(user)">X</button>
        </div>
    </li>
</ul>
```

The relevant section is as follows:

```
<div class="row text-center">
    <div class="col">
        <i class="fa fa-sync fa-spin fa-5x" aria-hidden="true"> </i>
    </div>
</div>
```

The result should be as shown in Figure 4-15.

Figure 4-15. *Loading*

We get a small animated image.

Now that we know that the installation was successful, let's create a component that displays while we wait for the data to load on the page:

```
ng g c components/shared/loading --style none
```

The --style none flag tells angular-cli not to create a style file for the component.

Let's replace the content of loading.component.html with:

```
<div class="row text-center">
    <div class="col">
        <i class="fa fa-sync fa-spin fa-5x" aria-hidden="true "></i>
    </div>
</div>
```

We can include the component in our home.component.html:

```
<app-loading> </app-loading>

<div class="container" style="margin-top: 40px;">
    <ul class="user-list">
        <li *ngFor="let user of users">
            <img [src]="user.avatar">
            <p>{{user.first_name}} {{user.last_name}}</p>
```

```
        <div style="padding-top: 5px; width: 18rem;">
            <button
              class="btn btn-outline-primary btn-sm"
              (click)="userDetails(user.id)">
              Details
            </button>
        </div>
    </li>
  </ul>

  <app-pager (pageSelected)="setPage($event)" [config]="config">
  </app-pager>
</div>
```

Of course, the idea is that the component is only displayed while the data is being received. To do this, we will add a loading property in our HomeComponent.

In home.component.ts, add:

```
loading: boolean = false;
```

And then in our getUsers method, add:

```
getUsers() {
    this.loading = true;

    this.reqresService.getUsers().subscribe(
      (res: User[]) => {
        this.users = res;
        this.loading = false;
      },
      (err) => {
        console.error(err);
      }
    );
  }
```

loading takes the value true when the function is entered and changes to false when the data is available. Now, to manipulate the visibility of our component, we modify the line:

```
<app-loading *ngIf="loading"></app-loading>
```

It will only be displayed as long as the data has not been received. Similarly, the rest of our page should behave in reverse. We will enclose the rest of the code in a container:

```
<div class="container pt-5" *ngIf="!loading">
    <div class="btn-toolbar" role="toolbar">
        <div class="btn-group">
            <button class="btn btn-success" (click)="addUser()">Add
            User</button>
        </div>
    </div>
    <ul>
        <li *ngFor="let user of users">
            <img [src]="user.avatar">
            <p>{{ user.first_name }} {{ user.last_name }}</p>
            <div style="padding-top: 5px; width: 18rem;">
                <button class="btn btn-outline-primary btn-sm"
                (click)="userDetails(user.id)">
                    Details
                </button>
                <button class="btn btn-danger btn-sm" title="Delete user"
                (click)="deleteUser(user)">X</button>
            </div>
        </li>
    </ul>
</div>
```

In this way, we will have a load indicator while the data is received.

Pipes

Every nontrivial application will at some point receive data that it must present to the user, and it will be difficult for that data to arrive in the most appropriate way to display it. We will need to format the data in a way that makes sense for our application. And it is also to be expected that these formats will be repeated in different parts.

To do this, Angular has a tool called "pipes." Pipes are elements that allow us to transform the way data is presented in the user interface. Angular has a large number of default pipes, the list of which can be found in

```
https://angular.io/api?type=pipe
```

The syntax of a pipe is basically the following:

```
data | pipe:params
```

That is, the data is sent to the pipe using the | and also the pipe can receive parameters that are entered with ":".

But in addition to the default pipes, Angular gives us the possibility to define our own pipes. We even have a command to generate the skeleton necessary to build it.

The pipe that we will build will help us deal with cases in which a user does not have a profile image.

Instead of getting an error in the console, indicating that the resource is not available, we will show an alternative image. You can download the image from here (`https://drive.google.com/open?id=1yEuXM4iOnZj7dgNCE2DmUsoCx9buU9Q0`).

In our project, we have an assets directory. Let's create there a new directory called img and copy the image into it (Figure 4-16).

Figure 4-16. *Noimage*

Now we will create our pipe with the following command:

```
ng g p pipes/noimage
```

This should create a pipes directory at the same height as the components directory. Inside this folder, we will have a file noimage.pipe.ts with the following content:

```
import { Pipe, PipeTransform } from '@angular/core';

@Pipe({
 name: 'noimage'
})
```

```
export class NoimagePipe implements PipeTransform {

  transform(value: any, args?: any): any {
    return null;
  }

}
```

The value argument represents the data that is sent to the pipe to be transformed. We also have an optional argument args.

Let's modify the pipe like this:

```
import { Pipe, PipeTransform } from '@angular/core';

@Pipe({
  name: 'noimage'
})
export class NoimagePipe implements PipeTransform {

  transform(image: any, args?: any): string {
    if (!image) {
      return 'assets/img/noimage.png';
    }

    return image;
  }

}
```

What this pipe does is check if an image exists. If not, a string corresponding to the address of our default image is returned.

Now in user-detail.component.html, we can replace the line where the user's image is included with the following:

```
<img [src]="user.avatar | noimage"
  class="card-img-top img-thumb"
  [alt]="user.first_name">
```

We can verify that our pipe works by intentionally sending a null value through it:

```
<img [src]="null | noimage" class="card-img-top img-thumb" [alt]="user.
first_name">
```

This will give us the output shown in Figure 4-17.

George

Lorem ipsum dolor sit amet, consectetur adipiscing elit. Maecenas convallis sed elit ac sagittis. Integer facilisis scelerisque erat quis finibus. Nunc euismod molestie eros, id semper lacus euismod tempus. Nulla at justo id felis venenatis varius. Morbi eu rutrum nibh, at tempor quam. Aenean interdum eu sapien ac sodales. Aenean ut gravida eros, id tincidunt massa. Vivamus accumsan dolor nec malesuada sagittis. Sed lobortis sit amet ligula eu molestie. Nulla facilisi. Nam elit dui, rutrum nec massa nec, volutpat gravida ante. Nulla tempus odio et interdum tincidunt. Aliquam lacinia ultrices pretium. Phasellus convallis consequat lacus sed suscipit. Fusce molestie lobortis lorem nec convallis.

User List

Figure 4-17. *Pipe*

Having verified that it works, let's return the line to its previous value:

```
<img [src]="user.avatar | noimage"
  class="card-img-top img-thumb"
  [alt]="user.first_name">
```

Now we can also use our pipe in the user list. In home.component.html, add:

```
<img [src]="user.avatar | noimage">
```

And in case that there is no profile image, the list will look as shown in Figure 4-18.

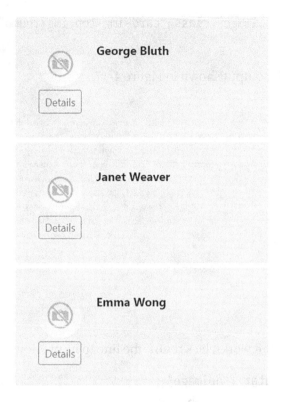

Figure 4-18. *Noimage*

Summary

In this chapter, we learned how to use npm to install Bootstrap. We also built a simple contact form, the logic to perform CRUD operations on our users, a loading component to improve the user experience, and a pipe to handle the case of missing user profile images. All this knowledge is a valuable piece that we can incorporate into projects of any complexity. And we have barely scratched the surface. In the next chapter, we will begin building a much more complex application.

CHAPTER 5

AuthApp

In practically all the applications that we develop, we must provide the registration and user login functionality.

This involves dealing with two concepts: authentication and authorization.

Authentication means recognizing if the user who tries to enter the application is who they claim to be. Authorization refers to restricting the user's access to certain parts of the application, according to their level of permission.

And it is also increasingly common – ubiquitous I would say – that both the login and the registration of users are done through social networks.

This functionality of the applications involves not a little time and effort if it is done from scratch. And everything becomes more tedious if we take into account that the code will be practically the same for each of these applications.

Therefore, having a way to standardize the authentication and authorization of users is a great advantage.

Fortunately, we have platforms that offer just that. And among them, Auth0 (`https://auth0.com/`) is probably the most widespread.

Auth0

According to its website, Auth0 provides a universal platform for authentication and authorization for applications, web, mobile, and legacy.

The use of the platform has a cost, but it has a free plan for up to 7000 active users with unlimited logins.

Creating an Account

Let's start creating an account by clicking SIGN UP (Figure 5-1).

© Victor Hugo Garcia 2023
V. H. Garcia, *Getting Started with Angular*, https://doi.org/10.1007/978-1-4842-9206-8_5

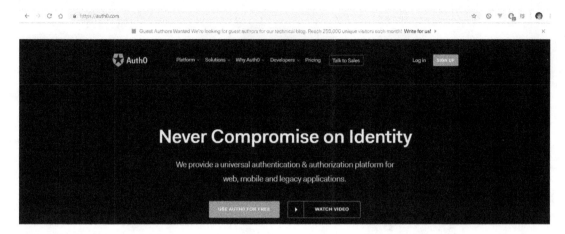

Figure 5-1. *Sign up*

By clicking SIGN UP, we will reach the screen shown in Figure 5-2.

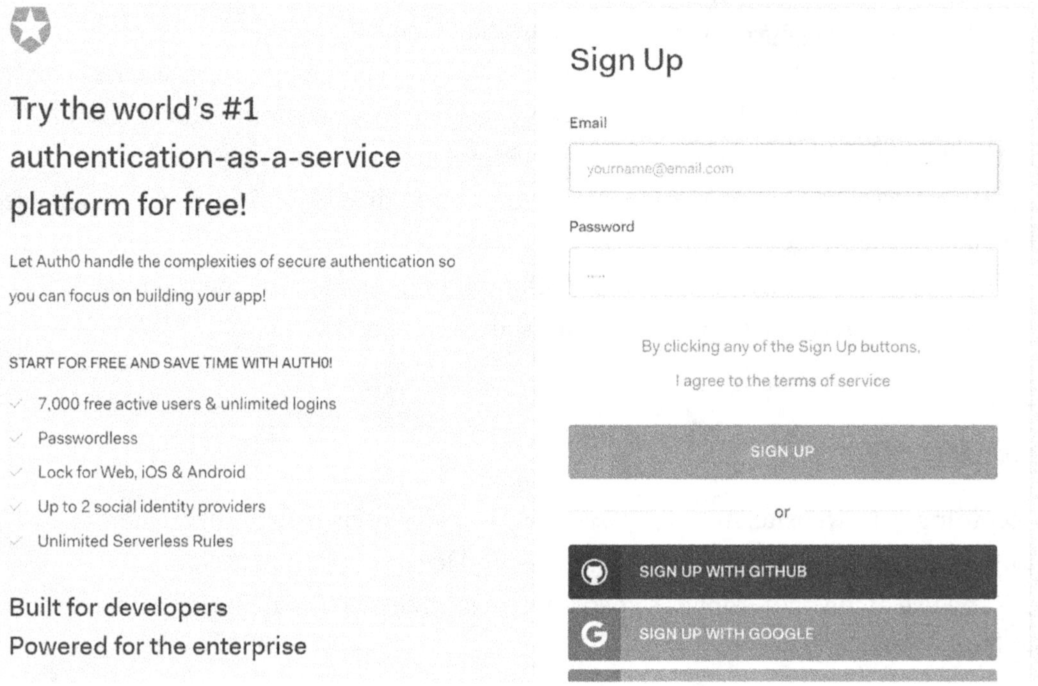

Figure 5-2. *Sign up*

We can register with our email and then choose a password or through one of the social networks.

The following screen will suggest a domain name that will be used as endpoints of the API of the clients of our applications. We can leave the one shown by default or enter our own (Figure 5-3).

Welcome to Auth0

Help us setup your first tenant and start authenticating.

STEP 1 OF 2

Figure 5-3. *Welcome*

The next step asks us for certain information about the type of account. We can leave the options as shown in Figure 5-4.

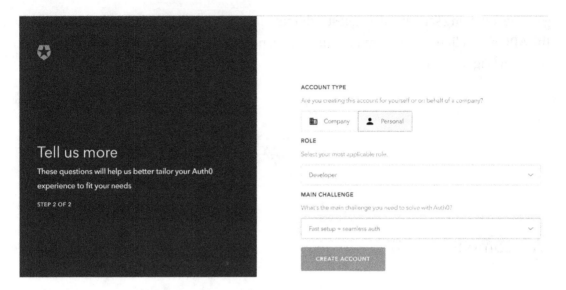

Figure 5-4. *Configuration*

Finally, we will be taken to our dashboard (Figure 5-5).

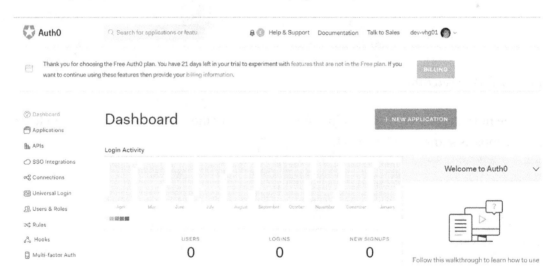

Figure 5-5. *Dashboard*

We click NEW APPLICATION, which leads to the next screen (Figure 5-6).

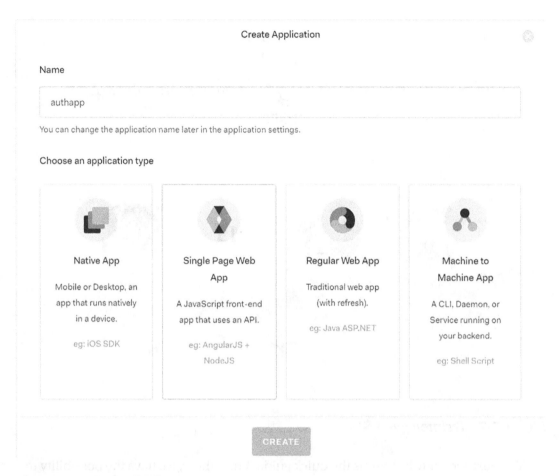

Figure 5-6. *New application*

Let's enter a name for our application. It is not something so important, we can change it later. We select CREATE, and we will see the following screen. We are asked what kind of technology we will use for the application, in order to show us a quick guide corresponding to the selected technology – in our case, Angular (Figure 5-7).

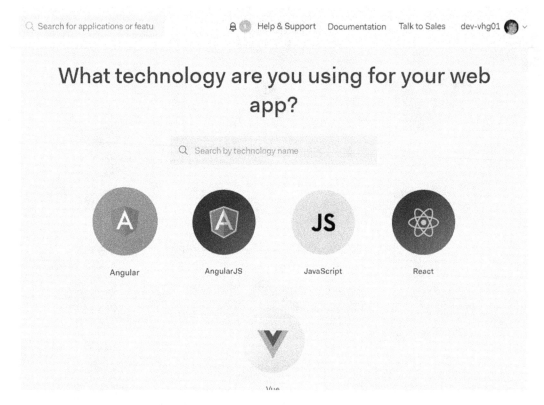

Figure 5-7. *Technology*

The next screen will show us the quick guide. From there, we have the possibility to download an example application, but in this case we will build it ourselves (Figure 5-8).

authapp

SINGLE PAGE APPLICATION

Quick Start   Settings   Addons   Connections   Client ID: 7O1Vuqfzd91N87yjtOVm7UXNinL8BPbA

Angular: Login

 By Andres Aguiar
○ Auth0

This tutorial demonstrates how to add user login to an Angular (versions 2 and above) application using Auth0.

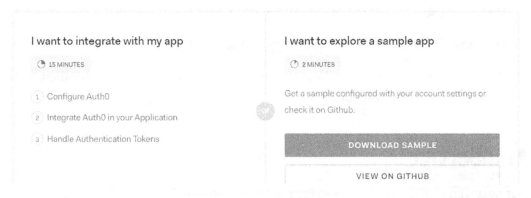

Figure 5-8. *Quickstart*

Our New App

Now, let's move on to create our new application with angular-cli. We have already seen how to do this, which should not present problems. Select **authapp** as the name of our application.

Our next step will be to install bootstrap, jQuery, and popper. This is something that we have already seen in previous chapters, so we will not repeat the steps here.

Then, we will install auth0 with the following command:

```
npm install --save auth0-js
```

As with bootstrap, jQuery, and popper, once the library is installed, we need to add the corresponding reference in the scripts array of the angular.json file:

```
"scripts": [
```

```
    "node_modules/popper.js/dist/umd/popper.min.js",
    "node_modules/jquery/dist/jquery.slim.min.js",
    "node_modules/bootstrap/dist/js/bootstrap.min.js",
    "node_modules/auth0-js/dist/auth0.js"
]
```

Alternatively, we could have simply included a reference to the library in our index.html:

```
<script type="text/javascript" src="node_modules/auth0-js/build/auth0.js">
</script>
```

We could also have loaded the library using a CDN:

```
<script src="https://cdn.auth0.com/js/auth0/9.10/auth0.min.js"> </script>
```

Personally, however, the installation using npm and the reference in the angular.json file is the alternative that I recommend.

AuthService

Our next step will be to create a service called simply "auth":

```
ng g s services/auth
```

Every time we go back to auth0.com, we will find our dashboard (Figure 5-9).

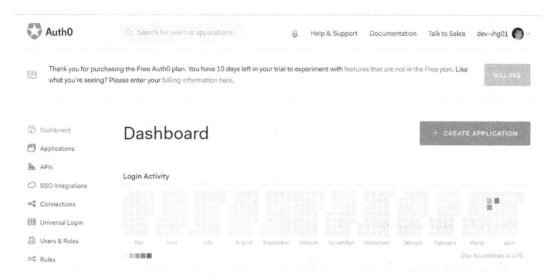

Figure 5-9. *Dashboard*

In the menu on the left, we can access the Applications option (Figure 5-10).

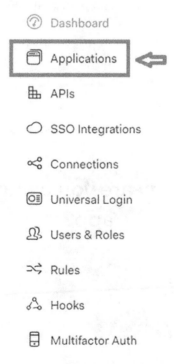

Figure 5-10. *Applications menu*

Here, we will see a list of all the applications we have created (Figure 5-11).

Applications

Setup a mobile, web or IoT application to use Auth0 for Authentication. Learn more ⌐

Figure 5-11. *Applications*

In this case, we can see our newly created authapp application. By clicking it, we access its details (Figure 5-12).

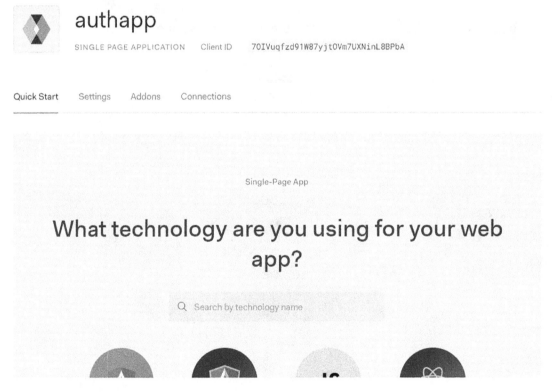

Figure 5-12. *Technology*

In the quickstart tab, we will always be presented with the technology choice option we saw at the time of creating our application. By selecting Angular, we will observe custom information for the framework.

In the section **Create an Authentication Service**, the following code is shown to be used in the service that we just created with angular-cli:

```
// src/app/auth/auth.service.ts

import { Injectable } from '@angular/core';
import { Router } from '@angular/router';
import * as auth0 from 'auth0-js';

@Injectable()
export class AuthService {

 private _idToken: string;
 private _accessToken: string;
 private _expiresAt: number;

 auth0 = new auth0.WebAuth({
   clientID: '[your-client-id]',
   domain: '[your-domain]',
   responseType: 'token id_token',
   redirectUri: 'http://localhost:3000/callback',
   scope: 'openid'
 });

 constructor(public router: Router) {
   this._idToken = '';
   this._accessToken = '';
   this._expiresAt = 0;
 }

 get accessToken(): string {
   return this._accessToken;
 }

 get idToken(): string {
   return this._idToken;
 }
```

```
  public login(): void {
    this.auth0.authorize();
  }

}
```

Let's copy it to our auth.service.ts file, but with a small change. The line

```
redirectUri: 'http://localhost:3000/callback',
```

must be replaced by

```
redirectUri: 'http://localhost:4200/callback',
```

As you may have guessed, this is because our server is running on port 4200.

You may also have seen that we do not have a route or a callback component yet, but we will take care of that later.

Following the documentation of the quickstart, we complete our service with the following methods. In auth.service.ts, add:

```
public handleAuthentication(): void {
    this.auth0.parseHash((err: any, authResult: any) => {
      if (authResult && authResult.accessToken && authResult.idToken) {
        window.location.hash = '';
        this.localLogin(authResult);
        this.router.navigate(['/home']);
      } else if (err) {
        this.router.navigate(['/home']);
        console.log(err);
      }
    });
}

private localLogin(authResult: any): void {
    // Set the time that the access token will expire at
    const expiresAt = (authResult.expiresIn * 1000) + Date.now();
    this._accessToken = authResult.accessToken;
    this._idToken = authResult.idToken;
    this._expiresAt = expiresAt;
}
```

```
public renewTokens(): void {
  this.auth0.checkSession({}, (err, authResult) => {
    if (authResult && authResult.accessToken && authResult.idToken) {
      this.localLogin(authResult);
    } else if (err) {
      alert(`Could not get a new token (${err.error}: ${err.error_
      description}) .`);
      this.logout();
    }
  });
}

public logout(): void {
  // Remove tokens and expiry time
  this._accessToken = '';
  this._idToken = '';
  this._expiresAt = 0;
  // Go back to the home route
  this.router.navigate(['/']);
}

public isAuthenticated(): boolean {
  // Check whether the current time is past the
  // access token's expiry time
  return this._accessToken && new Date.now() < this._expiresAt;
}
```

If you get the error "Could not find a declaration file for module 'auth0-js'", then you need to type:

```
npm install --save @types/auth0-js
```

at the terminal.

Although we have created our service, it will not be available until we add the corresponding reference in app.module.ts:

```
providers: [
  AuthService
],
```

and the corresponding import of course:

```
import { AuthService } from './services/auth.service';
```

At this point, we are now in a position to check that everything is going well so far. But before that, let's install bootstrap, jQuery, and popper. We have already seen how to do it, so I will skip that step and assume that the libraries have been installed correctly.

For this, we will have to add a couple of buttons that deal with the login and logout. These buttons will be in a navbar component, which we will create next.

NavbarComponent

Let's type:

```
ng g c components/navbar
```

With the following content in navbar.component.html:

```html
<nav class="navbar navbar-expand-lg navbar-light bg-light">
   <a class="navbar-brand" href="#">AuthApp</a>
   <button class="navbar-toggler" type="button" data-toggle="collapse"
data-target="#navbarText" aria-controls="navbarText"
aria-expanded="false" aria-label="Toggle navigation">
   <span class="navbar-toggler-icon"> </span>
 </button>
   <div class="collapse navbar-collapse" id="navbarText">
      <ul class="navbar-nav mr-auto">
         <li class="nav-item active">
            <a class="nav-link" href="#">
              Home <span class="sr-only">(current)</span>
            </a>
         </li>
         <li class="nav-item">
            <a class="nav-link" href="#">Features</a>
         </li>
```

```
        <li class="nav-item">
            <a class="nav-link" href="#">Pricing</a>
        </li>
    </ul>
    <span class="navbar-text">
      Navbar text with an inline element
    </span>
  </div>
</nav>
```

we are going to replace the text of the last span with a couple of buttons:

```
<button
  class="btn btn-primary btn-margin"
  *ngIf="!auth.isAuthenticated()" (click)="login()">
    Log In
</button>

<button
  class="btn btn-primary btn-margin"
  *ngIf="auth.isAuthenticated()" (click)="logout()">
    Log Out
</button>
```

Note that we are referring to a property, auth, that we have not yet defined. We are also invoking two methods, login and logout, which do not yet exist.

Let's replace the contents of navbar.component.ts with the following:

```
import { Component, OnInit } from '@angular/core';
import { AuthService } from 'src/app/services/auth.service';

@Component({
 selector: 'app-navbar',
 templateUrl: './navbar.component.html',
 styleUrls: ['./navbar.component.css']
})
export class NavbarComponent implements OnInit {
```

```
constructor( public auth: AuthService ) {}

ngOnInit() {
}

login() {
  this.auth.login();
}

logout() {
  this.auth.logout();
}

}
```

Before we can run the application in the browser, we create some other components: home, about, and private, all within the components directory.

Routing

Our next step is to create the routes file, app.routes.ts, and modify the navbar to add navigation to the new components. This is something that we have seen before.

The code of app.routes.ts will be as follows:

```
import { NgModule } from '@angular/core';
import { RouterModule, Routes } from '@angular/router';
import { HomeComponent } from './components/home/home.component';
import { AboutComponent } from './components/about/about.component';
import { PrivateComponent } from './components/private/private.component';

const routes: Routes = [
    { path: '', component: HomeComponent },
    { path: 'home', component: HomeComponent },
    { path: 'about', component: AboutComponent },
    { path: 'private', component: PrivateComponent },
    { path: '**', component: HomeComponent },
];
```

```
@NgModule({
    imports: [RouterModule.forRoot(routes)],
    exports: [RouterModule]
})
export class AppRoutingModule {}
```

As we have to remember, we have to add our new module in app.module.ts to be able to use it:

```
imports: [
    BrowserModule,
    AppRoutingModule
],
```

and its corresponding import:

```
import { AppRoutingModule } from './app.routes';
```

The navbar will be as follows:

```
<nav class="navbar navbar-expand-lg navbar-light bg-light">
    <a class="navbar-brand" href="#">AuthApp</a>
    <button class="navbar-toggler" type="button" data-toggle="collapse"
data-target="#navbarText" aria-controls="navbarText" aria-expanded="false"
aria-label="Toggle navigation">
    <span class="navbar-toggler-icon"> </span>
  </button>
    <div class="collapse navbar-collapse" id="navbarText">
        <ul class="navbar-nav mr-auto">
            <li class="nav-item" routerLinkActive="Active">
                <a class="nav-link" [routerLink]="['home']">
                  Home <span class="sr-only">(current)</span>
                </a>
            </li>
            <li class="nav-item" routerLinkActive="Active">
                <a class="nav-link" [routerLink]="['about']">About</a>
            </li>
```

```
                <li class="nav-item" routerLinkActive="Active">
                    <a class="nav-link" [routerLink]="['private']">Private</a>
                </li>
            </ul>
            <button
              class="btn btn-primary btn-margin"
              *ngIf="!auth.isAuthenticated()" (click)="login()">
                Log In
            </button>

            <button
              class="btn btn-primary btn-margin" *ngIf="auth.isAuthenticated()"
              (click)="logout()">
                Log Out
            </button>
        </div>
</nav>
```

And here's the corresponding file:

navbar.component.html

https://github.com/Apress/The-Beginning-Angular-by-Victor-Hugo-Garcia/blob/main/Chapter-05/03-navbar.component-v2.html

Now let's modify our app component:

```
<app-navbar> </app-navbar>

<div class="container">
    <router-outlet> </router-outlet>
</div>
```

Excellent. Now if we can open our application in the browser, we should see something like Figure 5-13.

AuthApp   Home   About   Private   Log In

home works!

Figure 5-13. *Home*

Do not click the login button yet. Let's return to the dashboard of our application on the site of auth0 and visit the Settings tab (Figure 5-14).

authapp
SINGLE PAGE APPLICATION

Quick Start   **Settings**   Addons   Connections

Figure 5-14. *Settings*

Auth0 Settings

There are two pieces of information that we must complete as shown in Figure 5-15.

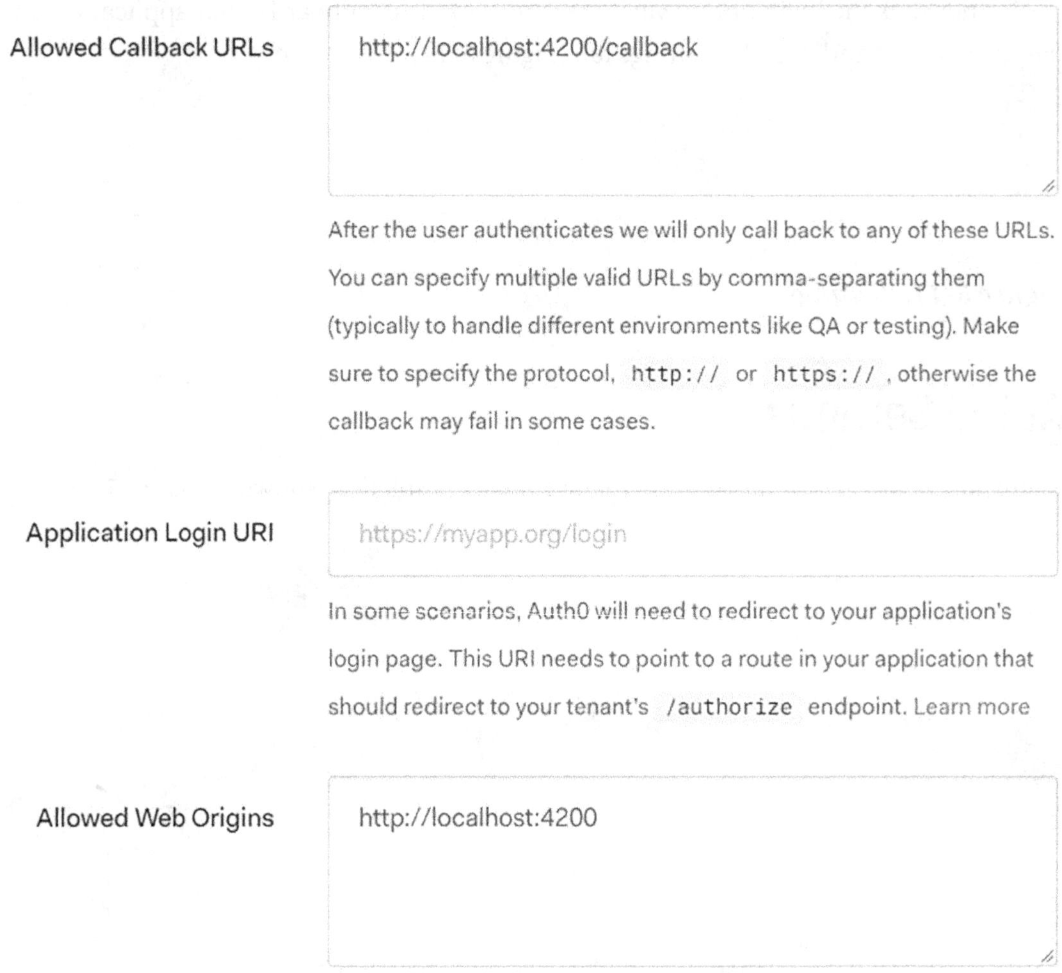

Allowed Callback URLs

http://localhost:4200/callback

After the user authenticates we will only call back to any of these URLs. You can specify multiple valid URLs by comma-separating them (typically to handle different environments like QA or testing). Make sure to specify the protocol, `http://` or `https://`, otherwise the callback may fail in some cases.

Application Login URI

https://myapp.org/login

In some scenarios, Auth0 will need to redirect to your application's login page. This URI needs to point to a route in your application that should redirect to your tenant's `/authorize` endpoint. Learn more

Allowed Web Origins

http://localhost:4200

Figure 5-15. *Settings*

Very well. Now if we click the Login button, we will see the screen shown in Figure 5-16.

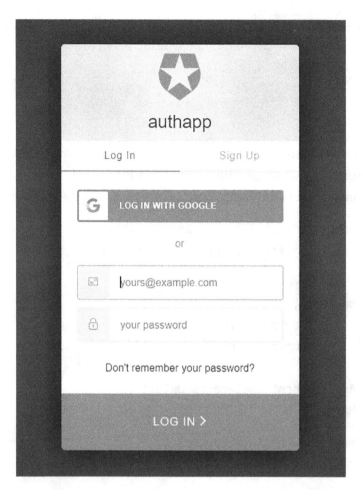

Figure 5-16. Login

Before trying to log in, however, we need to take a few more steps.

In our service, we have the following line:

```
redirectUri: 'http://localhost:4200/callback',
```

When a user logs in with Auth0, they are taken out of the application. Once the user is authenticated, it is returned to the application.

You can define any route to which the user returns. However, the auth0 documentation recommends creating a dedicated path.

We are going to create a new component called callback with the following content in its template:

```
<div class="loading">
   Loading
</div>
```

That's it. Instead of using a text, "Loading," we could use some indicator, for example, with Font Awesome or a vector graphic, but for now it's enough.

Finally, we must modify the code of app.component.ts in the following way:

```
import { Component, OnInit } from '@angular/core';
import { AuthService } from './services/auth.service';

@Component({
 selector: 'app-root',
 templateUrl: './app.component.html',
 styleUrls: ['./app.component.css']
})
export class AppComponent implements OnInit {
 title = 'authapp';

 constructor(public auth: AuthService) {
   auth.handleAuthentication();
 }

 ngOnInit() {
   if (this.auth.isAuthenticated()) {
     // this.auth.renewTokens ();
   }
 }
}
```

The line this.auth.renewTokens(); is commented out for the following reason.

If we make the login using a social network, for example, Google, we will get an error if the line is not commented out.

This happens because we are using auth0 with development keys, which allow us to test the application quickly. But using these development keys has important limitations that are explained here:

Auth0 Devkeys

`https://auth0.com/docs/authenticate/identity-providers/social-identity-providers/devkeys`

If we want to use the social login, we must register our application with the chosen social provider, as explained here (`https://auth0.com/docs/authenticate/identity-providers#social`).

For example, in the case of Google, you must follow the steps shown here (`https://marketplace.auth0.com/integrations/google-social-connection`).

For now, let's leave the commented line. Alternatively, we can register with an email account (Figure 5-17).

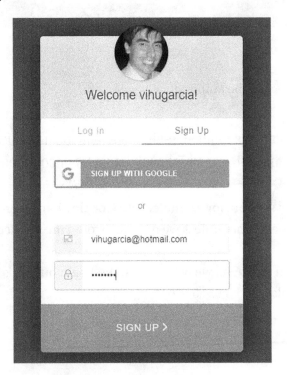

Figure 5-17. *Sign up*

We will be asked for authorization (Figure 5-18).

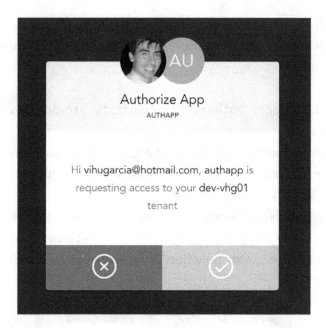

Figure 5-18. *Sign up*

After accepting, we will be automatically logged in.

Important   If we use this method, registration and login through user and password, the line this.auth.renewTokens(); must be uncommented.

But if we initiate a session, for example, with Google or another social provider, we will have to comment it out unless we have registered the application in the social provider.

If we now perform the login, we will see that the Login button is hidden and the Logout button is displayed (Figure 5-19).

Figure 5-19. *Log out*

We can navigate through our application, and the Logout button will also perform its work.

Very good, we are much closer. However, there is an important detail that some of you may have already noticed.

So far, we have followed the quickstart documentation to the letter. We can log in and browse the application. But what happens if after having logged in we refresh the page?

We will see how the Logout button disappears and the Login button appears again. What is happening?

Local Storage

The localLogin function at this time has the following form, in auth.service.ts:

```
private localLogin(authResult: any): void {
  // Set the time that the access token will expire at
  const expiresAt = (authResult.expiresIn * 1000) + Date.now();
  this._accessToken = authResult.accessToken;
  this._idToken = authResult.idToken;
  this._expiresAt = expiresAt;
}
```

As we can see, the data is being stored in variables in memory, so when you reload the application the values of these variables are lost.

Let's replace the code of the function in the following way:

```
private localLogin(authResult: any): void {
  const expiresAt = JSON.stringify(
    authResult.expiresIn * 1000 + new Date().getTime()
  );

  localStorage.setItem('access_token', authResult.accessToken);
  localStorage.setItem('id_token', authResult.idToken);
  localStorage.setItem('expires_at', expiresAt);
}
```

What we are doing is saving the value of the variables in the local storage.

We must also modify the isAuthenticated and logout methods as follows. In auth. service.ts, add:

```
public logout(): void {
```

```
  // Remove tokens and expiry time from localStorage
  localStorage.removeItem('access_token');
  localStorage.removeItem('id_token');
  localStorage.removeItem('expires_at');
  // Remove server SSO session
  this.router.navigate(['/']);
}

public isAuthenticated(): boolean {
  const expiresAt = JSON.parse(localStorage.getItem('expires_at')
  || '{}');
  return new Date().getTime() < expiresAt;
}
```

After logging in, we can see how the variables are stored in the localStorage using the Google developer tools (Figure 5-20).

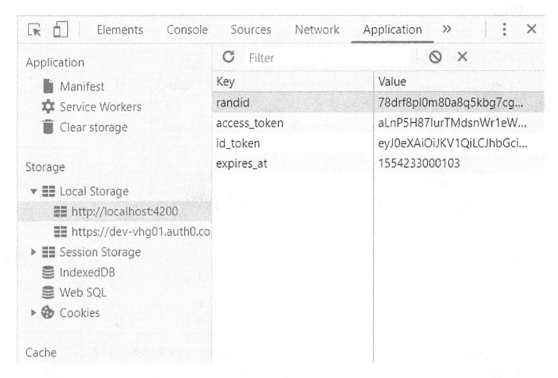

Figure 5-20. *Local storage*

These variables are removed when we perform the logout.

With these modifications made, our application will keep the session status started even when we refresh the page.

It is debatable if it is a good practice to keep variables in localStorage. A more secure alternative would be to perform the session management in the backend, for example, through a service developed in NodeJS.

In successive editions, we will see how to achieve this, but for the moment, we have made great progress, although there are still more things to see.

Securing Routes

Our application is working correctly. You can start and end a session. However, there is a page of our application, private, which is displayed whether the user has been identified or not (Figure 5-21).

Figure 5-21. *Protected route*

Our goal is to protect that route.

As a first step, we can make changes in our NavbarComponent, more precisely in navbar.component.html.

Let's change the lines:

```
<li class="nav-item" routerLinkActive="Active">
    <a class="nav-link" [routerLink]="['private']">Private</a>
</li>
```

to

```
<li *ngIf="auth.isAuthenticated()" class="nav-item"
  routerLinkActive="Active">
    <a class="nav-link" [routerLink]="['private']">Private</a>
</li>
```

We can now see that the link is not visible if the user has not been identified (Figure 5-22).

Figure 5-22. *Logged-in user*

However, this does not give us robust protection, since if the user knows the route, they can still visit it by typing the address in the browser (Figure 5-23).

Figure 5-23. *Private route*

We need a way to prevent the user from accessing routes for which it is not authorized, and fortunately we have a simple way to do it.

AuthGuard

Let's use the following command:

```
ng g guard services/auth`
```

With this command, we are generating a route guard. It is a mechanism that allows us to protect certain routes from unauthorized viewing. The command will give us the following content:

```
import { Injectable } from '@angular/core';
Import {
  CanActivate,
  ActivatedRouteSnapshot,
  RouterStateSnapshot
} from '@angular/router';
```

```
import { Observable } from 'rxjs';

@Injectable({
 providedIn: 'root'
})
export class AuthGuard implements CanActivate {
 canActivate(
   next: ActivatedRouteSnapshot,
   state: RouterStateSnapshot): Observable<boolean> | Promise<boolean> |
   boolean {
   return true;
 }
}
```

It is a simple class, with a single method: canActivate.

We will then deal with the parameters that it receives, but the important thing is to know that this method returns true or false, providing or denying access to a certain route. Of course, in this case we are simply returning true, so it is not very useful. Also, we have not yet applied it to a route.

We are going to do the latter. In the app.routes.ts file, change the line:

```
{ path: 'private', component: PrivateComponent },
```

to

```
{
     path: 'private',
     component: PrivateComponent,
     canActivate: [ AuthGuard ]
  },
```

Remember that we must include the corresponding import:

```
import { AuthGuard } from './services/auth.guard';
```

That is all. However, since the canActivate method always returns true, no change will be seen.

We can verify that by changing the return value true to false:

```
canActivate(
```

```
next: ActivatedRouteSnapshot,
state: RouterStateSnapshot): Observable<boolean> | Promise<boolean> |
boolean {
return false;
}
```

Now the user cannot visit the route. However, a method that does not have decision-making capacity is not useful. Let's fix that:

```
export class AuthGuard implements CanActivate {
 constructor( private auth: AuthService) {}

 canActivate(
   next: ActivatedRouteSnapshot,
   state: RouterStateSnapshot): Observable<boolean> | Promise<boolean> |
   boolean {
     if ( this.auth.isAuthenticated()) {
       return true;
     }

     return false;
 }
}
```

We also need the following import:

```
import { AuthService } from './auth.service';
```

With these changes, the route will now only be accessible when the user is identified.

Note   The route guards are only for the UI. They do not provide protection against access to an API. We must always force authentication and authorization in our APIs.

However, the route guards method does have utility when it comes to preventing non-authorized navigation.

To make sure everything is working correctly, I will provide the code for all the components and services.

CallbackComponent

callback.component.html

```
<div class="loading">
   Loading
</div>
```

callback.component.ts

```
import { Component, OnInit } from '@angular/core';

@Component({
 selector: 'app-callback',
 templateUrl: './callback.component.html',
 styleUrls: ['./callback.component.css']
})
export class CallbackComponent implements OnInit {

 constructor() {}

 ngOnInit() {
 }

}
```

File
https://github.com/Apress/The-Beginning-Angular-by-Victor-Hugo-Garcia/
blob/main/Chapter-05/02-callback.component.ts

NavbarComponent

navbar.component.html

```
<nav class="navbar navbar-expand-lg navbar-light bg-light">
   <a class="navbar-brand" href="#">AuthApp</a>
   <button class="navbar-toggler" type="button" data-toggle="collapse"
data-target="#navbarText" aria-controls="navbarText" aria-expanded="false"
aria-label="Toggle navigation">
   <span class="navbar-toggler-icon"> </span>
 </button>
   <div class="collapse navbar-collapse" id="navbarText">
       <ul class="navbar-nav mr-auto">
```

```
            <li class="nav-item" routerLinkActive="Active">
                <a class="nav-link" [routerLink]="['home']">
                  Home <span class="sr-only">(current)</span>
                </a>
            </li>
            <li class="nav-item" routerLinkActive="Active">
                <a class="nav-link" [routerLink]="['about']">
                  About
                </a>
            </li>
            <li
              *ngIf="auth.isAuthenticated()"
              class="nav-item" routerLinkActive="Active">
                <a class="nav-link" [routerLink]="['private']">Private</a>
            </li>
        </ul>
        <button
          class="btn btn-primary btn-margin"
          *ngIf="!auth.isAuthenticated()"
          (click)="login()">
            Log In
        </button>

        <button
          class="btn btn-primary btn-margin"
          *ngIf="auth.isAuthenticated()"
          (click)="logout ()">
            Log Out
        </button>
    </div>
</nav>
```

File
https://github.com/Apress/The-Beginning-Angular-by-Victor-Hugo-Garcia/
blob/main/Chapter-05/03-navbar.component-v2.html

navbar.component.ts

```
import { Component, OnInit } from '@angular/core';
import { AuthService } from 'src/app/services/auth.service';

@Component({
 selector: 'app-navbar',
 templateUrl: './navbar.component.html',
 styleUrls: ['./navbar.component.css']
})
export class NavbarComponent implements OnInit {

 constructor( public auth: AuthService ) {}

 ngOnInit() {
 }

 login() {
   this.auth.login();
 }

 logout() {
   this.auth.logout();
 }

}
```

File
https://github.com/Apress/The-Beginning-Angular-by-Victor-Hugo-Garcia/
blob/main/Chapter-05/04-navbar.component.ts

AuthService

auth.service.ts

```
// src/app/auth/auth.service.ts

import { Injectable } from '@angular/core';
import { Router } from '@angular/router';
import * as auth0 from 'auth0-js';
```

```
@Injectable()
export class AuthService {

 private _idToken: string;
 private _accessToken: string;
 private _expiresAt: number;

 auth0 = new auth0.WebAuth({
   clientID: '70IVuqfzd91W87yjtOVm7UXNinL8BPbA',
   domain: 'dev-vhg01.auth0.com',
   responseType: 'token id_token',
   redirectUri: 'http://localhost:4200/callback',
   scope: 'openid'
 });
 constructor(public router: Router) {
   this._idToken = '';
   this._accessToken = '';
   this._expiresAt = 0;
 }

 get accessToken(): string {
   return this._accessToken;
 }

 get idToken(): string {
   return this._idToken;
 }

 public login(): void {
   this.auth0.authorize();
 }

 public handleAuthentication(): void {
   this.auth0.parseHash((err: any, authResult: any) => {
     if (authResult && authResult.accessToken && authResult.idToken) {
       this.localLogin(authResult);
       this.router.navigate(['/home']);
     } else if (err) {
```

```
      this.router.navigate(['/home']);
      console.log(err);
      alert(`Error: ${err.error}. Check the console for further details.`);
    }
  });
}

private localLogin(authResult: any): void {
  const expiresAt = JSON.stringify(
    authResult.expiresIn * 1000 + new Date().getTime()
  );

  localStorage.setItem('access_token', authResult.accessToken);
  localStorage.setItem('id_token', authResult.idToken);
  localStorage.setItem('expires_at', expiresAt);
}

public renewTokens(): void {
  this.auth0.checkSession({}, (err, authResult) => {
    if (authResult && authResult.accessToken && authResult.idToken) {
      this.localLogin(authResult);
    } else if (err) {
      alert(`Could not get a new token (${err.error}: ${err.error_
      description}).`);
      this.logout();
    }
  });
}

public logout(): void {
  // Remove tokens and expiry time from localStorage
  localStorage.removeItem('access_token');
  localStorage.removeItem('id_token');
  localStorage.removeItem('expires_at');
  // Remove server SSO session
  this.router.navigate(['/']);
}
```

```
public isAuthenticated(): boolean {
    const expiresAt = JSON.parse(localStorage.getItem('expires_at')
    || '{}');
    return new Date().getTime() < expiresAt;
  }

}
```

File
https://github.com/Apress/The-Beginning-Angular-by-Victor-Hugo-Garcia/
blob/main/Chapter-05/05-auth.service.ts

AuthGuard

auth.guard.ts

```
import { Injectable } from '@angular/core';
import { CanActivate, ActivatedRouteSnapshot, RouterStateSnapshot }
from '@angular/router';
import { Observable } from 'rxjs';
import { AuthService } from './auth.service';

@Injectable({
 providedIn: 'root'
})
export class AuthGuard implements CanActivate {
 constructor( private auth: AuthService) {}

 canActivate(
   next: ActivatedRouteSnapshot,
   state: RouterStateSnapshot): Observable<boolean> | Promise<boolean> |
   boolean {
     if ( this.auth.isAuthenticated() ) {
       return true;
     }

     return false;
 }
}
```

File (https://github.com/Apress/The-Beginning-Angular-by-Victor-Hugo-
Garcia/blob/main/Chapter-05/06-auth.guard.ts)

Getting the User's Profile

We are going to complete this chapter by adding the functionality to obtain the user's profile.

Let's enter our Auth0 account. Once there, we will get to our board where we must select the Applications option from the left menu (Figure 5-24).

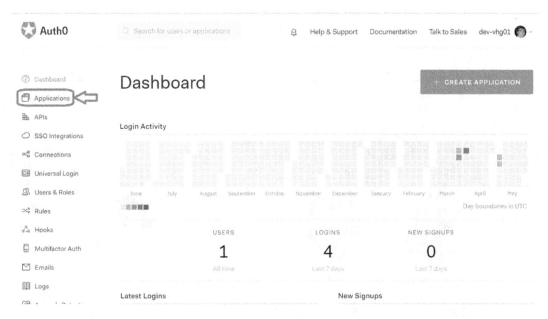

Figure 5-24. *Dashboard*

In the list of Applications, we will select our application **authapp** (Figure 5-25).

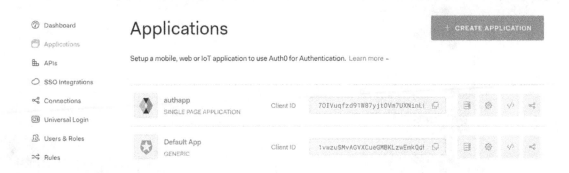

Figure 5-25. *Applications*

Then, in the Quickstart tab, we will again be asked to select the type of technology (Figure 5-26).

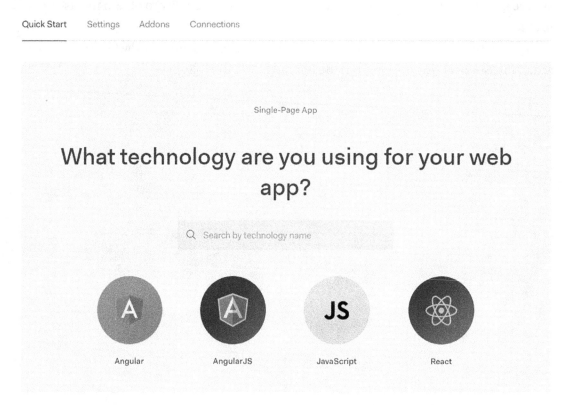

Figure 5-26. *Technology*

As always, select Angular. We will access the guide that has helped us to configure our service. At the bottom of the screen, we can see links to new tutorials (Figure 5-27).

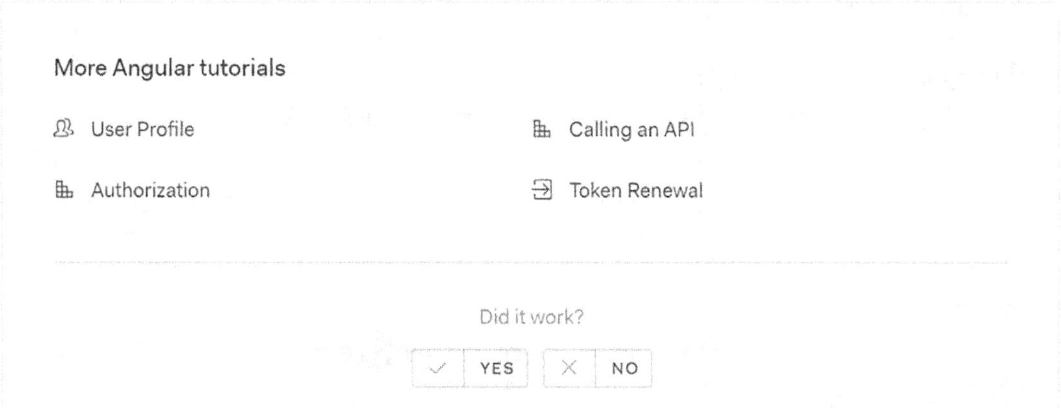

More Angular tutorials

🖧 User Profile   📖 Calling an API

📖 Authorization   ↪ Token Renewal

Did it work?

✓ YES   ✕ NO

Figure 5-27. *Tutorials*

Select User Profile. There we can see the steps to recover and display the user profile. Let's start.

We will make our first modification in our AuthService. There we have the following lines that initialize our auth object:

```
auth0 = new auth0.WebAuth({
   clientID: '[your-client-id]',
   domain: '[your-domain]',
   responseType: 'token id_token',
   redirectUri: 'http://localhost:4200/callback',
   scope: 'openid'
});
```

We must replace the line:

```
scope: 'openid'
```

by

```
scope: 'openid profile'
```

This will allow us to have access to the profile of the user who is logged in.

Next, let's add the following property:

```
userProfile: any;
```

and finally the following method:

```
public getProfile(cb: any): void {
    this._accessToken = localStorage.getItem('access_token') ?? '';
    if (!this._accessToken) {
      throw new Error('Access Token must exist to fetch profile');
    }

    const self = this;
    this.auth0.client.userInfo(this._accessToken, (err, profile) => {
      if (profile) {
        self.userProfile = profile;
      }
      cb(err, profile);
    });
  }
```

This method allows us to capture the profile information and save it in the userProfile property. But, where does this information come from? The answer is from the social provider that the user has used to log in.

Now, address to our PrivateComponent, at private.component.ts, and modify it as follows:

```
import { Component, OnInit } from '@angular/core';
import { AuthService } from '../../services/auth.service';

@Component({
  selector: 'app-private',
  templateUrl: './private.component.html',
  styleUrls: ['./private.component.css']
})
export class PrivateComponent implements OnInit {

  profile: any;

  constructor(public auth: AuthService) {}
```

```
ngOnInit() {
  if (this.auth.userProfile) {
    this.profile = this.auth.userProfile;
  } else {
    this.auth.getProfile((err: any, profile: any) => {
      this.profile = profile;
    });
  }
}

}
```

Let's follow the instructions in the quick guide and change the private.component. html code:

```
<div class="panel panel-default profile-area">
 <div class="panel-heading">
   <h3>Profile</h3>
 </div>
 <div class="panel-body">
   <img src="{{profile? .picture}}" class="avatar" alt="avatar">
   <div>
     <label> <i class="glyphicon glyphicon-user"> </i> Nickname</label>
     <h3 class="nickname">{{profile? .nickname}}</h3>
   </div>
   <pre class="full-profile">{{profile | json}}</pre>
 </div>
</div>
```

This will give us something like the one in Figure 5-28.

Profile

Nickname

vihugarcia

```
{
  "sub": "google-oauth2|104500265994329908528",
  "given_name": "Victor Hugo",
  "family_name": "Garcia",
  "nickname": "vihugarcia",
  "name": "Victor Hugo Garcia",
  "picture": "https://lh4.googleusercontent.com/-vxmDvnMvrFk/AAAAAAAAAAI/AAAAAAAAADE/z_6ys70sPwc/photo.jpg",
  "gender": "male",
  "locale": "es",
  "updated_at": "2019-05-04T18:02:03.170Z"
}
```

Figure 5-28. *Profile*

We can see all the information about the profile provided by the provider, in this case Google. It works, but it looks pretty bad.

Let's change the content to the following:

```
<div class="container" style="margin-top: 40px;">
    <div class="card" style="width: 100%;">
        <div class="card-body">
            <div class="row">
                <div class="col-4" style="text-align: center;">
                    <img
                        [src]="profile? .picture"
                        class="card-img-top img-thumb"
                        [alt]="profile? .nickname">
                    <h3>{{profile? .nickname}}</h3>
                </div>
                <div class="col-8">
                    <h5 class="card-title">{{profile? .name}}</h5>
                    <a [routerLink]="['/ home']" class="btn btn-
                    primary">Home</a>
```

```
            </div>
        </div>
    </div>
  </div>
</div>
```

That will give us the result shown in Figure 5-29.

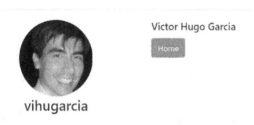

vihugarcia

Figure 5-29. *Profile*

In this way, we have concluded with the basics of Auth0. There are still many items to explore about this tool, but we have acquired the necessary knowledge to add robust authentication and authorization functionality to our application.

Just to be sure, here is our final AuthService:

autn.service.ts

```
// src/app/auth/auth.service.ts

import { Injectable } from '@angular/core';
import { Router } from '@angular/router';
import * as auth0 from 'auth0-js';

@Injectable()
export class AuthService {

  private _idToken: string;
  private _accessToken: string;
  private _expiresAt: number;

  userProfile: any;

  auth0 = new auth0.WebAuth({
    clientID: '[your-client-id]',
```

```
    domain: '[your-domain]',
    responseType: 'token id_token',
    redirectUri: 'http://localhost:4200/callback',
    scope: 'openid profile'
});

constructor(public router: Router) {
  this._idToken = '';
  this._accessToken = '';
  this._expiresAt = 0;
}

get accessToken(): string {
  return this._accessToken;
}

get idToken(): string {
  return this._idToken;
}

public login(): void {
  this.auth0.authorize();
}

public handleAuthentication(): void {
  this.auth0.parseHash((err: any, authResult: any) => {
    if (authResult && authResult.accessToken && authResult.idToken) {
      this.localLogin(authResult);
      this.router.navigate(['/home']);
    } else if (err) {
      this.router.navigate(['/home']);
      console.log(err);
      alert(`Error: ${err.error}. Check the console for further
      details.`);
    }
  });
}
```

```typescript
private localLogin(authResult: any): void {
  const expiresAt = JSON.stringify(
    authResult.expiresIn * 1000 + new Date().getTime()
  );

  localStorage.setItem('access_token', authResult.accessToken);
  localStorage.setItem('id_token', authResult.idToken);
  localStorage.setItem('expires_at', expiresAt);
}

public renewTokens(): void {
  this.auth0.checkSession({}, (err, authResult) => {
    if (authResult && authResult.accessToken && authResult.idToken) {
      this.localLogin(authResult);
    } else if (err) {
      alert(`Could not get a new token (${err.error}: ${err.error_
      description}).`);
      this.logout();
    }
  });
}

public logout(): void {
  // Remove tokens and expiry time from localStorage
  localStorage.removeItem('access_token');
  localStorage.removeItem('id_token');
  localStorage.removeItem('expires_at');
  // Remove server SSO session
  this.router.navigate(['/']);
}

public isAuthenticated(): boolean {
  const expiresAt = JSON.parse(localStorage.getItem('expires_at')
|| '{}');
  return new Date().getTime() < expiresAt;
}
```

```
public getProfile(cb: any): void {
  this._accessToken = localStorage.getItem('access_token') ?? '';
  if (!this._accessToken) {
    throw new Error('Access Token must exist to fetch profile');
  }

  const self = this;
  this.auth0.client.userInfo(this._accessToken, (err, profile) => {
    if (profile) {
      self.userProfile = profile;
    }
    cb(err, profile);
  });
 }

}
```

File
https://github.com/Apress/The-Beginning-Angular-by-Victor-Hugo-Garcia/ blob/main/Chapter-05/07-auth.service.ts

Exercise

As part of your practice, you can add sign-in with auth0 to the rest application in Chapter 4.

Summary

In this chapter, we have seen how to use auth0 to add authentication and authorization to our application. Although auth0 has a cost, it is well worth it if we take into account the robustness and security, as well as saving time by avoiding writing large amounts of code. In addition, we have obtained other tools such as sandbox, administration board, etc. We have thus acquired a fantastic tool for our arsenal as developers. And we have not seen anything yet. In the next chapters, we will develop applications with complex layouts, which interact with APIs to perform CRUD operations.

CHAPTER 6

Blog App Part 1

In this chapter, we will go further, building an application that interacts with a database through a backend. We will use MongoDB as the database, and the API of our backend will be developed with NodeJS. Now, this book is focused on Angular, so we will not dwell in great detail on Node's learning; however, we will learn enough to not feel lost.

MongoDB

MongoDB is a scalable and flexible NoSQL document database. Instead of saving the data in the form of records, MongoDB saves them in documents in BSON format, which is similar to JSON, which allows them to be more easily integrated into different applications.

First of all, we will download the installers from this link: `www.mongodb.com/try/download/community` (Figure 6-1).

© Victor Hugo Garcia 2023
V. H. Garcia, *Getting Started with Angular*, https://doi.org/10.1007/978-1-4842-9206-8_6

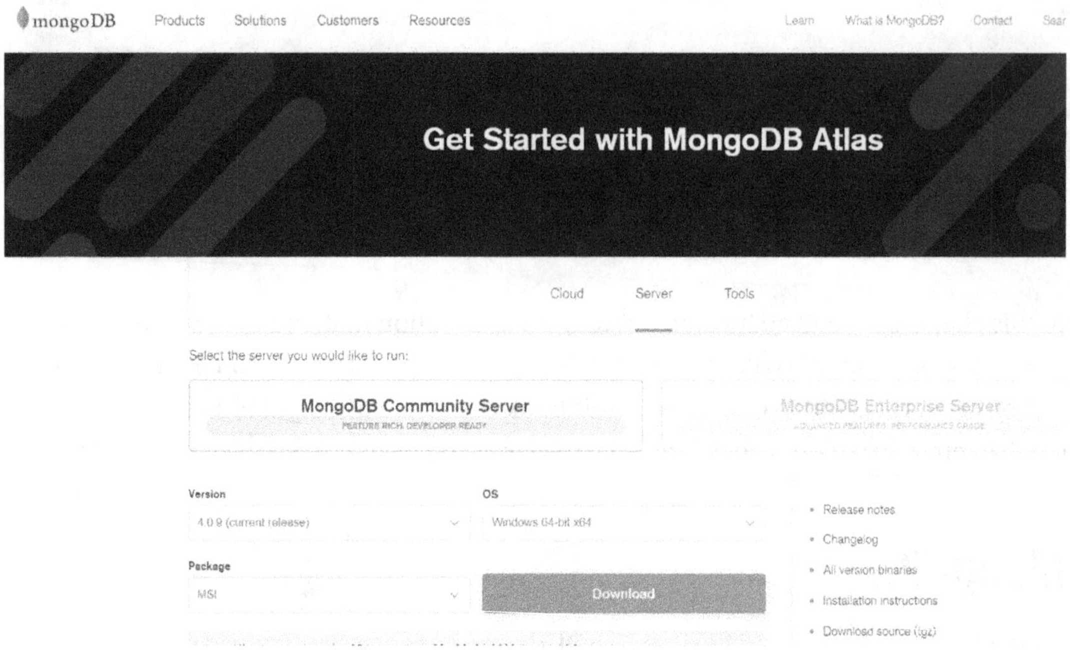

mongoDB   Products   Solutions   Customers   Resources

Learn   What is MongoDB?   Contact   Sear

Get Started with MongoDB Atlas

Cloud   Server   Tools

Select the server you would like to run:

MongoDB Community Server
FEATURE RICH, DEVELOPER READY

MongoDB Enterprise Server
ADVANCED FEATURES, PERFORMANCE GRADE

Version
4.0.9 (current release)

OS
Windows 64-bit x64

Package
MSI

Download

- Release notes
- Changelog
- All version binaries
- Installation instructions
- Download source (tgz)

Figure 6-1. *MongoDB download*

This will install the MongoDB service, but we will need a GUI tool in order to explore our documents. So, we also need to download MongoDB Compass, which is the GUI for MongoDB.

Once downloaded and installed, we can run the MongoDB Compass. The first time the screen will look similar to Figure 6-2.

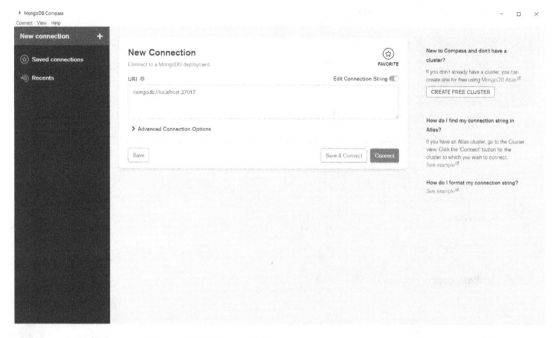

Figure 6-2.   *Connecting with MongoDB*

In this screen, we can establish a new connection, leaving in this case the default values. Note that the server will be listening on port 27017. Another point to keep in mind is that for this example we will not use any type of database authentication, which of course is not in any way advisable in a real environment.

If you wish, however, you can choose a user-based authentication and password in the Authentication tab visible in the **Advanced Connection Options**. You can access these tabs by clicking **Advanced Connection Options** in the previous screen (Figure 6-3).

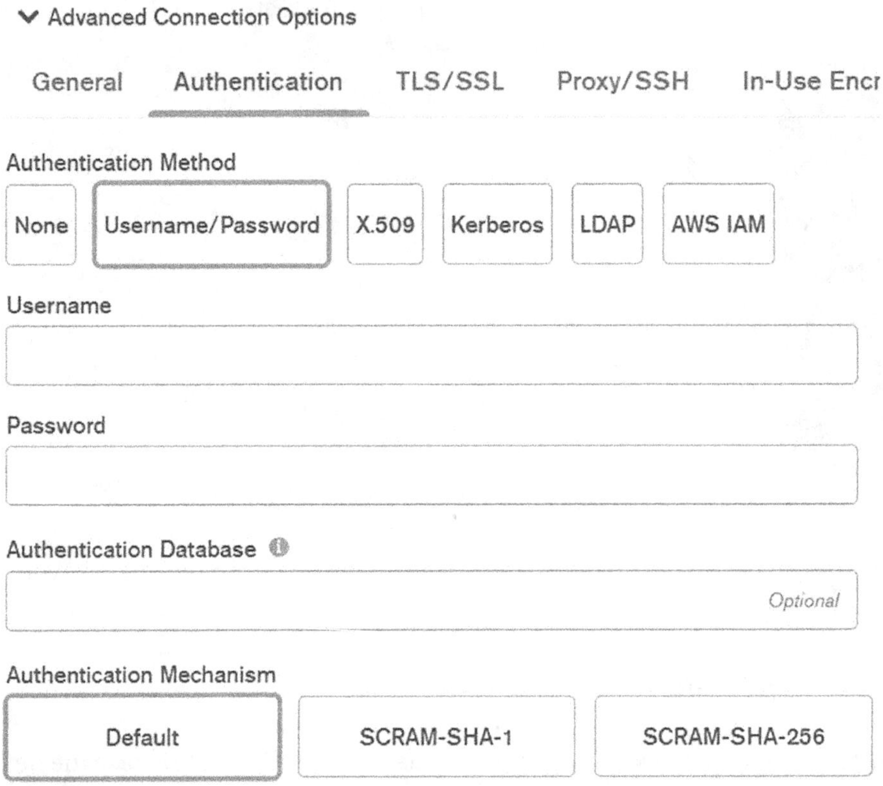

∨ Advanced Connection Options

| General | Authentication | TLS/SSL | Proxy/SSH | In-Use Encr |

Authentication Method

| None | Username/Password | X.509 | Kerberos | LDAP | AWS IAM |

Username

Password

Authentication Database ⓘ

Optional

Authentication Mechanism

| Default | SCRAM-SHA-1 | SCRAM-SHA-256 |

Figure 6-3. *Authentication*

At this point, if we try to connect, we could get the error shown in Figure 6-4.

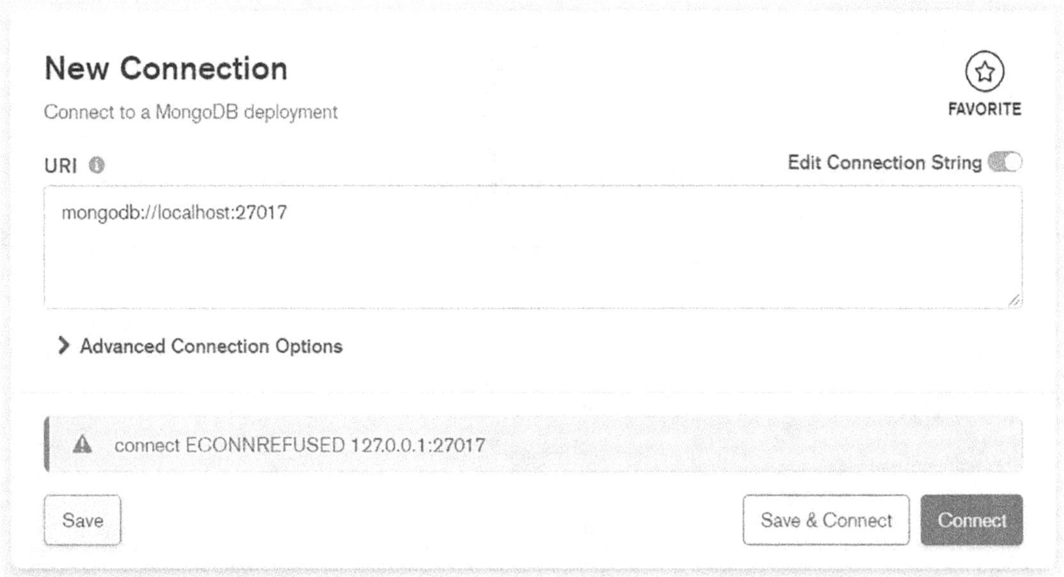

New Connection

Connect to a MongoDB deployment

FAVORITE

URI ⓘ

Edit Connection String ⬤

mongodb://localhost:27017

❯ Advanced Connection Options

⚠   connect ECONNREFUSED 127.0.0.1:27017

Save

Save & Connect   Connect

Figure 6-4. *Connection refused*

This is because we need to make sure that the MongoDB service is running. Now, the method to start a service differs from operating system to operating system. In Windows, you can access the services by typing Services and then looking for MongoDB Server (Figure 6-5).

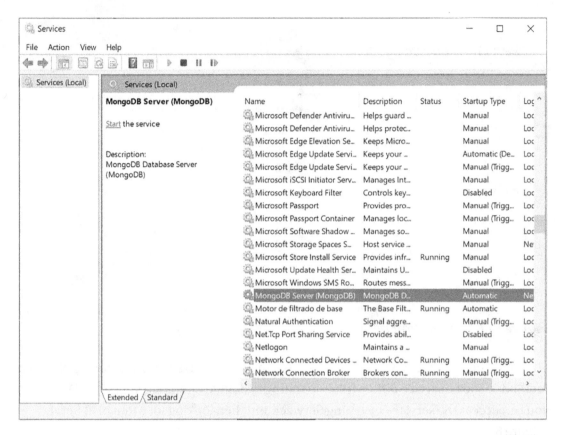

Figure 6-5. *MongoDB Server*

After starting the service, we should be able to connect.

Once connected, we will have access to the server's default databases (Figure 6-6).

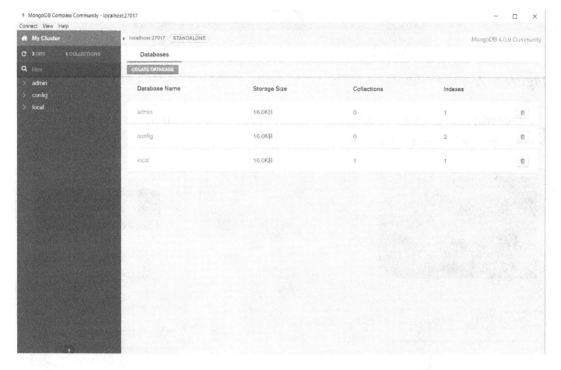

Figure 6-6. *Databases*

We will not use this interface to create a new database, although we could do it. We will simply leave the server running. We will have to start it every time our application exchanges data with the backend.

What We Will Be Doing

Our application will represent a blog, which will allow us to show how to perform CRUD operations on a backend.

For the graphical interface, we will not start from scratch, but we will use the base provided by bootstrap, in particular, version 4.6 of the framework.

In the website, we will find a link called Examples in this link: https:// getbootstrap.com/docs/4.6/examples/ (Figure 6-7).

Figure 6-7. *Examples*

This will take us to a grid with a good number of templates that exemplify the bootstrap capabilities (Figure 6-8).

Figure 6-8. *Sign-in*

We have the appropriate template for our blog, as well as the one we will use for the login.

All these examples can be downloaded so that we can use them (Figure 6-9).

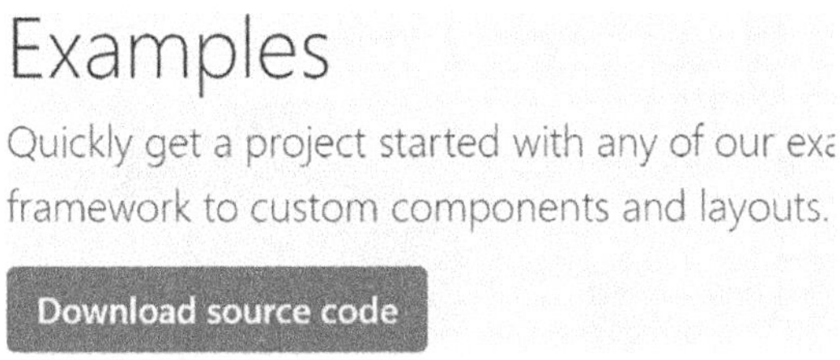

Examples

Quickly get a project started with any of our exa
framework to custom components and layouts.

Download source code

Figure 6-9. *Source of examples*

When unzipping the file, we will obtain a directory called
bootstrap.4.xx
where xx represents numbers of patches and minor versions that might be different
at the time you download the code.

Within this main directory, we have one called **site**, and within this one called **docs**.
Here, there will be a new directory of the form 4.x, which corresponds to the version of
the documentation at the time of download. Finally, inside, you will find the samples
directory.

In my particular case, the route is as follows:

bootstrap-4.6.2\site\content\docs\4.6\examples

Here are all the examples that illustrate the most important capabilities of
bootstrap4, including **blog** and **sign in**, which will serve as our starting point
(Figure 6-10).

album	13/2/2019 13:01	Carpeta de archivos
blog	13/2/2019 13:01	Carpeta de archivos
carousel	13/2/2019 13:01	Carpeta de archivos
checkout	13/2/2019 13:01	Carpeta de archivos
cover	13/2/2019 13:01	Carpeta de archivos
dashboard	13/2/2019 13:01	Carpeta de archivos
floating-labels	13/2/2019 13:01	Carpeta de archivos
grid	13/2/2019 13:01	Carpeta de archivos
jumbotron	13/2/2019 13:01	Carpeta de archivos
navbar-bottom	13/2/2019 13:01	Carpeta de archivos
navbar-fixed	13/2/2019 13:01	Carpeta de archivos
navbars	13/2/2019 13:01	Carpeta de archivos
navbar-static	13/2/2019 13:01	Carpeta de archivos
offcanvas	13/2/2019 13:01	Carpeta de archivos
pricing	13/2/2019 13:01	Carpeta de archivos
product	13/2/2019 13:01	Carpeta de archivos
sign-in	13/2/2019 13:01	Carpeta de archivos
starter-template	13/2/2019 13:01	Carpeta de archivos
sticky-footer	13/2/2019 13:01	Carpeta de archivos
sticky-footer-navbar	13/2/2019 13:01	Carpeta de archivos
.stylelintrc	13/2/2019 13:01	Archivo STYLELINT...
index.html	13/2/2019 13:01	Chrome HTML Do...

Figure 6-10. Directory of examples

Starting the Project

Now we create a new folder called blog. Standing inside the blog folder, let's create our new Angular project:

ng new frontend

At the same level as the frontend directory, let's add another new one called backend, which will contain the code of Node.js corresponding to our APIs.

212

We will then finally have these two directories (Figure 6-11).

backend

frontend

Figure 6-11. *Project structure*

Let's open the frontend folder directory in our IDE. We will see something like Figure 6-12.

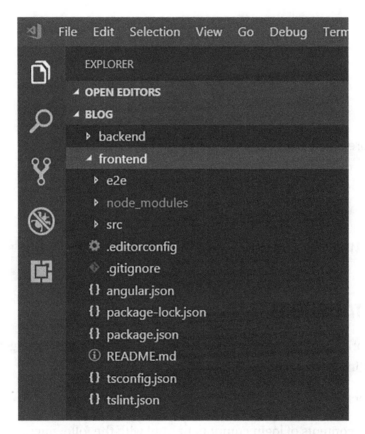

Figure 6-12. *Project structure*

Installing Bootstrap

Next, let's add bootstrap to our application. We have already seen how to do this in previous chapters, so you can refer to them if necessary.

In addition, we must install jQuery and popper.js, which has also been covered previously.

Now let's open a console inside the frontend directory and run the Angular server:

```
ng serve -o
```

We will see the screen to which we must already be accustomed (Figure 6-13).

Welcome to frontend!

Here are some links to help you start:

- Tour of Heroes
- CLI Documentation
- Angular blog

Figure 6-13. *Welcome screen*

Login Component

We will now work on the component that we will use for the login. First, generate it with the command line:

```
ng g c components/login
```

Replace the contents of login.component.html with the following:

```
<div class="main">
    <form class="form-signin">
        <h1 class="h3 mb-3 font-weight-normal">Please sign in</h1>
        <label for="inputEmail" class="sr-only">Email address</label>
        <input type="email" id="inputEmail" class="form-control"
placeholder="Email address" required autofocus>
```

```
    <label for="inputPassword" class="sr-only">Password</label>
    <input type="password" id="inputPassword" class="form-control"
placeholder="Password" required>
    <div class="checkbox mb-3">
        <label>
    <input type="checkbox" value="remember-me"> Remember me
  </label>
    </div>
    <button class="btn btn-lg btn-primary btn-block" type="submit">
        Sign in
    </button>
    <p class="mt-5 mb-3 text-muted">& copy; 2017 - {{date | date:
    "yyyy"}}</p>
  </form>
</div>
```

The previous code is the one that is present in the bootstrap sign-in example, which we downloaded earlier, with some modifications.

We have to add the date variable inside login.component.ts:

```
date = new Date();
```

Now, let's add the styles in login.component.css:

```
.main {
   text-align: center! important;
   display: -ms-flexbox;
   display: flex;
   -ms-flex-align: center;
   align-items: center;
   padding-top: 40px;
   padding-bottom: 40px;
}

.form-signin {
   width: 100%;
   max-width: 330px;
   padding: 15px;
```

```
    margin: auto;
}

.form-signin .checkbox {
    font-weight: 400;
}

.form-signin .form-control {
    position: relative;
    box-sizing: border-box;
    height: auto;
    padding: 10px;
    font-size: 16px;
}

.form-signin .form-control: focus {
    z-index: 2;
}

.form-signin input[type="email"] {
    margin-bottom: -1px;
    border-bottom-right-radius: 0;
    border-bottom-left-radius: 0;
}

.form-signin input[type="password"] {
    margin-bottom: 10px;
    border-top-left-radius: 0;
    border-top-right-radius: 0;
}
```

To verify that it works, let's replace the content of app.component.html to include our new component:

```
<app-login> </app-login>
```

The output will be as shown in Figure 6-14.

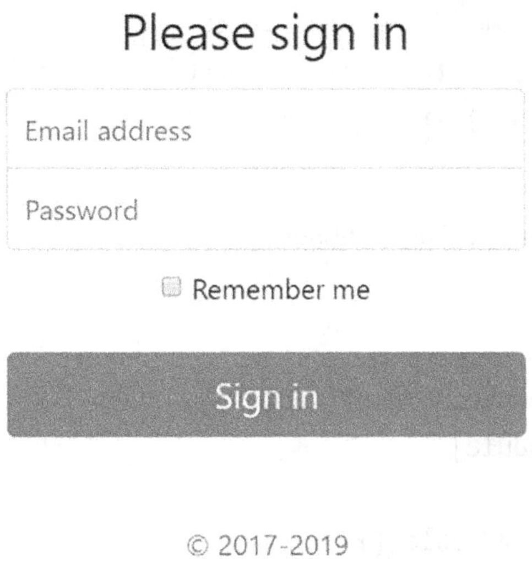

Please sign in

Email address

Password

☐ Remember me

Sign in

© 2017-2019

Figure 6-14. *Login component*

To be sure that everything is correct, I will give you the links to the source code of the login component:

login.component.html

https://github.com/Apress/The-Beginning-Angular-by-Victor-Hugo-Garcia/
blob/main/Chapter-06/01-login.component.html

login.component.css

https://github.com/Apress/The-Beginning-Angular-by-Victor-Hugo-Garcia/
blob/main/Chapter-06/02-login.component.css

login.component.ts

https://github.com/Apress/The-Beginning-Angular-by-Victor-Hugo-Garcia/
blob/main/Chapter-06/03-login.component-v1.ts

Routes of the Application

So far, we have managed to show the login screen in our application; however, we have not yet defined any route.

From previous chapters, we will remember that we use the approach of employing a module to define the routes of the application.

At the same level as our app.module.ts file, let's define a file named app.routes.ts with the following content:

```
import { NgModule } from '@angular/core';
import { RouterModule, Routes } from '@angular/router';
import { LoginComponent } from './components/login/login.component';

const routes: Routes = [
    { path: '', component: LoginComponent },
];

@NgModule({
    imports: [RouterModule.forRoot(routes)],
    exports: [RouterModule]
})
export class AppRoutingModule {}
```

In order for our module to be usable, we must add it in the imports array of app.
module.ts:

```
imports: [
    BrowserModule,
    AppRoutingModule
 ],
```

So we should also add the following line:

```
import { AppRoutingModule } from './app.routes';
```

Now we can replace the content of our app.component.html with the following:

```
<router-outlet> </router-outlet>
```

User Model

Our login screen is already displayed, but still it is not functional. The idea is that we will
send a username and password through it, and that user and password will be validated
in the server, which will return a response to see if the user can be admitted to the
application or not.

Now we will concentrate on creating a user model, a simple class that is responsible
for saving the user and password that will be sent.

Create a directory called **models** inside the **app** folder, and within this models directory, create a user.model.ts file with the following content:

```
export class User {
    private username = '';
    private password = '';

    constructor(username: string, password: string) {
        this.username = username;
        this.password = password;
    }
}
```

As we mentioned, it's a very simple class, with two properties: username and password. We could have reduced it even more in the following way:

```
export class User {
    public username = '';
    public password = '';

    constructor() {}
}
```

In this way, by declaring username and password as public properties, we could manipulate them directly from outside the class. But as we mentioned in the chapter where the classes were introduced, it is not a good idea that the properties of an object can be manipulated directly from a code external to the object itself, so we will keep our first option.

Login Service

We need a service that makes requests to the backend (which we do not yet have), sending the user and password to be validated. We use:

```
ng g s services/login
```

As a result of this command, we will obtain a services directory and a login.service.ts file with the following content:

```
import { Injectable } from '@angular/core';

@Injectable({
  providedIn: 'root'
})
export class LoginService {

  constructor() {}
}
```

As a first step, add a login method, which will receive an object of type User, and a logout method. We will not develop the logic of these methods yet:

```
login(user: User) {

  }

  logout() {}
```

Of course, we must have the corresponding import of the user model:

```
import { User } from '../models/user.model';
```

For now, this is enough. Now we will make the necessary changes in our login component to be able to use the service.

Adding the Logic of the Form

At this point, we are going to modify our form to capture the data entered by the user.

We will be using what is known in Angular as Reactive Forms. This is one of two approaches that Angular allows when we refer to the handling of forms.

Through Reactive Forms, we can keep track of changes to a model easily. This is all we need to know for now.

Modify the content of login.component.ts in the following way:

```
import { Component, OnInit } from '@angular/core';
import { FormBuilder, FormGroup, Validators } from '@angular/forms';
import { LoginService } from '../../services/login.service';
import { User } from '../../models/user.model';
```

```
@Component({
  selector: 'app-login',
  templateUrl: './login.component.html',
  styleUrls: ['./login.component.css']
})
export class LoginComponent implements OnInit {
  date = new Date();
  loginForm: FormGroup;
  submitted = false;
  loading = false;
  user: User = new User('', '');
  error: string = '';

constructor(
    private formBuilder: FormBuilder,
    private loginService: LoginService
) {
  this.loginForm = this.formBuilder.group({
    username: ['', Validators.required],
    password: ['', Validators.required]
  });
}

  ngOnInit() {}

  get f() { return this.loginForm.controls; }

  onSubmit() {
    this.submitted = true;

    // stop here if form is invalid
    if (this.loginForm.invalid) {
        return;
    }

    this.loading = true;
```

```
        this.user = new User(this.f['username'].value,
        this.f['password'].value);

        console.log( this.user );
    }
}
```

There are many changes, but we are going to analyze them one by one. First, we have the following new import:

```
import { FormBuilder, FormGroup, Validators } from '@angular/forms';
import { LoginService } from '../../services/login.service';
import { User } from '../../models/user.model';
```

The first three allow us to define a form programmatically, as well as perform validations on form fields.

To be more specific, FormBuilder makes it easier to create FormGroups, which represent groups of grouped form objects.

Then we import our service and the user model, which we will need to communicate with the API.

The following properties are then entered:

```
loginForm: FormGroup;
submitted = false;
loading = false;
user: User = new User('', '');
error: string = '';
```

loginForm will be the variable by which we identify the group of controls in our form. In more complex forms, we would have more than one group of controls, but in this case, it is not necessary since we have only two.

The variable submitted is a flag that is set to true when the form is submitted, and loading will be true while waiting for the response from the server. Then we have the model, and error will show any error returned by the API.

```
constructor(
    private formBuilder: FormBuilder,
    private loginService: LoginService
) {}
```

```
ngOnInit() {
  this.loginForm = this.FormBuilder.group({
    username: ['', Validators.required],
    password: ['', Validators.required]
  });
}
```

We must declare two properties in our constructor, one for our FormBuilder and one for our LoginService.

Then, in the OnInit function, we instantiate our FormBuilder, passing it as a parameter two fields, which will be mandatory.

Then we have a getter:

```
get f() { return this.LoginForm.controls; }
```

The purpose of this function is to allow us to reference the controls of the form by means of the identifier **f**.

Finally, the onSubmit function is executed when the button of the form is clicked. There, a validation is carried out on the required fields, and if this fails, the process will stop. Otherwise, in this case we will simply show the values per console.

It is important to make the following changes in our app.module.ts. First, add the following import:

```
import { ReactiveFormsModule, FormsModule } from '@angular/forms';
```

Then, in the array of imports, we must add the imported modules:

```
imports: [
  BrowserModule,
  FormsModule,
  ReactiveFormsModule,
  AppRoutingModule
]
```

If we do not make these changes in our app.module.ts, we will get errors.

Now let's modify the content of login.component.html as follows:

```
<div class="main">
    <div *ngIf="error" class="alert alert-danger">{{error}}</div>
```

```
<form [formGroup]="loginForm" (ngSubmit)="onSubmit ()"
class="form-signin">
    <h1 class="h3 mb-3 font-weight-normal">Please sign in</h1>
    <label for="username" class="sr-only">Username</label>
    <input type="text" formControlName="username"
class="form-control"
 placeholder="Username"
[ngClass]="{'is-invalid': submitted && f['username'].errors}" />
    <div *ngIf="submitted && f['username'].errors" class="invalid-
    feedback">
        <div *ngIf="f['username'].errors['required']">Username is
        required</div>
    </div>

    <label for="password" class="sr-only">Password</label>
    <input type="password" formControlName="password"
class="form-control"
 placeholder="Password"
[ngClass]="{'is-invalid': submitted && f['password'].errors}" />
    <div *ngIf="submitted && f['password'].errors" class="invalid-
    feedback">
        <div *ngIf="f['password'].errors['required']">Password is
        required</div>
    </div>

    <div class="form-group">
        <button [disabled]="loading"
class="btn btn-lg btn-primary btn-block">
            <span *ngIf="loading"
class="spinner-border spinner-border-sm mr-1">
 </span>
            Sign in
        </button>
    </div>
</form>
</div>
```

Notice in the first text box:

```
formControlName="username"
```

We are linking the text box with the username control of our FormGroup. If instead of using the Reactive Forms approach, we have used a Template approach, we would have something like this:

```
[(ngModel)] ="username"
```

where username would refer to a property of our login.component.ts.

With these changes, now our login looks almost the same as before (Figure 6-15).

Figure 6-15. *Login form*

But if we try to log in without entering the username or password, we will see the corresponding errors (Figure 6-16).

Figure 6-16. *Required fields*

If, on the contrary, we enter a username and password, we will obtain the expected console output (Figure 6-17).

Figure 6-17. *Console output*

That is, everything works as expected up to now.

Let's now add two methods in our user model:

```
getUserName() {
    return this.username;
}

getPassword() {
    return this.password;
}
```

Now we can complete the definition of the login method in login.service.ts. But before that, we need to declare a private property in our constructor method:

```
constructor( private http: HttpClient ) { }
```

and of course the corresponding import:

```
import { HttpClient } from '@angular/common/http';
```

Finally, we can modify the login method as follow:

```
login(user: User) {
    return this.http.post('/api/user/login', {
        username : user.getUserName(),
```

```
        password : user.getPassword()
    });
 }
```

Of course, we have not written the API yet, but we will do it soon. The login method will return an observable, to which we can subscribe from our login component. Here is the onSubmit method of login.component.ts:

```
onSubmit() {
    this.submitted = true;

    // stop here if form is invalid
    if (this.loginForm.invalid) {
        return;
    }

    this.loading = true;

    this.user = new User(this.f.username.value, this.f.password.value);

    this.loginService.login( this.user ).subscribe({
      next: (result) => console.log(result),
      error: (e) => console.error(e),
      complete: () => console.info('complete')
    });
 }
```

However, we must also add a new import in the imports array of our app.module.ts:

```
HttpClientModule
```

and the corresponding line:

```
import { HttpClientModule } from '@angular/common/http';
```

If we do not do this, we will get the error shown in Figure 6-18.

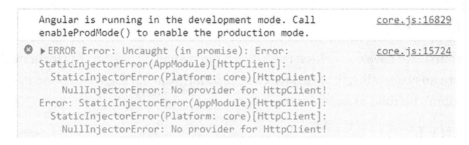

Figure 6-18. *HttpClientModule not imported*

If everything is correct, we will see the login screen. If we enter a username and password, we will get the error shown in Figure 6-19.

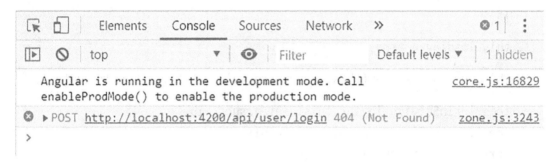

Figure 6-19. *Path not found*

However, this is an expected error, since the api/user/login path does not exist. But it tells us that the request is being made.

To finish with this first part, I will provide links to the code of our components, models, services, and modules, in order to make sure that everything is working correctly.

Application Code

LoginComponent

login.component.ts

https://github.com/Apress/The-Beginning-Angular-by-Victor-Hugo-Garcia/
blob/main/Chapter-06/04-login.component-v2.ts

login.component.html

https://github.com/Apress/The-Beginning-Angular-by-Victor-Hugo-Garcia/
blob/main/Chapter-06/05-login.component-v2.html

User Model

user.model.ts

https://github.com/Apress/The-Beginning-Angular-by-Victor-Hugo-Garcia/
blob/main/Chapter-06/06-user.model.ts

LoginService

login.service.ts

https://github.com/Apress/The-Beginning-Angular-by-Victor-Hugo-Garcia/
blob/main/Chapter-06/07-login.service.ts

Routes

app.routes.ts

https://github.com/Apress/The-Beginning-Angular-by-Victor-Hugo-Garcia/
blob/main/Chapter-06/08-app.routes.ts

AppModule

app.module.ts

https://github.com/Apress/The-Beginning-Angular-by-Victor-Hugo-Garcia/
blob/main/Chapter-06/09-app.module.ts

Summary

In this chapter, we have laid the foundations of our application. By far, this will be
the most complex application built so far by us, but it will undoubtedly help us to put
together all the concepts seen so far. In the next chapter, we will work with the backend
by writing the API to authenticate the user. It will be developed in NodeJS and will
communicate with a database in MongoDB.

CHAPTER 7

Blog App Part 2

In the previous chapter, we began to define the frontend of our application. We created the component to perform the login, and we defined the services that will be communicating with the API. In this chapter, we will focus on the backend, using NodeJS, Express, and MongoDB for it. We'll build our home component, which will be the central screen of our application. In addition, we'll establish the mechanisms to persist the user's session.

NodeJS

NodeJS is an execution environment for JavaScript oriented to asynchronous events. It allows us to build scalable network applications, which support multiple simultaneous connections. It uses separate execution threads for this.

NodeJS undoubtedly deserves a book by itself, but we will see here enough to give life to a simple but robust API.

To make things even easier, we will use Express.

Express

Express is a framework that works on the Node execution environment. It facilitates the creation of applications, shortening the development time.

MongoDB

We already talked about MongoDB in the previous chapter. In this, we will connect to a MongoDB database using Mongoose.

© Victor Hugo Garcia 2023
V. H. Garcia, *Getting Started with Angular*, https://doi.org/10.1007/978-1-4842-9206-8_7

Mongoose

Mongoose is an Object Document Mapper written in JavaScript, which allows us to define and manipulate in a simple way dynamic objects in a MongoDB database, mapping those objects to documents.

These tools will allow us to build a robust and efficient API, which will serve as an excellent backend for our application.

Starting the Project on the Server

We have two folders in our project: frontend and backend. The frontend folder is the one that hosts our Angular project.

Let's open the console in the backend folder and execute the following command:

```
npm init
```

When executing this command, we will be asked a series of questions. We can simply leave the default values by pressing enter on each of the options.

As a result of the process, we will obtain a file called package.json with the following content:

```
{
 "name": "backend",
 "version": "1.0.0",
 "description": "",
 "main": "index.js",
 "scripts": {
   "test": "echo \"Error: no test specified\" && exit 1"
 },
 "author": "",
 "license": "ISC"
}
```

In this file, we can change any option that we consider necessary.

Now install the express framework running:

```
npm install express --save
```

At the end, we will have a new directory, node_modules, with all the framework packages (Figure 7-1).

Figure 7-1. *Install Express*

At the same level as the directory, we create a file called index.js with the following content:

```
const express = require('express');
const app = express();

app.get('/api/user/login', (req, res) => {
   res.send('Hello World!')
});

app.listen(3000, () => console.log('Listening on port 3000'));
```

The code is simple. We are defining a path: /api/user/login, which will receive a GET request, and that will simply return a text message.

At the same time, we are indicating that the requests will be heard on port 3000. We could have used another port, as long as it was unoccupied.

Now, from the console, and always standing inside the backend directory, let's run the command:

```
node index.js
```

We'll see a message indicating that the app is listening on port 3000 (Figure 7-2).

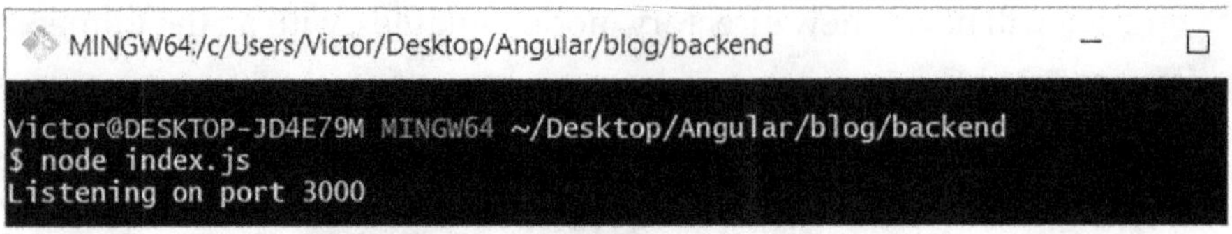

MINGW64:/c/Users/Victor/Desktop/Angular/blog/backend   —   □

Victor@DESKTOP-JD4E79M MINGW64 ~/Desktop/Angular/blog/backend
$ node index.js
Listening on port 3000

Figure 7-2. *Node index.js*

If we now point the browser to http://localhost:3000/api/user/login, we will
see the welcome message (Figure 7-3).

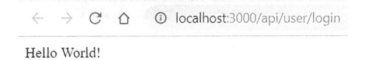

Hello World!

Figure 7-3. *Hello World backend*

We now need to install two new packages:

npm install body-parser --save

This package will allow you to extract parameters from the requests received by the
server. Then let's run:

npm install mongoose --save

As we mentioned before, this package will allow you to easily interact with the
MongoDB database.

Creating the Database

We have the packages installed, but we do not have a database yet. First, we must start
the MongoDB server and connect. We can do it easily using MongoDB Compass, which
we downloaded and installed in the previous chapter (Figure 7-4).

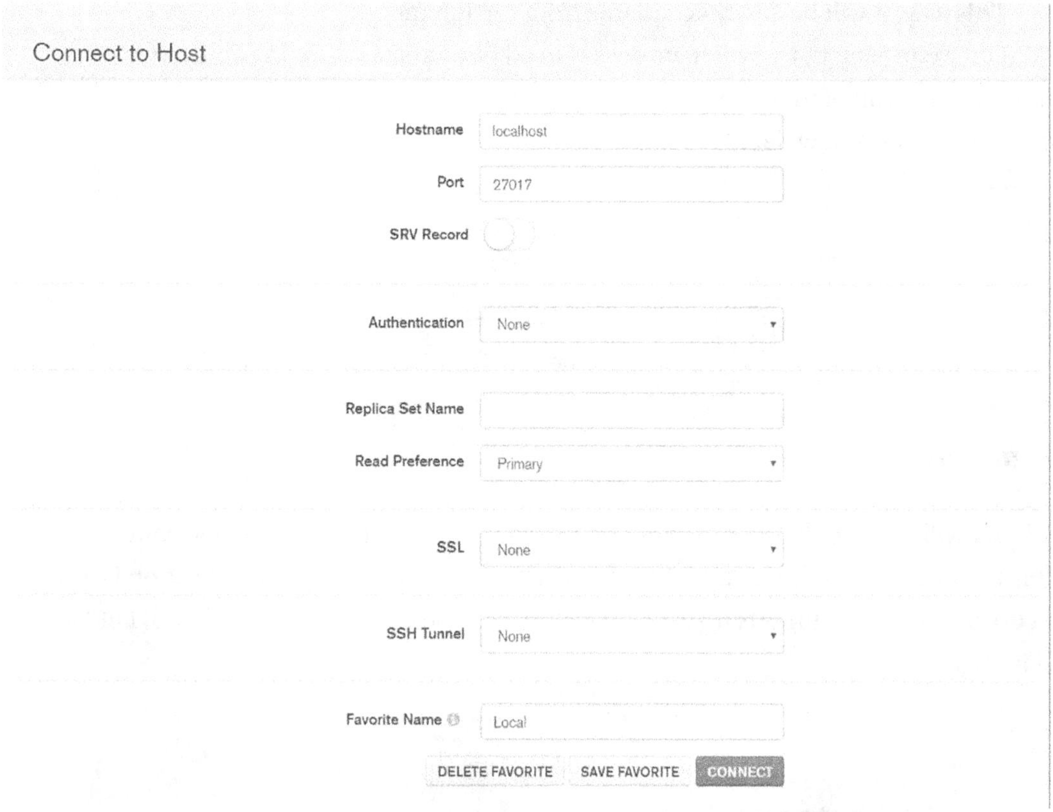

Figure 7-4. *Connect to host*

If we wish, we can save this connection as one of our favorites (Figure 7-5).

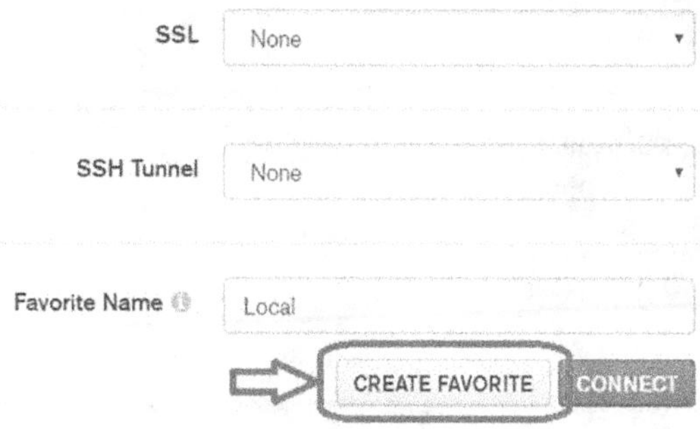

Figure 7-5. *Create favorite*

This way, it will be easily accessible from the left menu.

Once connected, we will have access to all our databases, being able to perform operations on all of them and even create new ones.

Let's create a new database (Figure 7-6).

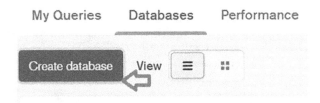

Figure 7-6. *Create database*

We will need to define the name of the database and the name of one collection. It is tempting to assimilate the concept of collection to a table, but a collection is a set of documents. Documents inside a collection can have a different number of fields (Figure 7-7).

Create Database

Database Name

blog

Collection Name

user

> Advanced Collection Options (e.g. Time-Series, Capped, Clustered collections)

Cancel   Create Database

Figure 7-7. *Create database*

Go ahead and type blog as the database name and user as the collection, then click **Create Database**.

Note that we have not had to specify any type of structure for the collection, but we don't need to. We can see the newly added database (Figure 7-8).

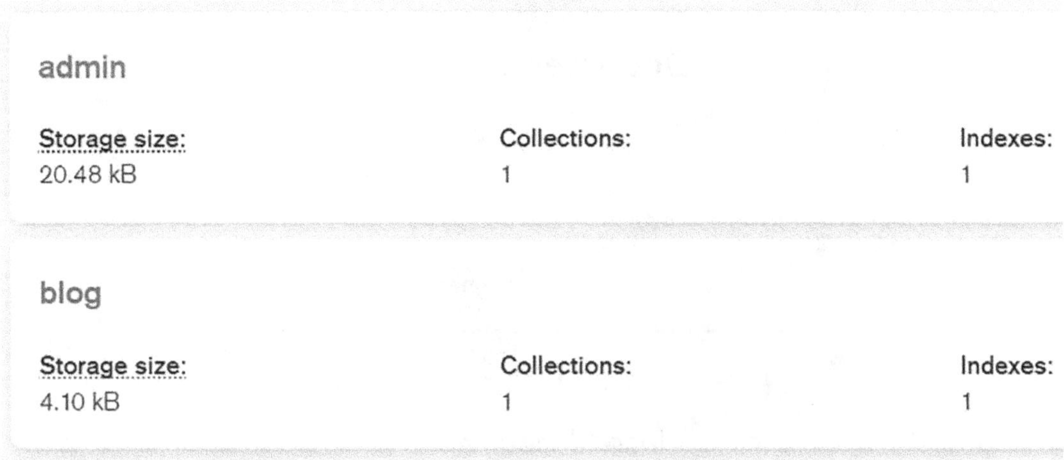

admin

Storage size:	Collections:	Indexes:
20.48 kB	1	1

blog

Storage size:	Collections:	Indexes:
4.10 kB	1	1

Figure 7-8. *New DB*

Click the name of the database; we'll see the only collection (Figure 7-9).

Create collection   View   ≡   ∷

user

Storage size:	Documents:
4.10 kB	0

Figure 7-9. *New collection*

Click the collection. Then select the option **Insert Document** from the **ADD DATA** list (Figure 7-10).

Figure 7-10. Insert document

We'll be presented with a pop-up window. Replace the content with the following:

```
{
  "name": "Administrator",
  "username": "Admin",
  "password": "1234"
}
```

Then click Insert. We can see the newly added document (Figure 7-11).

Figure 7-11. User inserted

We have in this way a user against whom we can test the login, but we still have to take some steps to connect the frontend with the backend.

```
{
   "/api/*": {
      "target": "http://localhost:3000",
      "secure": "false"
   }
}
```

Now, let's open the angular.json file. In it, we will find the following section:

```
"serve": {
         "builder": "@angular-devkit/build-angular:dev-server",
         "configurations": {
           "production": {
             "browserTarget": "frontend:build:production"
           },
           "development": {
             "browserTarget": "frontend:build:development"
           }
         },
         "defaultConfiguration": "development"
       },
```

Replace it with:

```
"serve": {
         "builder": "@angular-devkit/build-angular:dev-server",
         "configurations": {
           "production": {
             "browserTarget": "frontend:build:production"
           },
           "development": {
             "browserTarget": "frontend:build:development",
             "proxyConfig": "src/proxy.json"
           }
         },
```

```
                "defaultConfiguration": "development"
},
```

We have just added the line:

```
"proxyConfig": "src/proxy.json"
```

This step is necessary because we are hosting our client application and the server within the same parent directory.

If we had already executed:

```
ng serve -o
```

We must stop the Angular server with Ctrl+C and restart it.

Let's go back to the backend folder again and create a directory called models there. Let's add a file named user.js with the following content:

```
const mongoose = require('mongoose');
const Schema = mongoose.Schema;

// create a schema
const userSchema = new Schema({
    username: { type: String, required: true, unique: true },
    password: { type: String, required: true },
    name: { type: String }
}, { collection: 'user' });

const User = mongoose.model('User', userSchema);

module.exports = User;
```

Now we rewrite the content of index.js in the following way:

```
const express = require('express');
const bodyParser = require('body-parser');
const app = express();
const mongoose = require('mongoose');
const url = 'mongodb://localhost/blog';
const User = require('./models/user');
```

```
mongoose.set('strictQuery', true);

app.use(bodyParser.json());
app.use(bodyParser.urlencoded({ extended: false }));

app.post('/api/user/login', (req, res) => {
    mongoose.connect(url, { },
function(err) {
        if (err) throw err;
        User.find({
            username: req.body.username,
            password: req.body.password
        }, function(err, user) {
            if (err) throw err;
            if (user.length === 1) {
                return res.status(200).json({
                    status: 'success',
                    data: user
                })
            } else {
                return res.status(200).json({
                    status: 'fail',
                    message: 'Login Failed'
                })
            }

        })
    });
});

app.listen(3000, () => console.log('Listening on port 3000'));
```

Let's analyze the changes:

```
const bodyParser = require('body-parser');
const mongoose = require('mongoose');
const url = 'mongodb://localhost/blog';
const User = require('./model/user');
```

We are requiring the body-parser module to obtain the parameters that are sent in the requests to the server. Then we require mongoose because we will work with a MongoDB database. We also define a constant that will reference the url of our database, and finally we require our user model to interact with the collection of the same name.

We will not analyze the rest of the code in detail, but what it does is search the user collection for a user whose username and password match the one received.

If we had previously started the server with:

```
node index.js
```

we will need to halt the execution and start the server again.

If now we try to log in, and assuming that we enter as user Admin and password 1234, we will see the output by console (Figure 7-12).

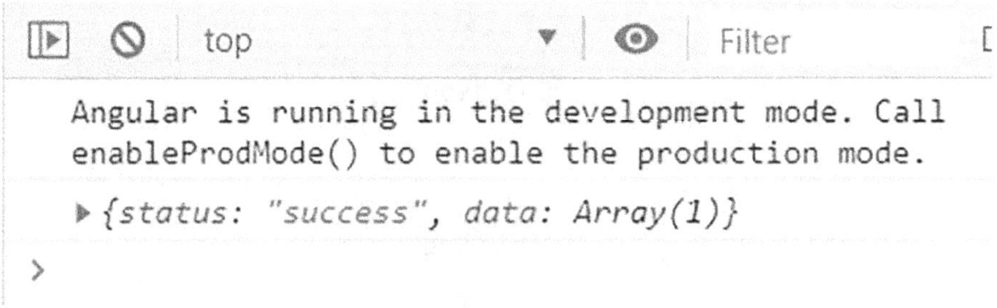

Figure 7-12. *Login success*

It is to be expected, since in our login component we are simply sending the result received from the server to the console. What we should do is redirect the user to the main page, which we do not have yet.

Home Component

Go ahead and create a component called **home**; we have already done this several times.

Let's replace the contents of home.component.html with the following. It's a lot of content, so it's probably better to use this file:

https://github.com/Apress/The-Beginning-Angular-by-Victor-Hugo-Garcia/ blob/main/Chapter-07/01-home.component-v1.html

```
<div class="container">
    <header class="blog-header py-3">
```

```
    <div class="row flex-nowrap justify-content-between align-
    items-center">
        <div class="col-4 pt-1">
            <a class="text-muted" href="#">Subscribe</a>
        </div>
        <div class="col-4 text-center">
            <a class="blog-header-logo text-dark" href="#">Large</a>
        </div>
        <div class="col-4 d-flex justify-content-end align-
        items-center">
            <a class="text-muted" href="#">
                <svg xmlns="http://www.w3.org/2000/svg" width="20"
                height="20"
fill="none" stroke="currentColor" stroke-linecap="round" stroke-
linejoin="round"
stroke-width="2" class="mx-3" role="img" viewBox="0 0 24 24"
focusable="false">
<title>Search</title>
<circle cx="10.5" cy="10.5" r="7.5"/> <path d="M21 21l-5.2-5.2"/>
                </svg>
            </a>
            <a class="btn btn-sm btn-outline-secondary" href="#">
Sign up</a>
        </div>
    </div>
  </header>

  <div class="nav-scroller py-1 mb-2">
    <nav class="nav d-flex justify-content-between">
        <a class="p-2 text-muted" href="#">World</a>
        <a class="p-2 text-muted" href="#">US</a>
        <a class="p-2 text-muted" href="#">Technology</a>
        <a class="p-2 text-muted" href="#">Design</a>
        <a class="p-2 text-muted" href="#">Culture</a>
        <a class="p-2 text-muted" href="#">Business</a>
        <a class="p-2 text-muted" href="#">Politics</a>
```

243

```
            <a class="p-2 text-muted" href="#">Opinion</a>
            <a class="p-2 text-muted" href="#">Science</a>
            <a class="p-2 text-muted" href="#">Health</a>
            <a class="p-2 text-muted" href="#">Style</a>
            <a class="p-2 text-muted" href="#">Travel</a>
        </nav>
    </div>

    <div class="jumbotron p-4 p-md-5 text-white rounded bg-dark">
        <div class="col-md-6 px-0">
            <h1 class="display-4 font-italic">
              Title of a longer featured blog post
            </h1>
            <p class="lead my-3">Multiple lines of text that form the
lede, informing new readers quickly and about what's
most interesting in this post's contents.</p>
            <p class="lead mb-0">
              <a href="#" class="text-white font-weight-bold">
                Continue reading ...
              </a>
            </p>
        </div>
    </div>

    <div class="row mb-2">
        <div class="col-md-6">
            <div class="row no-gutters border rounded overflow-hidden
flex-md-row mb-4 shadow-sm h-md-250 position-relative">
                <div class="col p-4 d-flex flex-column position-static">
                    <strong class="d-inline-block mb-2 text-
                    primary">World</strong>
                    <h3 class="mb-0">Featured post</h3>
                    <div class="mb-1 text-muted">Nov 12</div>
                    <p class="card-text mb-auto">
This is a larger card with supporting text below
as a natural lead-in to additional content.</p>
```

```
                <a href="#" class="stretched-link">
                  Continue reading
                </a>
              </div>
              <div class="col-auto d-none d-lg-block">
                <svg class="bd-placeholder-img"
width="200" height="250" xmlns="http://www.w3.org/2000/svg"
preserveAspectRatio="xMidYMid slice" focusable="false"
role="img" aria-label="Placeholder: Thumbnail">
  <title>Placeholder</title>
  <rect width="100%" height="100%" fill="# 55595c"> </rect>
  <text x="50%" y="50%" fill="#eceeef" dy=".3em">Thumbnail</text>
                </svg>
              </div>
          </div>
        </div>
        <div class="col-md-6">
            <div
                class="row no-gutters border rounded
overflow-hidden flex-md-row mb-4 shadow-sm
h-md-250 position-relative">
                <div class="col p-4 d-flex flex-column position-static">
                    <strong class="d-inline-block mb-2 text-
                    success">Design</strong>
                    <h3 class="mb-0">Post title</h3>
                    <div class="mb-1 text-muted">Nov 11</div>
                    <p class="mb-auto">This is a larger card with
supporting text below as a natural lead-in to additional content.</p>
                    <a href="#" class="stretched-link">Continue reading</a>
                </div>
                <div class="col-auto d-none d-lg-block">
                    <svg class="bd-placeholder-img"
width="200" height="250" xmlns="http://www.w3.org/2000/svg"
preserveAspectRatio="xMidYMid slice" focusable="false"
role="img" aria-label="Placeholder: Thumbnail">
```

```
<title>Placeholder</title>
<rect width="100%" height="100%" fill="# 55595c"> </rect>
<text x="50%" y="50%" fill="#eceeef" dy=".3em">Thumbnail</text>
                </svg>
            </div>
        </div>
    </div>
</div>

<main role="main" class="container">
    <div class="row">
        <div class="col-md-8 blog-main">
            <h3 class="pb-4 mb-4 font-italic border-bottom">
                From the Firehose
            </h3>

            <div class="blog-post">
                <h2 class="blog-post-title">Sample blog post</h2>
                <p class="blog-post-goal">January 1, 2014 by <a
                href="#">Mark</a> </p>

                <p>This blog post shows a few different types of
content that is supported and styled with Bootstrap.
Basic typography, images, and code are all supported.</p>
                <hr>
                <p>Cum sociis natoque penatibus et magnis
<a href="#">dis parturient montes</a>, nascetur ridiculus mus.
Aenean eu leo quam. Pellentesque ornare sem lacinia quam
venenatis vestibulum. Sed posuere consectetur est at
lobortis. Cras mattis consectetur
                purus sit amet fermentum.</p>
                <blockquote>
                    <p>Curabitur blandit tempus porttitor.
<strong>Nullam quis risus eget urn mollis</strong>
ornare vel eu leo. Nullam id pain id nibh ultricies
vehicula ut id elit.</p>
```

```
        </blockquote>
        <p>Etiam carries
<em>sem embarrassed magna</em> mollis euismod.
Cras mattis consectetur purus sit amet fermentum.
Aenean lacinia bibendum nulla sed consectetur.</p>
        <h2>Heading</h2>
        <p>Vivamus sagittis lacus vel augue
laoreet rutrum faucibus pain auctor. Duis mollis,
est non commodo luctus, nisi erat porttitor ligula,
eget lacinia hate sem nec elit. Morbi leo risus,
porta ac consectetur ac,
vestibulum at eros.</p>
        <h3>Sub-heading</h3>
        <p>Cum sociis natoque penatibus
et magnis dis parturient montes, nascetur ridiculus mus.</p>
        <pre> <code>Example code block</code> </pre>
        <p>Aenean lacinia bibendum nulla sed consectetur.
Etiam carries sem embarrassment magna mollis euismod.
Fusce dapibus, tellus ac cursus commodo, tortor
mauris condimentum nibh, ut fermentum massa.</p>
        <h3>Sub-heading</h3>
        <p>Cum sociis natoque penatibus et magnis dis
parturient montes, nascetur ridiculus mus. Aenean lacinia
bibendum nulla sed consectetur. Etiam carries sem embarrassment
magna mollis euismod. Fusce dapibus, tellus ac cursus commodo,
tortor mauris condimentum nibh, ut fermentum massa just sit
amet risus.</p>
        <ul>
            <li>Praesent commodo cursus magna, vel
scelerisque nisl consectetur et.</li>
            <li>Donec id elit non my gravida at eget metus.</li>
            <li>Nulla vitae elit libero, a pharetra augue.</li>
        </ul>
        <p>Donec ullamcorper nulla non metus auctor fringilla.
Nulla vitae elit libero, to pharetra augue.</p>
```

```
        <ol>
            <li>Vestibulum id ligula porta felis euismod
semper.</li>
            <li>Cum sociis natoque penatibus et magnis dis
parturient montes, nascetur ridiculus mus.</li>
            <li>Maecenas sed diam eget risus varius blandit
sit amet non magna.</li>
        </ol>
        <p>Cras mattis consectetur purus sit amet fermentum.
Sed posuere consectetur est at lobortis.</p>
    </div>
    <! - /.blog-post ->

    <div class="blog-post">
        <h2 class="blog-post-title">Another blog post</h2>
        <p class="blog-post-goal">
          December 23, 2013 by <a href="#">Jacob</a>
        </p>

        <p>Cum sociis natoque penatibus et magnis
<a href="#">dis parturient montes</a>, nascetur ridiculus mus.
Aenean eu leo quam. Pellentesque ornare sem lacinia quam
venenatis vestibulum. Sed posuere consectetur est at lobortis.
Cras mattis consectetur purus sit amet fermentum.</p>
        <blockquote>
            <p>Curabitur blandit tempus porttitor.
<strong>Nullam quis risus eget urn mollis</strong> ornare vel
eu leo. Nullam id pain id nibh ultricies vehicula ut id elit.</p>
        </blockquote>
        <p>Etiam carries <em>sem embarrassed magna</em>
 mollis euismod. Cras mattis consectetur purus sit amet
fermentum. Aenean lacinia bibendum nulla sed consectetur.</p>
        <p>Vivamus sagittis lacus vel augue laoreet
rutrum faucibus pain auctor. Duis mollis, est non commodo luctus,
nisi erat porttitor ligula, eget lacinia hate sem nec elit.
Morbi leo risus, porta ac consectetur ac, vestibulum at eros.</p>
```

```
    </div>
    <! - /.blog-post ->

    <div class="blog-post">
        <h2 class="blog-post-title">New feature</h2>
        <p class="blog-post-goal">
          December 14, 2013 by <a href="#">Chris</a>
        </p>

        <p>Cum sociis natoque penatibus et magnis dis
parturient montes, nascetur ridiculus mus. Aenean lacinia bibendum
nulla sed consectetur. Etiam carries sem embarrassment magna
mollis euismod. Fusce dapibus, tellus ac cursus commodo, tortor
mauris condimentum nibh, ut fermentum massa just sit amet risus.</p>
            <ul>
                <li>Praesent commodo cursus magna, vel scelerisque
nisl consectetur et.</li>
                <li>Donec id elit non my gravida at eget metus.</li>
                <li>Nulla vitae elit libero, a pharetra augue.</li>
            </ul>
            <p>Etiam carries <em>sem embarrassed magna</em>
mollis euismod. Cras mattis consectetur purus sit amet fermentum.
Aenean lacinia bibendum nulla sed consectetur.</p>
            <p>Donec ullamcorper nulla non metus auctor fringilla.
Nulla vitae elit libero, to pharetra augue.</p>
        </div>
        <! - /.blog-post ->

        <nav class="blog-pagination">
            <a class="btn btn-outline-primary" href="#">Older</a>
            <a class="btn btn-outline-secondary disabled"
href="#" tabindex="-1" aria-disabled="true">Newer</a>
        </nav>

    </div>
    <! - /.blog-main ->

    <aside class="col-md-4 blog-sidebar">
```

```
        <div class="p-4 mb-3 bg-light rounded">
            <h4 class="font-italic">About</h4>
            <p class="mb-0">Etiam carries <em>sem malaise magna</em>
mollis euismod. Cras mattis consectetur purus sit amet fermentum.
Aenean lacinia bibendum nulla sed consectetur.</p>
        </div>

        <div class="p-4">
            <h4 class="font-italic">Archives</h4>
            <ol class="list-unstyled mb-0">
                <li> <a href="#">March 2014</a> </li>
                <li> <a href="#">February 2014</a> </li>
                <li> <a href="#">January 2014</a> </li>
                <li> <a href="#">December 2013</a> </li>
                <li> <a href="#">November 2013</a> </li>
                <li> <a href="#">October 2013</a> </li>
                <li> <a href="#">September 2013</a> </li>
                <li> <a href="#">August 2013</a> </li>
                <li> <a href="#">July 2013</a> </li>
                <li> <a href="#">June 2013</a> </li>
                <li> <a href="#">May 2013</a> </li>
                <li> <a href="#">April 2013</a> </li>
            </ol>
        </div>

        <div class="p-4">
            <h4 class="font-italic">Elsewhere</h4>
            <ol class="list-unstyled">
                <li> <a href="#">GitHub</a> </li>
                <li> <a href="#">Twitter</a> </li>
                <li> <a href="#">Facebook</a> </li>
            </ol>
        </div>
    </aside>
    <! - /.blog-sidebar ->

</div>
```

```
    <! - /.row ->
</main>
<! - /.container ->

<footer class="blog-footer">
    <p>Blog template built for
<a href="https://getbootstrap.com/">Bootstrap</a> by
<a href="https://twitter.com/mdo">@mdo</a>.</p>
    <p>
        <a href="#">Back to top</a>
    </p>
</footer>
```

Again, it's a very large portion of code, so it's probably best that you use the following file: https://github.com/Apress/The-Beginning-Angular-by-Victor-Hugo-Garcia/ blob/main/Chapter-07/01-home.component-v1.html.

Now add the following content to home.component.css:

```
/* stylelint-disable selector-list-comma-newline-after */

.blog-header {
    line-height: 1;
    border-bottom: 1px solid #e5e5e5;
}

.blog-header-logo {
    font-family: "Playfair Display", Georgia, "Times New Roman", serif;
    font-size: 2.25rem;
}

.blog-header-logo: hover {
    text-decoration: none;
}

h1,
h2,
h3,
h4,
```

```
h5,
h6 {
    font-family: "Playfair Display", Georgia, "Times New Roman", serif;
}

.display-4 {
    font-size: 2.5rem;
}

@media (min-width: 768px) {
    .display-4 {
        font-size: 3rem;
    }
}

.nav-scroller {
    position: relative;
    z-index: 2;
    height: 2.75rem;
    overflow-y: hidden;
}

.nav-scroller .nav {
    display: -ms-flexbox;
    display: flex;
    -ms-flex-wrap: nowrap;
    flex-wrap: nowrap;
    padding-bottom: 1rem;
    margin-top: -1px;
    overflow-x: auto;
    text-align: center;
    white-space: nowrap;
    -webkit-overflow-scrolling: touch;
}

.nav-scroller .nav-link {
    padding-top: .75rem;
    padding-bottom: .75rem;
```

```
    font-size: .875rem;
}

.card-img-right {
    height: 100%;
    border-radius: 0 3px 3px 0;
}

.flex-auto {
    -ms-flex: 0 0 auto;
    flex: 0 0 auto;
}

.h-250 {
    height: 250px;
}

@media (min-width: 768px) {
    .h-md-250 {
        height: 250px;
    }
}
/*
 * Blog name and description
 */

.blog-title {
    margin-bottom: 0;
    font-size: 2rem;
    font-weight: 400;
}

.blog-description {
    font-size: 1.1rem;
    color: #999;
}
```

```
@media (min-width: 40em) {
    .blog-title {
        font-size: 3.5rem;
    }
}

/* Pagination */

.blog-pagination {
    margin-bottom: 4rem;
}

.blog-pagination>.btn {
    border-radius: 2rem;
}

/*
 * Blog posts
 */

.blog-post {
    margin-bottom: 4rem;
}

.blog-post-title {
    margin-bottom: .25rem;
    font-size: 2.5rem;
}

.blog-post-meta {
    margin-bottom: 1.25rem;
    color: #999;
}

/*
 * Footer
 */

.blog-footer {
```

```
    padding: 2.5rem 0;
    color: #999;
    text-align: center;
    background-color: #f9f9f9;
    border-top: .05rem solid #e5e5e5;
}

.blog-footer p: last-child {
    margin-bottom: 0;
}
```

Again, just to be sure here is the file (https://github.com/Apress/The-Beginning-Angular-by-Victor-Hugo-Garcia/blob/main/Chapter-07/03-home.component-v1.css).

Now, we have a page to redirect the user after they have started a session. However, we must add the corresponding path in our app.routes.ts:

```
{ path: 'home', component: HomeComponent }
```

and its corresponding import:

```
import { HomeComponent } from './components/home/home.component';
```

The page and the route are ready. But to be able to perform the redirection, we have to add a new import in our login.component.ts:

```
import { Router } from '@angular/router';
```

And we will modify the constructor to create a private variable of type Router:

```
constructor(
  private formBuilder: FormBuilder,
  private loginService: LoginService,
  private router: Router
) {}
```

Now we will rewrite the call to the login service within the onSubmit method:

```
this.loginService.login( this.user ).subscribe({
    next: (result: any) => {
      if (result['status'] === 'success') {
        this.router.navigate(['/home']);
      } else {
```

```
      this.error = 'Wrong username password';
    }
  },
  error: (e) => {
    this.error = e;
    this.loading = false;
  },
  complete: () => console.info('complete')
});
```

If everything went well, when we log in we will see the screen shown in Figure 7-13.

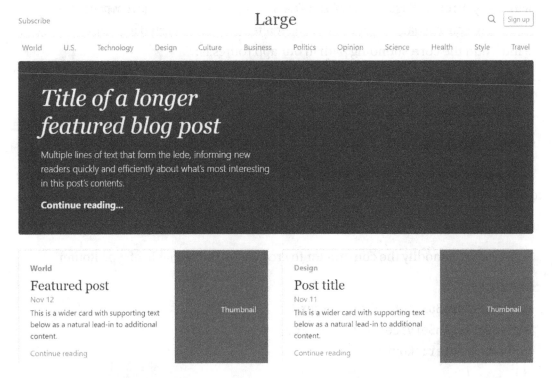

Figure 7-13. *Home template*

At this point, we have fulfilled the goal of initially showing a login screen to the user and then redirecting it to the home once they have entered their username and password.

However, as you may have noticed, that is not the desired behavior. What we should do is allow our users to see the home and require the login for any other functionality other than viewing content, for example, create, edit, and delete posts.

In addition, at this time, the application has no memory that a user has logged in.

Fortunately, we have seen how to deal with these concepts when we work on the chapter related to Auth0, so get down to work!

AuthService: Saving the User in the Session

When it was just the login, it made sense to call our LoginService service. However, now it will perform more functions, so it makes sense to change its name to AuthService.

Rename the login.service.ts file as auth.service.ts. Now, in the file, we must change:

```
export class LoginService
```

by

```
export class AuthService
```

In login.component.ts, we must replace the line:

```
import { LoginService } from '../../services/login.service';
```

by

```
import { AuthService } from '../../services/auth.service';
```

Now we must change the signature of our constructor as follows:

```
constructor(
  private formBuilder: FormBuilder,
  private authService: AuthService,
  private router: Router
) {}
```

And then change the call to the service:

```
this.loginService.login
```

by

```
this.authService.login
```

With these changes, everything should work as before.

Now let's go to our AuthService and add two new methods:

```
setCurrentUser(user: User) {
    localStorage.setItem('currentUser', user.getUserName ());
}

isAuthenticated() {
    const currentUser = localStorage.getItem('currentUser');

    if (currentUser) {
      return true;
    }

    return false;
}
```

And let's complete the definition of the logout method:

```
logout() {
    localStorage.removeItem('currentUser');
}
```

Now let's go to our login.component.ts and modify the call to the login method of the service as follows:

```
this.authService.login( this.user ).subscribe({
    next: (result: any) => {
      if (result['status'] === 'success') {
        this.authService.setCurrentUser(this.user);
        this.router.navigate(['/home']);
      } else {
        this.error = 'Wrong username password';
      }
    },
    error: (e: any) => {
      this.error = e;
      this.loading = false;
    },
```

```
    complete: () => console.info('complete')
  });
```

We have just added the line:

```
this.authService.setCurrentUser(this.user);
```

After logging in, using the Application tab of the Chrome developer console, we can see that the logged user's data has been saved in our local storage (Figure 7-14).

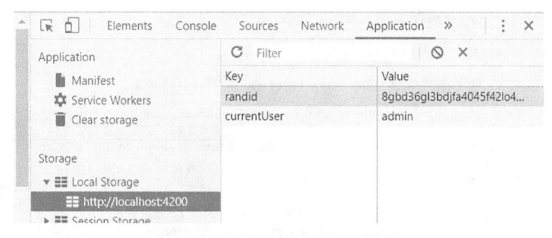

Figure 7-14. *Local storage*

Okay, but what happens if the user goes back to the home page? Then you will be presented with the login screen again.

We are going to correct that. In the constructor of our login component, let's add the following verification:

```
constructor(
  private formBuilder: FormBuilder,
  private authService: AuthService,
  private router: Router
) {
  this.loginForm = this.formBuilder.group({
  username: ['', Validators.required],
  password: ['', Validators.required]
  });
```

```
  if (this.authService.isAuthenticated()) {
    this.router.navigate(['/home']);
  }
}
```

If the user is authenticated – which is equivalent to checking if their data is in the local storage – then we simply redirect to the home.

Now, in our home.component.ts, we initialize a private variable of type AuthService:

```
constructor( public authService: AuthService ) {}
```

adding the corresponding import:

```
import { AuthService } from '../../services/auth.service';
```

Then, in our home.component.html, look for the following line:

```
<a class="btn btn-sm btn-outline-secondary" href="#">Sign up</a>
```

And replace it with:

```
<button *ngIf="!this.authService.isAuthenticated()"
class="btn btn-sm btn-outline-secondary">Login</button>
<button *ngIf="this.authService.isAuthenticated()"
class="btn btn-sm btn-outline-secondary">Logout</button>
```

Buttons are displayed when appropriate, but still do not perform any function.
Let's start with the Logout button.

```
<button  *ngIf="this.authService.isAuthenticated()"
(click)="logout()" class="btn btn-sm btn-outline-secondary">
Logout</button>
```

Now let's write the logout method of our home component. The purpose of this function is very simple: call the authentication method of the AuthService, and redirect to the login page.

For this, we need to first import the Router:

```
import { Router } from '@angular/router';
```

And then instantiate it in the constructor:

```
constructor(
  public authService: AuthService,
  public router: Router
) {}
```

Finally, we can define the logout method:

```
logout() {
  this.authService.logout();
  this.router.navigate(['']);
}
```

If we now click the Logout button, we will be redirected to the login, at the same time that the user will be removed from the local storage.

We can visit the home without having logged in, but now we will see the Login button instead of Logout (Figure 7-15).

Figure 7-15. *Login button*

Let's add the action for that button:

```
<button *ngIf="!this.authService.isAuthenticated()"
(click)="this.router.navigate([''])"
class="btn btn-sm btn-outline-secondary">Login</button>
```

This is simply to direct to the login page, which we have set in our app.routes.ts to answer the route:

```
([''])
```

The redirection is a single line, so we don't need a function.

With this, we have concluded this chapter. In the next, we will start to write the logic to retrieve the posts from the database and display them in our application. To make sure everything works correctly, I will provide the gists for each piece of code.

Source Code

LoginComponent

login.component.html

https://github.com/Apress/The-Beginning-Angular-by-Victor-Hugo-Garcia/blob/main/Chapter-07/04-login.component.html

login.component.ts

https://github.com/Apress/The-Beginning-Angular-by-Victor-Hugo-Garcia/blob/main/Chapter-07/05-login.component.ts

login.component.css

https://github.com/Apress/The-Beginning-Angular-by-Victor-Hugo-Garcia/blob/main/Chapter-07/06-login.component.css

HomeComponent

home.component.html

https://github.com/Apress/The-Beginning-Angular-by-Victor-Hugo-Garcia/blob/main/Chapter-07/07-home.component-v3.html

home.component.ts

https://github.com/Apress/The-Beginning-Angular-by-Victor-Hugo-Garcia/blob/main/Chapter-07/08-home.component.ts

home.component.css

https://github.com/Apress/The-Beginning-Angular-by-Victor-Hugo-Garcia/blob/main/Chapter-07/09-home.component-v2.css

AuthService

auth.service.ts

https://github.com/Apress/The-Beginning-Angular-by-Victor-Hugo-Garcia/blob/main/Chapter-07/10-auth.service.ts

Summary

In this chapter, we built our home component, which will be the central screen of our application. In addition, we established the mechanisms to persist the user's session.

In the next chapter, we will add the necessary logic to show the posts that are stored in the database.

CHAPTER 8

Blog App Part 3: Showing Posts

Our goal in this chapter is to build a component that represents an individual post, which will be displayed on the home page. This also implies adding a collection in our database that allows hosting these posts.

Modifying the User Class

At the moment, we have a user class in our frontend with the following form:

```
export class User {
    private username = '';
    private password = '';

    constructor(username: string, password: string) {
        this.username = username;
        this.password = password;
    }

    getUserName() {
        return this.username;
    }

    getPassword() {
        return this.password;
    }
}
```

© Victor Hugo Garcia 2023
V. H. Garcia, *Getting Started with Angular*, https://doi.org/10.1007/978-1-4842-9206-8_8

In this class, we have two fields, username and password. However, in order to establish a relationship between users and the posts they publish, our user needs to have an id that uniquely identifies them.

When an object is inserted in a collection, MongoDB is responsible for assigning an id, as we can see after a user has logged in (Figure 8-1).

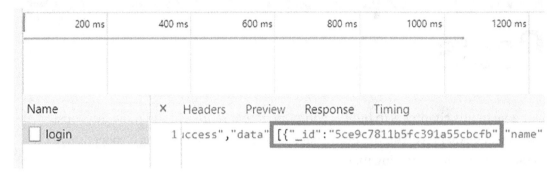

Figure 8-1. *User id*

We can see that the ids are shown as hexadecimal text strings. Strictly speaking, in the context of MongoDB, an _id is of type ObjectId, but we do not need to delve into too many details.

With this in mind, let's modify our user class in the following way:

```
export class User {
    private id = '';
    private username = '';
    private password = '';

    constructor (username: string, password: string) {
        this.username = username;
        this.password = password;
    }

    getUserName() {
        return this.username;
    }

    getPassword() {
        return this.password;
    }
```

```
    setId(id: string ) {
        this.id = id;
    }

    getId() {
        return this.id;
    }
}
```

Now, in login.component.ts, let's add a single line in the call to the AuthService Login:

```
this.authService.login( this.user ).subscribe({
    next: (result: any) => {
      if (result['status'] === 'success') {
        this.user.setId(result['data'][0]._id);
        this.authService.setCurrentUser(this.user);
        this.router.navigate(['/home']);
      } else {
        this.error = 'Wrong username password';
      }
    },
    error: (e: any) => {
      this.error = e;
      this.loading = false;
    },
    complete: () => console.info('complete')
  });
```

The line in question is the following:

```
this.user.setId(result['data'][0]._id);
```

Now let's modify two methods in our AuthService:

```
setCurrentUser(user: User) {
  const loggedInUser = {
    id: user.getId(),
    username: user.getUserName()
```

```
  };
  localStorage.setItem('currentUser', JSON.stringify(loggedInUser));
}

isAuthenticated() {
  const currentUser =
JSON.parse(localStorage.getItem('currentUser') as string);

  if (currentUser) {
    return true;
  }

  return false;
}
```

We use the JSON.stringify method to convert the loggedInUser object into a JSON text string.

Conversely, the JSON parse method allows you to convert the JSON text string into an object.

Post Component

From the command line, create a new component called post:

```
ng g c components/post
```

This component will represent a single post of our application. Let's start with the template. The code will be extracted from home.component.html. Modify the post.component.html code:

```
<h2 class="blog-post-title">Sample blog post</h2>
<p class="blog-post-goal">January 1, 2014 by <a href="#">Mark</a> </p>

<p>This blog post shows a few different types of content that
is supported and styled with Bootstrap. Basic typography, images,
and code are all supported.</p>
<hr>
<p>Cum sociis natoque penatibus et magnis
<a href="#">dis parturient montes</a>, nascetur
```

ridiculus mus. Aenean eu leo quam. Pellentesque ornare
sem lacinia quam venenatis vestibulum. Sed posuere
consectetur est at lobortis. Cras mattis consectetur purus
    sit amet fermentum.</p>
<blockquote>
    <p>Curabitur blandit tempus porttitor.
      <strong>Nullam quis risus eget urn mollis</strong>
        ornare vel eu leo. Nullam id pain id nibh ultricies
vehicula ut id elit.</p>
</blockquote>
<p>Etiam carries <em>sem embarrassment magna</em>
mollis euismod. Cras mattis consectetur purus sit amet fermentum.
Aenean lacinia bibendum nulla sed consectetur.</p>
<h2>Heading</h2>
<p>Vivamus sagittis lacus vel augue laoreet rutrum faucibus dolor
auctor. Duis mollis, est non commodo luctus, nisi erat porttitor
ligula, eget lacinia hate sem nec elit. Morbi leo risus, porta
ac consectetur ac, vestibulum at eros.</p>
<h3>Sub-heading</h3>
<p>Cum sociis natoque penatibus et magnis dis parturient
montes, nascetur ridiculus mus.</p>
<pre> <code>Example code block</code> </pre>
<p>Aenean lacinia bibendum nulla sed consectetur.
Etiam carries sem embarrassment magna mollis euismod.
Fusce dapibus, tellus ac cursus commodo, tortor mauris
condimentum nibh, ut fermentum massa.</p>
<h3>Sub-heading</h3>
<p>Cum sociis natoque penatibus et magnis dis parturient montes,
nascetur ridiculus mus. Aenean lacinia bibendum nulla sed
consectetur. Etiam carries sem embarrassment magna mollis euismod.
Fusce dapibus, tellus ac cursus commodo, tortor mauris
condimentum nibh, ut fermentum massa just sit amet risus.</p>
<ul>
    <li>Praesent commodo cursus magna, vel scelerisque nisl
consectetur et.</li>

```
    <li>Donec id elit non my gravida at eget metus.</li>
    <li>Nulla vitae elit libero, a pharetra augue.</li>
</ul>
<p>Donec ullamcorper nulla non metus auctor fringilla.
Nulla vitae elit libero, to pharetra augue.</p>
<ol>
    <li>Vestibulum id ligula porta felis euismod semper.</li>
    <li>Cum sociis natoque penatibus et magnis dis parturient
montes, nascetur ridiculus mus.</li>
    <li>Maecenas sed diam eget risus varius blandit sit amet
non magna.</li>
</ol>
<p>Cras mattis consectetur purus sit amet fermentum. Sed posuere
consectetur est at lobortis.</p>
```

Here is the corresponding file:
https://github.com/Apress/The-Beginning-Angular-by-Victor-Hugo-Garcia/
blob/main/Chapter-08/01-post.component.html

In our home component, we can now replace the series of example posts with the component call:

```
<div class="blog-post">
    <app-post> </app-post>
</div>
```

Since it is a considerable amount of code, I will provide the file (https://github.com/Apress/The-Beginning-Angular-by-Victor-Hugo-Garcia/blob/main/Chapter-08/02-home.component-v1.html) instead of presenting the code here.

Our home page has not changed radically, only now a single post is shown.

Creating the Post Collection

Now it's time to create our post collection, we already saw how to do it in the previous chapter.

Then, we will insert a document. Paste the following code in the pop-up:

```
{
  "title": "Sample Post",
```

```
    "text": "Lorem ipsum dolor sit amet, consectetur adipiscing elit.)
Duis et tortor
condimentum, accumsan metus at, hendrerit metus, Lorem ipsum dolor sit
amet, consectetur adipiscing elit, Donec dictum eros vitae eros
vulputate, in
maximus sem egestas, Maecenas egestas pharetra gravida, Vestibulum nec
lectus feugiat, finibus ante eget, convallis arcu, Nam ligula erat,
fermentum ac
tortor nec, efficienur facilisis eros Nulla elementum felis ut my consequat
sagittis
Cras viverra enim mi, vel condimentum est dignissim quis Pellentesque
ut libero
lobortis, porta mauris non, blandit velit Aenean cursus blandit
scelerisque Donec
bibendum massa ut tellus euismod, ut euismod arcu gravida Integer dignissim
sem hare, vel suscipit sem faucibus id Nulla nec nibh est Vestibulum
convallis
magna vitae placerat eleifend Duis lacinia rhoncus elit, a sodales mauris
sollicitudin eu.Proin tincidunt finibus cursus. ",
    "author_id": {
      "$oid": "6345f87e429dc42f97964406"
    }
}
```

It's probably better if you use this file:

https://github.com/Apress/The-Beginning-Angular-by-Victor-Hugo-Garcia/blob/main/Chapter-08/03-post-insert.txt

It is important to pay attention to the line:

```
author_id: ObjectId ('5ce9c7811b5fc391a55cbcfb')
```

The author_id field is of the ObjectId type since it will contain references to a user in the **user** collection. The text string that is passed as a parameter must therefore correspond to the id of a document in the user collection.

At this moment, we have a single user identified as **admin**, and the corresponding id is the one we keep in the local storage after the user has logged in (Figure 8-2).

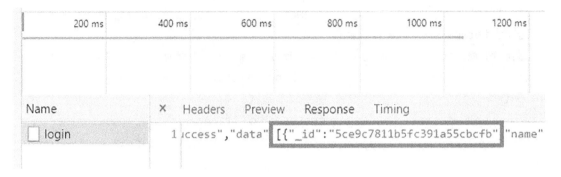

Figure 8-2. *User id*

You must use the value that shows up there.

To have more data, insert another pair of records repeating the same procedure.

Using MongoDB Compass, we can see something like the one shown in Figure 8-3 after the insertions.

Figure 8-3. *Documents*

Now we are going to define a Post model. Let's create a file called post.js with the following code:

```
const mongoose = require('mongoose');
const Schema = mongoose.Schema;

// create a schema
```

```
const postSchema = new Schema({
    title: { type: String, required: true },
    text: { type: String, required: true },
    author_id: { type: Schema.Types.ObjectId, ref: 'User' }
}, { collection: 'post' });

const Post = mongoose.model('Post', postSchema);

module.exports = Post;
```

The line

```
author_id: { type: Schema.Types.ObjectId, ref: 'User' }
```

is what determines that there is a relationship between the "Post" scheme and the "User" scheme. This allows retrieving data from related documents when a query is made.

Our next step will be to add the endpoint to recover the posts in our index.js:

```
app.post('/api/post/getAllPost', (req, res) => {
    mongoose.connect(url, { }, function(err) {
        if (err) throw err;
        Post.find({}, [], { sort: { _id: -1 } }, (err, Doc) => {
            if (err) throw err;
            return res.status(200).json({
                status: 'success',
                data: Doc
            })
        })
    });
});
```

For this to work, we need to import the model. Let's add the line:

```
const Post = require('./models/post');
```

after

```
const User = require('./models/user');
```

So far, the complete index.js should look like this:

```
const express = require('express');
const bodyParser = require('body-parser');
const app = express();
const mongoose = require('mongoose');
const url = 'mongodb://localhost/blog';
const User = require('./models/user');
const Post = require('./models/post');

mongoose.set ('strictQuery', true);

app.use(bodyParser.json());
app.use(bodyParser.urlencoded({ extended: false }));

app.post('/api/user/login', (req, res) => {
   mongoose.connect(url, { },
function(err) {
      if (err) throw err;
      User.find({
         username: req.body.username,
         password: req.body.password
      }, function(err, user) {
         if (err) throw err;
         if (user.length === 1) {
            return res.status(200).json({
               status: 'success',
               data: user
            })
         } else {
            return res.status(200).json({
               status: 'fail',
               message: 'Login Failed'
            })
         }
      })
   });
});
```

```
app.post('/api/post/getAllPost', (req, res) => {
    mongoose.connect(url, { }, function(err) {
        if (err) throw err;
        Post.find({}, [], { sort: { _id: -1 } }, (err, Doc) => {
            if (err) throw err;
            return res.status(200).json({
                status: 'success',
                data: Doc
            })
        })
    });
});

app.listen(3000, () => console.log('Listening on port 3000'));
```

To make sure everything is fine, here is the file of our index.js:

https://github.com/Apress/The-Beginning-Angular-by-Victor-Hugo-Garcia/blob/main/Chapter-08/04-index-v1.js

---

Important   Remember, in order for the new endpoint to work, you need to stop the server and restart it.

That's all from the side of our backend. Now we can return to our frontend and work on a new service to recover the posts.

Post Service

Create a new service called **post**:

```
ng g s services/post
```

In the post.service.ts file, copy the following content:

```
import { Injectable } from '@angular/core';
import { HttpClient } from '@angular/common/http';
```

```
@Injectable({
 providedIn: 'root'
})
export class PostService {

 constructor( private http: HttpClient ) {}

 getAllPost() {
   return this.http.post('/api/post/getAllPost', {});
 }
}
```

This service will be used by our home component, since that is where we will show the posts.

First of all, we need to import the service:

```
import { PostService } from '../../services/post.service';
```

Then, let's define a property to contain the posts received from the API:

```
posts: any[] = [];
```

And then we must modify the constructor:

```
constructor(
  private authService: AuthService,
  private router: Router,
  private postService: PostService
) {}
```

Let's add a method to get the posts:

```
getPosts() {
    this.postService.getAllPost().subscribe({
      next: (result: any) => {
        this.posts = result['data'];
        console.log( this.posts );
      }
    });
  }
```

Finally, we can call the getPosts method in the OnInit method:

```
ngOnInit() {
   this.getPosts();
 }
```

Post Component

It is time to work on our Post Component.

Modify post.component.ts as follows:

```
import { Component, OnInit, Input } from '@angular/core';

@Component({
 selector: 'app-post',
 templateUrl: './post.component.html',
 styleUrls: ['./post.component.css']
})
export class PostComponent implements OnInit {
 @Input() post: any = {};

 constructor() {}

 ngOnInit() {
 }

}
```

We have already seen the use of @Input to receive data from a parent component. Now let's modify the post.component.html file as follows:

```
<h2 class="blog-post-title">{{post.title}}</h2>
<p class="blog-post-goal">
   January 1, 2014 by <a href="#">Mark</a>
</p>

<div class="text-white p-4 mb-3 bg-secondary rounded">
   {{post.text}}
</div>
```

Now, in home.component.html, we can rewrite the call to the component as follows:

```
<div class="blog-post" *ngFor="let post of posts">
    <app-post [post]="post"></app-post>
</div>
```

There is nothing new there, a loop to display posts, where each of them is passed as a parameter to the child component.

The output will be like Figure 8-4.

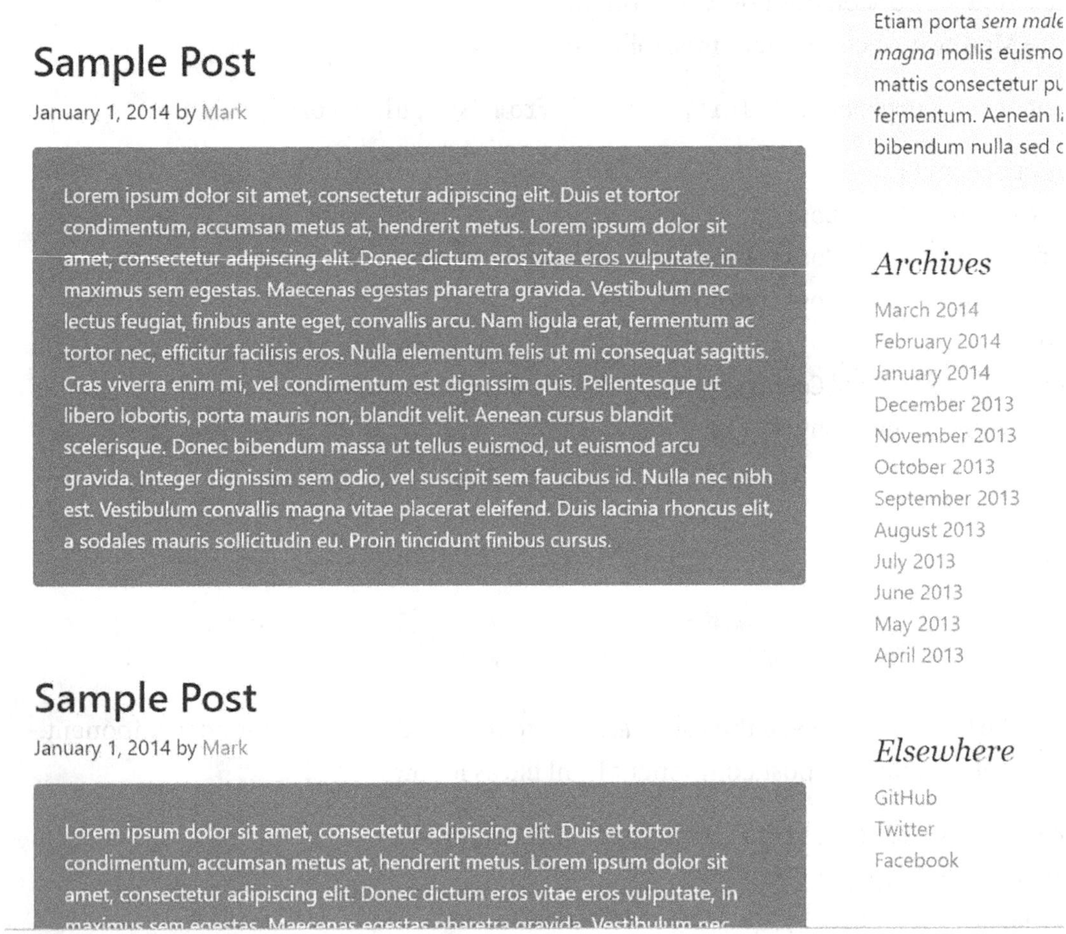

Etiam porta *sem male*
magna mollis euismo
mattis consectetur pt
fermentum. Aenean l;
bibendum nulla sed c

Sample Post

January 1, 2014 by Mark

Lorem ipsum dolor sit amet, consectetur adipiscing elit. Duis et tortor
condimentum, accumsan metus at, hendrerit metus. Lorem ipsum dolor sit
amet, consectetur adipiscing elit. Donec dictum eros vitae eros vulputate, in
maximus sem egestas. Maecenas egestas pharetra gravida. Vestibulum nec
lectus feugiat, finibus ante eget, convallis arcu. Nam ligula erat, fermentum ac
tortor nec, efficitur facilisis eros. Nulla elementum felis ut mi consequat sagittis.
Cras viverra enim mi, vel condimentum est dignissim quis. Pellentesque ut
libero lobortis, porta mauris non, blandit velit. Aenean cursus blandit
scelerisque. Donec bibendum massa ut tellus euismod, ut euismod arcu
gravida. Integer dignissim sem odio, vel suscipit sem faucibus id. Nulla nec nibh
est. Vestibulum convallis magna vitae placerat eleifend. Duis lacinia rhoncus elit,
a sodales mauris sollicitudin eu. Proin tincidunt finibus cursus.

Archives

March 2014
February 2014
January 2014
December 2013
November 2013
October 2013
September 2013
August 2013
July 2013
June 2013
May 2013
April 2013

Sample Post

January 1, 2014 by Mark

Lorem ipsum dolor sit amet, consectetur adipiscing elit. Duis et tortor
condimentum, accumsan metus at, hendrerit metus. Lorem ipsum dolor sit
amet, consectetur adipiscing elit. Donec dictum eros vitae eros vulputate, in
maximus sem egestas. Maecenas egestas pharetra gravida. Vestibulum nec

Elsewhere

GitHub
Twitter
Facebook

Figure 8-4. *Posts*

It doesn't look bad, but one problem is that we are showing the full text of the post. Let's remedy that:

```
<h2 class="blog-post-title">{{post.title}}</h2>
<p class="blog-post-goal">January 1, 2014 by <a href="#">Mark</a> </p>

<div class="text-white p-4 mb-3 bg-secondary rounded">
   {{(post.text.length> 300) ? (post.text | slice:0:300) + '...' :
   ( post.text)}}
</div>
```

We are using the pipe **slice** to limit the size of the text displayed to 300 characters. Now, the home will look like Figure 8-5.

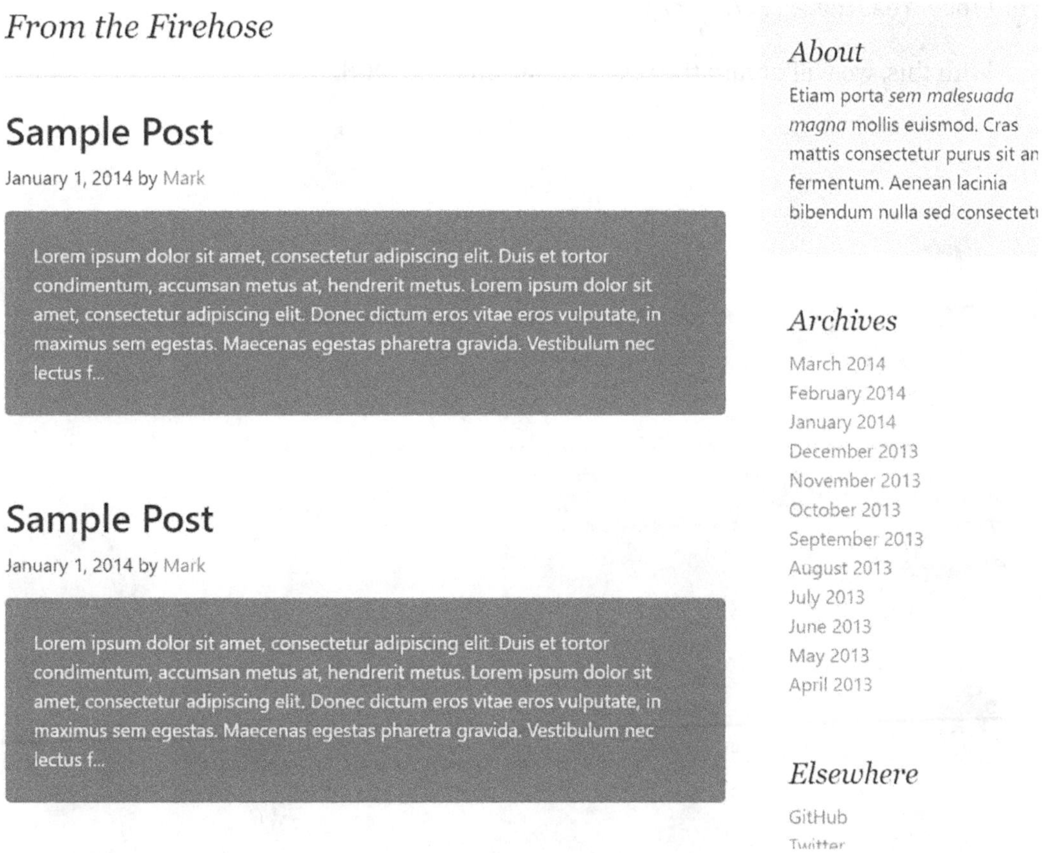

From the Firehose

Sample Post

January 1, 2014 by Mark

Lorem ipsum dolor sit amet, consectetur adipiscing elit. Duis et tortor condimentum, accumsan metus at, hendrerit metus. Lorem ipsum dolor sit amet, consectetur adipiscing elit. Donec dictum eros vitae eros vulputate, in maximus sem egestas. Maecenas egestas pharetra gravida. Vestibulum nec lectus f...

Sample Post

January 1, 2014 by Mark

Lorem ipsum dolor sit amet, consectetur adipiscing elit. Duis et tortor condimentum, accumsan metus at, hendrerit metus. Lorem ipsum dolor sit amet, consectetur adipiscing elit. Donec dictum eros vitae eros vulputate, in maximus sem egestas. Maecenas egestas pharetra gravida. Vestibulum nec lectus f...

About

Etiam porta *sem malesuada magna* mollis euismod. Cras mattis consectetur purus sit an fermentum. Aenean lacinia bibendum nulla sed consectetu

Archives

March 2014
February 2014
January 2014
December 2013
November 2013
October 2013
September 2013
August 2013
July 2013
June 2013
May 2013
April 2013

Elsewhere

GitHub
Twitter

Figure 8-5. *Posts*

Much better. Of course, we could use a custom pipe so that the cut always occurs at the end of a complete word, but for now it is enough.

Let's give it a final touch including a link to read the full post:

```
<h2 class="blog-post-title">{{post.title}}</h2>
<p class="blog-post-goal">January 1, 2014 by <a href="#">Mark</a> </p>

<div class="text-white p-4 mb-3 bg-secondary rounded">
    {{(post.text.length> 300) ? (post.text | slice:0:300) + '...' :
    ( post.text)}}
</div>
<p class="lead mb-0 border-bottom"> <a href="#"
class="text-black-50 font-weight-bold">
Continue reading ...</a> </p>
```

With this, we will obtain the result shown in Figure 8-6.

Sample Post

January 1, 2014 by Mark

Lorem ipsum dolor sit amet, consectetur adipiscing elit. Duis et tortor condimentum, accumsan metus at, hendrerit metus. Lorem ipsum dolor sit amet, consectetur adipiscing elit. Donec dictum eros vitae eros vulputate, in maximus sem egestas. Maecenas egestas pharetra gravida. Vestibulum nec lectus f...

Continue reading...

Sample Post

January 1, 2014 by Mark

Lorem ipsum dolor sit amet, consectetur adipiscing elit. Duis et tortor condimentum, accumsan metus at, hendrerit metus. Lorem ipsum dolor sit amet, consectetur adipiscing elit. Donec dictum eros vitae eros vulputate, in maximus sem egestas. Maecenas egestas pharetra gravida. Vestibulum nec lectus f...

Continue reading...

Etiam porta *sem malesuad* *magna* mollis euismod. Cra mattis consectetur purus s fermentum. Aenean lacinia bibendum nulla sed conse

Archives

March 2014
February 2014
January 2014
December 2013
November 2013
October 2013
September 2013
August 2013
July 2013
June 2013
May 2013
April 2013

Elsewhere

GitHub
Twitter
Facebook

Figure 8-6. *Posts*

We have many things to improve, but for the moment, we have fulfilled our goal. As always, to ensure that everything works correctly, I will provide the gists of each component and service.

Backend Source Code

Model post (in backend/models)

post.js

https://github.com/Apress/The-Beginning-Angular-by-Victor-Hugo-Garcia/ blob/main/Chapter-08/05-post.js

API

index.js

https://github.com/Apress/The-Beginning-Angular-by-Victor-Hugo-Garcia/
blob/main/Chapter-08/06-index-v2.js

Frontend Source Code

Home Component

home.component.html

https://github.com/Apress/The-Beginning-Angular-by-Victor-Hugo-Garcia/
blob/main/Chapter-08/07-home.component-v2.html

home.component.ts

https://github.com/Apress/The-Beginning-Angular-by-Victor-Hugo-Garcia/
blob/main/Chapter-08/08-home.component.ts

home.component.css

https://github.com/Apress/The-Beginning-Angular-by-Victor-Hugo-Garcia/
blob/main/Chapter-08/09-home.component.css

LoginComponent

login.component.html

https://github.com/Apress/The-Beginning-Angular-by-Victor-Hugo-Garcia/
blob/main/Chapter-08/10-login.component.html

login.component.ts

https://github.com/Apress/The-Beginning-Angular-by-Victor-Hugo-Garcia/
blob/main/Chapter-08/11-login.component.ts

login.component.css

https://github.com/Apress/The-Beginning-Angular-by-Victor-Hugo-Garcia/
blob/main/Chapter-08/12-login.component.css

Post Component

post.component.html

https://github.com/Apress/The-Beginning-Angular-by-Victor-Hugo-Garcia/
blob/main/Chapter-08/13-post.component.html

post.component.ts

https://github.com/Apress/The-Beginning-Angular-by-Victor-Hugo-Garcia/
blob/main/Chapter-08/14-post.component.ts

User Model

user.model.ts

https://github.com/Apress/The-Beginning-Angular-by-Victor-Hugo-Garcia/
blob/main/Chapter-08/15-user.model.ts

Auth Service

auth.service.ts

https://github.com/Apress/The-Beginning-Angular-by-Victor-Hugo-Garcia/
blob/main/Chapter-08/16-auth.service.ts

Post Service

post.service.ts

https://github.com/Apress/The-Beginning-Angular-by-Victor-Hugo-Garcia/
blob/main/Chapter-08/17-post.service.ts

AppModule

app.module.ts

https://github.com/Apress/The-Beginning-Angular-by-Victor-Hugo-Garcia/
blob/main/Chapter-08/18-app.module.ts

Routes

app.routes.ts

https://github.com/Apress/The-Beginning-Angular-by-Victor-Hugo-Garcia/
blob/main/Chapter-08/19-app.routes.ts

Summary

In this chapter, we have seen how to recover the posts stored in a collection of our database.

We modified the home to present the posts thanks to a new component. If we analyze our application until now, it presents a series of problems that many of you will surely have noticed. One of them, and not unimportant, is that of security. User passwords are saved as plain text in the **user** collection. This is not only bad practice, but inadmissible. In later chapters, we will solve this and other issues, but for now we will continue advancing until the application performs all CRUD operations on the posts.

CHAPTER 9

Blog App Part 4: Filtering Posts

In this chapter, we will focus on building a board from which users who have logged in will be able to manage their own posts. We'll also make changes to improve the interface.

Dashboard Component

Let's create a new component called dashboard:

```
ng g c components/dashboard
```

Let's replace the content of dashboard.component.html with the following:

```
<nav class="navbar navbar-dark fixed-top bg-dark flex-md-nowrap p-0
shadow">
    <a class="navbar-brand col-sm-3 col-md-2 mr-0" href="#">Company name</a>
    <input class="form-control form-control-dark w-100" type="text"
placeholder="Search" aria-label="Search">
    <ul class="navbar-nav px-3">
        <li class="nav-item text-nowrap">
            <a class="nav-link" href="#">Sign out</a>
        </li>
    </ul>
</nav>

<div class="container-fluid">
    <div class="row">
        <nav class="col-md-2 d-none d-md-block bg-light sidebar">
            <div class="sidebar-sticky">
```

© Victor Hugo Garcia 2023
V. H. Garcia, *Getting Started with Angular*, https://doi.org/10.1007/978-1-4842-9206-8_9

```
            <ul class="nav flex-column">
                <li class="nav-item">
                    <a class="nav-link active" href="#">
                        <span data-feather="home"></span>
Dashboard <span class="sr-only">(current)</span>
                    </a>
                </li>
                <li class="nav-item">
                    <a class="nav-link" href="#">
                        <span data-feather="file"></span> Posts
                    </a>
                </li>
                <li class="nav-item">
                    <a class="nav-link" href="#">
                        <span data-feather="shopping-cart"></span>
                        Comments
                    </a>
                </li>
            </ul>
        </div>
    </nav>

    <main role="main" class="col-md-9 ml-sm-auto col-lg-10 px-4">
        <div class="d-flex justify-content-between flex-wrap flex-
        md-nowrap
align-items-center pt-3 pb-2 mb-3 border-bottom">
            <h1 class="h2">Dashboard</h1>
            <div class="btn-toolbar mb-2 mb-md-0">
                <div class="btn-group mr-2">
                    <button type="button"
class="btn btn-sm btn-outline-secondary">Add Post</button>
                </div>
                <button type="button"
class="btn btn-sm btn-outline-secondary dropdown-toggle">
                    <span data-feather="calendar"></span>
                    This week
```

```
            </button>
        </div>
    </div>

    <h2 class="border-bottom text-center">My Posts</h2>
    <div *ngFor="let post of posts">
        <app-post [post]="post"></app-post>
    </div>
  </main>
 </div>
</div>
```

And here is the link to the file dashboard.component.html: `https://github.com/` `Apress/The-Beginning-Angular-by-Victor-Hugo-Garcia/blob/main/Chapter-09/10-` `post.service.ts`.

Now, let's change the contents of dashboard.component.ts:

```
import { Component, OnInit } from '@angular/core';
import { PostService } from '../../services/post.service';

@Component({
 selector: 'app-dashboard',
 templateUrl: './dashboard.component.html',
 styleUrls: ['./dashboard.component.css']
})
export class DashboardComponent implements OnInit {
 posts: any[] = [];

 constructor( private postService: PostService ) { }

 ngOnInit() {
   this.getPosts();
 }

 getPosts() {
   this.postService.getAllPost().subscribe({
    next: (result: any) => {
      this.posts = result['data'];
```

```
    console.log( this.posts );
  }
 });
 }

}
```

Next, we need to add the route in our app.routes.ts:

```
{ path: 'dashboard', component: DashboardComponent }
```

Don't forget the import sentence:

```
import { DashboardComponent } from './components/dashboard/dashboard.
component';
```

If we now visit `http://localhost:4200/dashboard`, we should see something like Figure 9-1.

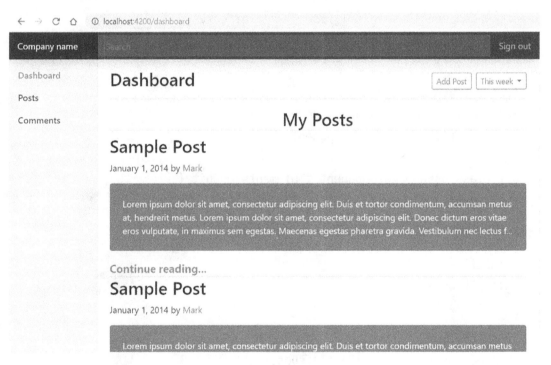

Figure 9-1. *Dashboard*

The route is visible even when we have not logged in, and this is something that we must change.

In the chapter where we worked with Auth0, we saw the concept of a route guardian, and that is the resource we will use to protect this route from unauthorized access.

Let's execute the following command:

```
ng g g services/auth
```

If you see a prompt, just leave CanActivate selected. This will create a file called auth. guard.ts, inside the services directory. Let's replace the contents of the file as follows:

```
import { Injectable } from '@angular/core';
import {
CanActivate,
ActivatedRouteSnapshot,
RouterStateSnapshot
} from '@angular/router';
import { Observable } from 'rxjs';
import { AuthService } from './auth.service';

@Injectable({
 providedIn: 'root'
})
export class AuthGuard implements CanActivate {
 constructor( private auth: AuthService ) {}

 canActivate(
   next: ActivatedRouteSnapshot,
   state: RouterStateSnapshot): Observable<boolean> | Promise<boolean> |
   boolean {

     if ( this.auth.isAuthenticated() ) {
       return true;
     }
   return false;
 }
}
```

Here is the link to the file auth.guard.ts: https://github.com/Apress/The-Beginning-Angular-by-Victor-Hugo-Garcia/blob/main/Chapter-09/02-auth.guard.ts.

And just to be sure, here is the code of the AuthService that is imported in the guard:

```
import { Injectable } from '@angular/core';

import { User } from '../models/user.model';

import { HttpClient } from '@angular/common/http';

@Injectable({
  providedIn: 'root'
})
export class AuthService {

  constructor(private http: HttpClient) { }

  login(user: User) {
    return this.http.post('/api/user/login', {
      username : user.getUserName(),
      password : user.getPassword()
    });
  }

  logout() {
    localStorage.removeItem('currentUser');
  }

  setCurrentUser(user: User) {
    const loggedInUser = {
      id: user.getId(),
      username: user.getUserName()
    };
    localStorage.setItem('currentUser', JSON.stringify(loggedInUser));
  }

  isAuthenticated() {
    const currentUser = JSON.parse(localStorage.getItem('currentUser') as
    string);

    if (currentUser) {
      return true;
    }
```

```
    return false;
  }
}
```

Remember that the purpose of a guard is to protect the routes of our application, so only authorized people can visit them. Think about routes for administering users, for example, you wouldn't want every person being able to change other users' data.

The canActivate method returns true or false to indicate whether or not you have access to a route. We are in charge of specifying the conditions that will cause a true value to be returned and therefore authorize access to the route. In this case, it is sufficient that the user has been identified.

In order for the guard to take effect for our route, we must change the definition of the route in app.routes.ts in the following way:

```
{
    path: 'dashboard',
    component: DashboardComponent,
    canActivate: [AuthGuard]
}
```

Of course, we need to import our AuthGuard:

```
import { AuthGuard } from './services/auth.guard';
```

If we now try to access the dashboard route, we will find a blank page.

Instead of returning false if the user is not authenticated, we can redirect it to the login page. Let's do that:

```
import { Injectable } from '@angular/core';
import {
    CanActivate,
    ActivatedRouteSnapshot,
    RouterStateSnapshot,
    Router,
    UrlTree
} from '@angular/router';
import { Observable } from 'rxjs';
import { AuthService } from './auth.service';
```

```
@Injectable({
 providedIn: 'root'
})
export class AuthGuard implements CanActivate {
 constructor(
   private auth: AuthService,
   private router: Router
) {}

 canActivate(
   next: ActivatedRouteSnapshot,
  state: RouterStateSnapshot
): Observable<boolean> | Promise<boolean> | boolean | UrlTree {

   if ( this.auth.isAuthenticated() ) {
     return true;
   }

   return this.router.parseUrl('');
 }
}
```

Now before the attempt to access the route without having logged in, we will be redirected to the login page.

Post Component

The posts are showing on our dashboard, but we need to make some modifications. For example, the "Continue reading" link does not make sense on our post management page.

In our Post class, let's add the following property:

```
@Input() read = true;
```

Now let's modify the link in post.component.html as follows:

```
<p class="lead mb-0 border-bottom">
<a *ngIf="read" href="#"
class="text-black-50 font-weight-bold">Continue reading...</a>
</p>
```

Now let's modify the link in dashboard.component.html as follows:

```
<app-post [post]="post" [read]="false"></app-post>
```

In this way, the link will have disappeared in the dashboard (Figure 9-2).

Dashboard

My Posts

Sample Post

January 1, 2014 by Mark

Lorem ipsum dolor sit amet, consectetur adipiscing elit. Duis et tortor condimentum, accumsan metus at, hendrerit metus. Lorem ipsum dolor sit amet, consectetur adipiscing elit. Donec dictum eros vitae eros vulputate, in maximus sem egestas. Maecenas egestas pharetra gravida. Vestibulum nec lectus f...

Sample Post

January 1, 2014 by Mark

Lorem ipsum dolor sit amet, consectetur adipiscing elit. Duis et tortor condimentum, accumsan metus at, hendrerit metus. Lorem ipsum dolor sit amet, consectetur adipiscing elit. Donec dictum eros vitae

Figure 9-2. *Dashboard posts*

We will now make other modifications, such as showing buttons to edit and delete in each post of the dashboard.

Let's start by installing Font Awesome. From a console, let's execute:

```
npm install --save-dev @fortawesome/fontawesome-free
```

Then we must include the file in the angular.json file:

```
"styles": [
"src/styles.css",
"node_modules/bootstrap/dist/css/bootstrap.min.css",
"node_modules/@fortawesome/fontawesome-free/css/all.css"
]
```

For the changes to take effect, we must stop the angular-cli server by pressing Ctrl+C and then restart it.

Let's make the following changes to post.component.html:

```
<div class="text-right">
   <i title="Edit" class="fas fa-edit" aria-hidden="true"
style="cursor: pointer"></i>
   <i title="Delete" class="fas fa-trash-alt" aria-hidden="true"
style="cursor: pointer"></i>
</div>
<h2 class="blog-post-title">{{ post.title }}</h2>
<p class="blog-post-meta">January 1, 2014 by <a href="#">Mark</a></p>

<div class="text-white p-4 mb-3 bg-secondary rounded">
   {{ (post.text.length>300)? (post.text | slice:0:300)+'...':(post.
   text) }}
</div>
<p class="lead mb-0 border-bottom">
<a *ngIf="read" href="#"
class="text-black-50 font-weight-bold">Continue reading...</a></p>
```

Now we can see the result in Figure 9-3.

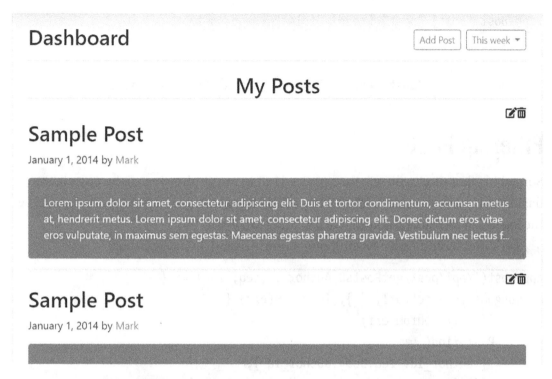

Figure 9-3. *Edit and delete icons*

However, if we now go to home, the buttons to edit and delete posts will be visible. We are going to solve it by making use of a new property:

```
@Input() admin = false;
```

And now we can control the visibility of the div that contains the buttons as follows:

```
<div class="text-right" *ngIf="admin">
  <i title="Edit" class="fas fa-edit" aria-hidden="true"
style="cursor: pointer"></i>
  <i title="Delete" class="fas fa-trash-alt" aria-hidden="true"
style="cursor: pointer"></i>
</div>
```

In dashboard.component.html, we need to change this line:

```
<app-post [post]="post" [read]="false"></app-post>
```

to

```
<app-post [post]="post" [read]="false" [admin]="true"></app-post>
```

Filtering Posts

Something that surely you will have noticed is that we are showing all the posts in the dashboard indiscriminately, when what should happen is that only the posts created by the logged-in user are displayed. We are going to solve it.

Let's start by adding a new endpoint in the backend. In index.js, add:

```
app.post('/api/post/getPostsByAuthor', (req, res) => {
    mongoose.connect(url, { }, function(err) {
        if (err) throw err;
        Post.find(
          { author_id: req.body.author_id },
          [], { sort: { _id: -1 } }, (err, doc) => {
            if (err) throw err;
            return res.status(200).json({
                status: 'success',
                data: doc
            })
        })
    })
});
```

So in order for the changes made to index.js to be registered, we will have to stop the server and restart it again with **node index.js**.

The code is very similar to the getAllPost method. But we will worry about refactoring later.

Now, let's go back to the frontend and add the following method in post.service.ts:

```
getPostsByAuthor() {
  const currentUser = JSON.parse(
    localStorage.getItem('currentUser') as string
  );

  return this.http.post('/api/post/getPostsByAuthor',
  { author_id: currentUser.id });
}
```

And now let's modify the getPosts method of dashboard.component.ts as follows:

```
getPosts() {
  this.postService.getPostsByAuthor().subscribe({
    next: (result: any) => {
      this.posts = result['data'];
      console.log( this.posts );
    }
  });
}
```

We will not see any changes in the frontend, but that's fine, since we do not have any other registered users.

We can use MongoDB Compass to quickly enter a new user (Figures 9-4 and 9-5).

Figure 9-4. *Insert document*

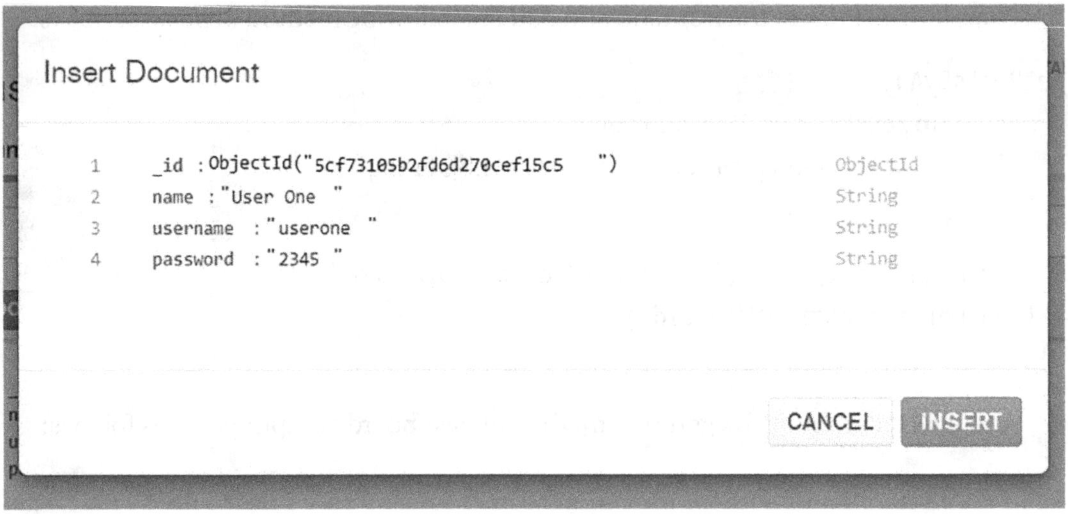

Insert Document

```
1      _id : ObjectId("5cf73105b2fd6d270cef15c5   ")        ObjectId
2      name : "User One "                                    String
3      username : "userone "                                 String
4      password : "2345 "                                    String
```

CANCEL   INSERT

Figure 9-5. *Insert user*

Now, we can see the post collection and use the clone function to insert a new document, replacing the id of the author with the id of the new user (Figures 9-6 and 9-7).

```
> _id: ObjectId("5cf2b74d862746a62ab083ca")
  title: "Sample Post"
  text: "Lorem ipsum dolor sit amet, consectetur adipiscing elit. Duis et torto..."
  author_id: ObjectId("5ce9c7811b5fc391a55cbcfb")
```

Clone Document

Figure 9-6. *Clone document*

Insert Document

```
1      title : "Sample Post   "                                          String
2      text : "Lorem ipsum dolor sit amet, consectetur … "              String
3      author_id  : ObjectId(" 5cf73105b2fd6d270cef15c5   ")             ObjectId
```

CANCEL   INSERT

Figure 9-7. *Clone document*

If we return to the home, close the session, and reenter with the data of the new user and we go again to the dashboard, we will see only one post.

Sharpening Details

We are going to make some small changes. First of all, we will replace the link **Sign Out** of the dashboard with a link that shows the text **Logout** that allows to effectively close the session.

It's something we've seen before, so we'll do it quickly. First, let's replace the line:

```
<a class="nav-link" href="#">Sign out</a>
```

by

```
<button class="btn btn-outline-primary" (click)="logout()">
Logout
</button>
```

Now the screen should look like Figure 9-8.

Figure 9-8. *Logout button*

We need to rewrite the constructor of our Dashboard Component:

```
constructor( private postService: PostService,
private auth: AuthService,
private router: Router ) { }
```

Don't forget the imports:

```
import { AuthService } from '../../services/auth.service';
import { Router } from '@angular/router';
```

And then add the logout method:

```
logout() {
    this.auth.logout();
    this.router.navigate(['']);
 }
```

Now we can close the session from the dashboard.

Our next step will be to get rid of the **This week** button. It is about eliminating the following lines:

```
<button type="button" class="btn btn-sm btn-outline-secondary
dropdown-toggle">
    <span data-feather="calendar"></span>
    This week
</button>
```

With these small changes, our dashboard is closer to being finished.

In the next chapter, we will focus on the functionality needed to add posts. But now, as always, I will provide the gists to ensure that everything works correctly.

Backend Source Code

index.js
    https://github.com/Apress/The-Beginning-Angular-by-Victor-Hugo-Garcia/
blob/main/Chapter-09/03-index.js

Frontend Source Code

Home Component

home.component.html

https://github.com/Apress/The-Beginning-Angular-by-Victor-Hugo-Garcia/blob/main/Chapter-09/04-home.component.html

home.component.ts

https://github.com/Apress/The-Beginning-Angular-by-Victor-Hugo-Garcia/blob/main/Chapter-09/05-home.component.ts

Dashboard Component

dashboard.component.html

https://github.com/Apress/The-Beginning-Angular-by-Victor-Hugo-Garcia/blob/main/Chapter-09/06-dashboard.component.html

dashboard.component.ts

https://github.com/Apress/The-Beginning-Angular-by-Victor-Hugo-Garcia/blob/main/Chapter-09/07-dashboard.component.ts

Post Component

post.component.html

https://github.com/Apress/The-Beginning-Angular-by-Victor-Hugo-Garcia/blob/main/Chapter-09/08-post.component.html

post.component.ts

https://github.com/Apress/The-Beginning-Angular-by-Victor-Hugo-Garcia/blob/main/Chapter-09/09-post.component.ts

Post Service

post.service.ts

https://github.com/Apress/The-Beginning-Angular-by-Victor-Hugo-Garcia/blob/main/Chapter-09/10-post.service.ts

Summary

In this chapter, we modified the logic of the dashboard to show only the posts published by the user who has logged in. We also made changes to improve the interface. We are closer to having our application finished. In the next chapter, we will add the necessary functionality to register posts.

CHAPTER 10

Blog App Part 5: Adding Posts

In this chapter, we will add the necessary functionality to register new posts. For this, we will design a simple form, with two fields to complete: the title and text of the post. In addition, as part of the data that will be sent to the backend, we will include the user id so that they can be filtered when the user enters their dashboard.

AddPost Component

Generate a new component:

ng g c components/addPost

Replace the content of add-post.component.ts with the following:

```
import { Component, OnInit } from '@angular/core';
import { FormBuilder, FormGroup, Validators } from '@angular/forms';

@Component({
  selector: 'app-add-post',
  templateUrl: './add-post.component.html',
  styleUrls: ['./add-post.component.css']
})
export class AddPostComponent implements OnInit {
  postForm: FormGroup;
  submitted = false;

  constructor( private formBuilder: FormBuilder ) {
    this.postForm = this.formBuilder.group({
```

© Victor Hugo Garcia 2023
V. H. Garcia, *Getting Started with Angular*, https://doi.org/10.1007/978-1-4842-9206-8_10

```
      title: ['', Validators.required],
      text: ['', Validators.required]
   });
 }

 ngOnInit () {}

 get f() { return this.postForm.controls; }

 onSubmit() {
    this.submitted = true;

    // stop here if form is invalid
    if (this.postForm.invalid) {
        return;
    }
 }

}
```

This should already be familiar to us given our experience with the login form. We import the modules needed to build the form:

```
import { FormBuilder, FormGroup, Validators } from '@angular/forms';
```

Then we initialize a pair of properties:

```
postForm: FormGroup;
submitted = false;
```

postForm will reference our group of form controls. Again, for such a simple form, we will only have one group.

submitted will be our flag to indicate when the form has been sent.

Then we have the constructor:

```
constructor( private formBuilder: FormBuilder ) {
    this.postForm = this.FormBuilder.group({
      title: ['', Validators.required],
      text: ['', Validators.required]
    });
}
```

We declare a private property that will reference our form and initialize it. We declare two controls, title and text, which will be mandatory.

For the moment, our onSubmit method does nothing but return if the form is invalid. Here is the link to the file:

https://github.com/Apress/The-Beginning-Angular-by-Victor-Hugo-Garcia/ blob/main/Chapter-10/01-add-post.component.ts

Now let's replace the content of add-post.component.html as follows:

```
<div class="modal fade" id="exampleModal" tabindex="-1" role="dialog"
aria-labelledby="exampleModalLabel" aria-hidden="true">
   <div class="modal-dialog" role="document">
       <div class="modal-content">
           <div class="modal-header">
               <h5 class="modal-title" id="exampleModalLabel">
Modal title</h5>
               <button type="button" #closeBtn class="close"
data-dismiss="modal" aria-label="Close">
           <span aria-hidden="true">x</span>
         </button>
         </div>
         <div class="modal-body">

             <form [formGroup]="postForm" (ngSubmit)="onSubmit ()">
                 <label for="title" class="sr-only">Title</label>
                 <input type="text"
formControlName="title"
class="form-control"
placeholder="Title"
[ngClass]="{'is-invalid': submitted && f['title'].errors}" />
                 <div *ngIf="submitted && f['title'].errors"
class="invalid-feedback">
                     <div *ngIf="f['title'].errors['required']">
Title is required</div>
                 </div>
```

```
            <div class="form-group">
                <label for="text" class="sr-only">Text</label>
                <textarea formControlName="text"
class="form-control" placeholder="Text"
[ngClass]="{'is-invalid': submitted && f['text'].errors}">
                </textarea>
                <div *ngIf="submitted && f['text'].errors"
class="invalid-feedback">
                    <div *ngIf="f['text'].errors['required']">
Text is required</div>
                </div>
            </div>

            <button class="btn btn-primary">Add</button>
        </form>

      </div>
    </div>
  </div>
</div>
```

And again here is the link to the file: https://github.com/Apress/The-Beginning-Angular-by-Victor-Hugo-Garcia/blob/main/Chapter-10/02-add-post.component.html

Now we can use our new component in our dashboard. In dashboard.component.html:

```
<main role="main" class="col-md-9 ml-sm-auto col-lg-10 px-4">
        <div class="d-flex justify-content-between flex-wrap
flex-md-nowrap align-items-center pt-3 bp-2 mb-3 border-bottom">
            <h1 class="h2">Dashboard</h1>
            <div class="btn-toolbar mb-2 mb-md-0">
                <div class="btn-group mr-2">
                    <button type="button"
```

```
class="btn btn-sm btn-outline-secondary"
data-toggle="modal"
data-target="#exampleModal">Add Post</button>
                    </div>
                </div>
            </div>

            <h2 class="border-bottom text-center">
My Posts</h2>
            <div *ngFor="let post of posts">
                <app-post [post]="post" [read]="false" [admin]="true">
                </app-post>
            </div>
        </main>
        <app-add-post> </app-add-post>
```

Notice where the component tag has been added.

Also, notice how the definition of the **Add Post** button has changed:

```
<button type="button"
class="btn btn-sm btn-outline-secondary"
data-toggle="modal"
data-target="#exampleModal">Add Post</button>
```

Just to be sure, here is the link to the dashboard.component.html: https://github.com/Apress/The-Beginning-Angular-by-Victor-Hugo-Garcia/blob/main/Chapter-10/03-dashboard.component.html.

Now, clicking the **Add Post** button, we should see the modal window appear as shown in Figure 10-1.

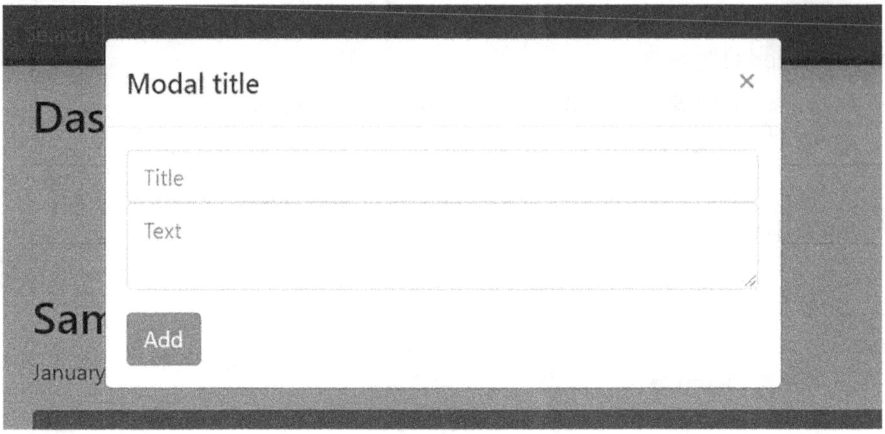

Figure 10-1. *Add modal*

And if we try to send the form without completing the fields, we will get errors (Figure 10-2).

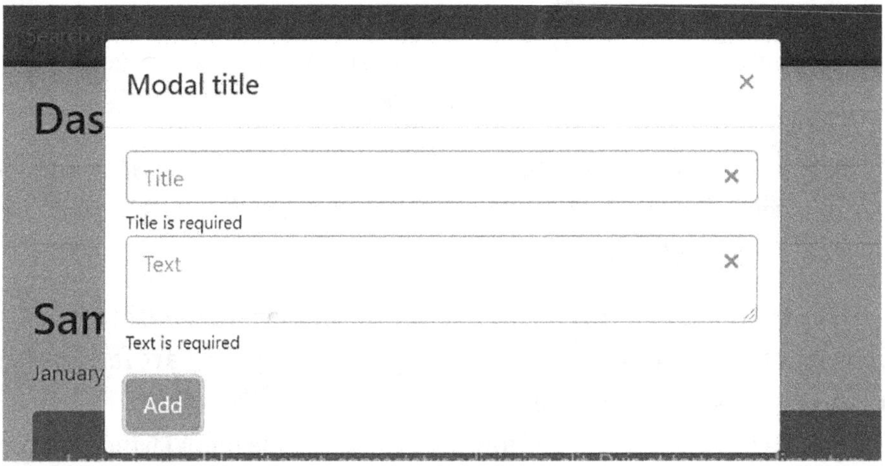

Figure 10-2. *Add modal errors*

With the frontend acceptably finished, let's concentrate now on our API, where we will include the endpoint in charge of inserting the posts in the database.

At this point, I will make a recommendation.

As you may have noticed, every time we make changes to our API, that is, we modify our index.js file from the backend, we are forced to stop the server with Ctrl+C and restart it with node index.js so that the changes are visible.

This can be tedious, but fortunately we have a way of avoiding it. We can install a utility called nodemon (https://nodemon.io/), which will monitor the changes made to our source code and automatically restart the server. In this way, we need only to start the server once, and then we can work on our code and see the changes reflected automatically. It is not mandatory to install this tool, but is very convenient.

To install it, we can simply enter the following from a terminal:

npm install -g nodemon

The -g flag indicates that we want to install the tool globally. Now, from our backend directory, it is only a matter of starting the server using the nodemon command instead of the node command (Figure 10-3).

MINGW64:/c/Users/Victor/Desktop/Angular/blog/backend

```
Victor@DESKTOP-JD4E79M MINGW64 ~/Desktop/Angular/blog/backend
$ nodemon index.js
[nodemon] 1.18.9
[nodemon] to restart at any time, enter `rs`
[nodemon] watching: *.*
[nodemon] starting `node index.js`
Listening on port 3000
```

Figure 10-3. *Nodemon*

This is not absolutely necessary, but it is convenient.

Now let's continue working on our API.

createPost method

Add the following method to index.js:

```
app.post('/api/post/createPost', (req, res) => {
    mongoose.connect(url, { }, function(err) {
        if (err) throw err;
        const post = new Post({
            title: req.body.title,
            text: req.body.text,
            author_id: mongoose.Types.ObjectId(req.body.author_id)
        });
```

307

```
    post.save((err, Doc) => {
        if (err) throw err;
        return res.status(200).json({
            status: 'success',
            data: Doc
        })
    })
  });
});
```

Here's the corresponding code snippet: https://github.com/Apress/The-Beginning-Angular-by-Victor-Hugo-Garcia/blob/main/Chapter-10/04-index.js.

That's it from the backend side. Now let's go back to the frontend and start by adding a post model.

Post Model

In our models directory, add a post.model.ts file with the following content:

```
export class Post {
    private id = '';
    private title;
    private text;
    private author_id = '';

    constructor(title: string, text: string) {
        this.title = title;
        this.text = text;
    }

    getTitle() {
        return this.title;
    }

    getText() {
        return this.text;
    }
}
```

And here is the link to the corresponding file: https://github.com/Apress/The-Beginning-Angular-by-Victor-Hugo-Garcia/blob/main/Chapter-10/05-post.model-v1.ts.

It is a simple class. In the constructor, we set the values of title and text and add a pair of getters to obtain the values of these two properties. Also, we have a setter for the author_id.

We will now create a service called addPost:

```
ng g s services/addPost
```

This will give us an add-post.service.ts file. Let's replace the content with the following:

```
import { Injectable } from '@angular/core';
import { HttpClient } from '@angular/common/http';
import { Post } from '../models/post.model';

@Injectable({
 providedIn: 'root'
})
export class AddPostService {

 constructor(private http: HttpClient) {}

 addPost(post: Post) {
   const user = JSON.parse(localStorage.getItem('currentUser') as string);

   return this.http.post('/api/post/createPost', {
       title : post.getTitle(),
       text : post.getText(),
       author_id: user.id
   });
 }
}
```

Our next step will be to modify the add-post.component.ts file to make use of the service.

We add the necessary import:

```
import { AddPostService } from '../../services/add-post.service';
```

And we modify the constructor to add a reference to the service:

```
constructor(
private formBuilder: FormBuilder,
private addPostService: AddPostService
) {}
```

We also need to import our post model:

```
import { Post } from '../../models/post.model';
```

And initialize a property:

```
post: Post = new Post('', '');
```

Now we can modify the onSubmit method to make use of the service:

```
onSubmit() {
  this.submitted = true;

  // stop here if form is invalid
  if (this.postForm.invalid) {
      return;
  }

  this.post = new Post(this.f['title'].value, this.f['text'].value);

  this.addPostService.addPost( this.post ).subscribe({
    next: (result: any) => {
      if (result ['status'] === 'success') {
      } else {
        console.log( 'Error adding post' );
      }
    },
    error: (e: any) => {},
    complete: () => { console.info('complete') }
  });
}
```

Just to be sure, here is the complete code of the AddPost Component:

```
import { Component, OnInit } from '@angular/core';
import { FormBuilder, FormGroup, Validators } from '@angular/forms';
import { AddPostService } from '../../services/add-post.service';
import { Post } from '../../models/post.model';

@Component({
 selector: 'app-add-post',
 templateUrl: './add-post.component.html',
 styleUrls: ['./add-post.component.css']
})
export class AddPostComponent implements OnInit {
 postForm: FormGroup;
 submitted = false;
 post: Post = new Post('', '');

 constructor(
  private formBuilder: FormBuilder,
  private addPostService: AddPostService
  ) {
  this.postForm = this.formBuilder.group({
    title: ['', Validators.required],
    text: ['', Validators.required]
  });
 }

 ngOnInit() {}

 get f() { return this.postForm.controls; }

 onSubmit() {
  this.submitted = true;

  // stop here if form is invalid
  if (this.postForm.invalid) {
      return;
  }
```

```
this.post = new Post(this.f['title'].value, this.f['text'].value);

this.addPostService.addPost( this.post ).subscribe({
  next: (result: any) => {
    if (result ['status'] === 'success') {
    } else {
      console.log( 'Error adding post' );
    }
  },
  error: (e: any) => {},
  complete: () => { console.info('complete') }
});
}
}
```

With these changes applied, we can try adding a new post (Figure 10-4).

Figure 10-4. *Adding posts*

We can use MongoDB Compass to see that a new document has been inserted as shown in Figure 10-5 (it may be necessary to refresh the interface).

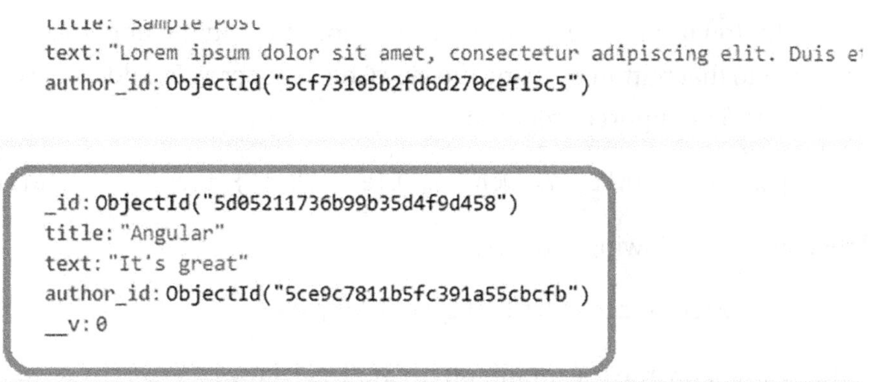

```
title: Sample Post
text: "Lorem ipsum dolor sit amet, consectetur adipiscing elit. Duis e
author_id: ObjectId("5cf73105b2fd6d270cef15c5")
```

```
_id: ObjectId("5d05211736b99b35d4f9d458")
title: "Angular"
text: "It's great"
author_id: ObjectId("5ce9c7811b5fc391a55cbcfb")
__v: 0
```

Figure 10-5. *New post in DB*

However, we can notice that the modal window is still in place. If we close and refresh the page, we will see the new post (Figure 10-6).

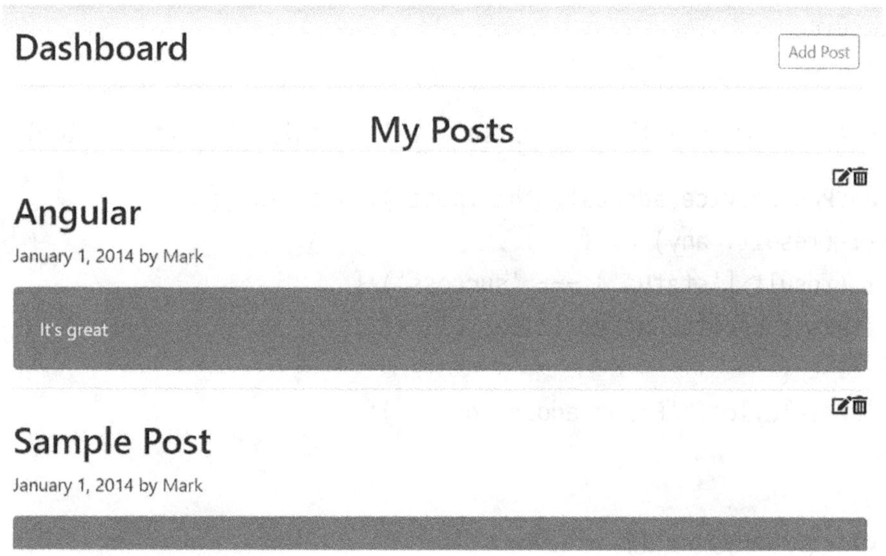

Dashboard · Add Post

My Posts

Angular
January 1, 2014 by Mark

> It's great

Sample Post
January 1, 2014 by Mark

Figure 10-6. *New post added*

Logically, leaving the modal window open is something we should avoid. To do this, we will use the viewChild decorator, which allows you to use a property to refer to an element of a component.

In add-post.component.html, we have the definition of the following button:

```
<button type="button" #closeBtn class="close"
data-dismiss="modal" aria-label="Close">
```

This is the button used to close the modal window, the x in the upper-right corner.

We can refer to that button by using the viewChild property. In add-post.component. ts, let's modify the first import as follows:

```
import { Component, OnInit, ViewChild, ElementRef } from '@angular/core';
```

And then add the following property:

```
@ViewChild('closeBtn') closeBtn!: ElementRef;
```

With this, we can rewrite the onSubmit method as follows:

```
onSubmit() {
  this.submitted = true;

  // stop here if form is invalid
  if (this.postForm.invalid) {
      return;
  }

  this.post = new Post(this.f['title'].value, this.f['text'].value);

  this.addPostService.addPost( this.post ).subscribe({
    next: (result: any) => {
      if (result ['status'] === 'success') {
        this.closeBtn.nativeElement.click();
      } else {
        console.log( 'Error adding post' );
      }
    },
    error: (e: any) => {},
    complete: () => { console.info('complete') }
  });
 }

}
```

Here is the code snippet: https://github.com/Apress/The-Beginning-Angular-by-Victor-Hugo-Garcia/blob/main/Chapter-10/07-add-post.component.ts.

Now, the modal window will be closed after the new post has been added. This is not the only use of viewChild. It can also be used to refer to a child component from a parent component, in order to be able to access the child's properties or methods.

We have solved a problem, but we still have the issue of updating the dashboard once a new post has been added. For this, we will use the power of the Observables.

Observables

Observables provide a form of message-based communication between a sender and one or more subscribers.

In response to an event, the sender sends a notification that is received by all subscribers. Application examples would be to detect when a user has registered and communicate the subscription to a component responsible for sending an email message.

First, we add a new service:

```
ng g s services/common
```

This generates a new common.service.ts file. Let's replace the content with the following:

```
import { Injectable } from '@angular/core';
import { Subject } from 'rxjs';

@Injectable({
 providedIn: 'root'
})
export class CommonService {

   public postAdded_Observable = new Subject();

   constructor() {

   }

   notifyPostAddition(msg: string) {
       this.postAdded_Observable.next(msg);
   }
}
```

Now let's modify our add-post.component.ts again. Add an import of the new service:

```
import { CommonService } from '../../services/common.service';
```

Then in the constructor, add:

```
builder(
    private formBuilder: FormBuilder,
    private addPostService: AddPostService,
    private commonService: CommonService
) {}
```

Finally, on the onSubmit method of add-post.component.ts, add:

```
onSubmit() {
  this.submitted = true;

  // stop here if form is invalid
  if (this.postForm.invalid) {
      return;
  }

  this.post = new Post(this.f['title'].value, this.f['text'].value);

  this.addPostService.addPost( this.post ).subscribe({
    next: (result: any) => {
      if (result ['status'] === 'success') {
        this.closeBtn.nativeElement.click();
        this.commonService.notifyPostAddition('');
      } else {
        console.log( 'Error adding post' );
      }
    },
    error: (e: any) => {},
    complete: () => { console.info('complete') }
  });
}
```

The notification is issued, but our Dashboard Component must react to it.

Add the following import to dashboard.component.ts:

```
import { CommonService } from '../../services/common.service';
```

Initialize a new property in the constructor:

```
constructor(
  private postService: PostService,
  private auth: AuthService,
  private router: Router,
  private commonService: CommonService
)
```

And now modify the ngOnInit method:

```
ngOnInit() {
  this.getPosts();

  this.commonService.postAdded_Observable.subscribe((res) => {
    this.getPosts();
  });
}
```

With these modifications, when adding a new post, we will see how the dashboard screen shows the new post added immediately.

As always, we're going to end the chapter with the gists that contain the source code to make sure everything works correctly.

Backend Source Code

index.js
    https://github.com/Apress/The-Beginning-Angular-by-Victor-Hugo-Garcia/
blob/main/Chapter-10/08-index.js

Frontend Source Code

add-post.component.ts

https://github.com/Apress/The-Beginning-Angular-by-Victor-Hugo-Garcia/ blob/main/Chapter-10/09-add-post.component.ts

dashboard.component.ts

https://github.com/Apress/The-Beginning-Angular-by-Victor-Hugo-Garcia/ blob/main/Chapter-10/10-dashboard.component.ts

common.service.ts

https://github.com/Apress/The-Beginning-Angular-by-Victor-Hugo-Garcia/ blob/main/Chapter-10/11-common.service.ts

post.model.ts

https://github.com/Apress/The-Beginning-Angular-by-Victor-Hugo-Garcia/ blob/main/Chapter-10/12-post.model-v2.ts

Summary

We have thus completed the necessary functionality to add posts. Of course, there are things that could definitely be improved. For example, at this time our posts do not support more than text format. But we are on the way to completing the basic CRUD operations. There will be time to make the necessary improvements.

In the next chapter, we will focus on editing posts.

CHAPTER 11

Blog App Part 6: Editing Posts

In this chapter, we will focus on editing posts, getting closer to finalizing the basic functionality of the application, although of course there will be details that we will have to deal with later.

Frontend Post Model

As a first step, we will add three new methods to our Post model. In the file post.model. ts, add:

```
setTitle(title: string) {
  this.title = title;
}

setText(text: string) {
  this.text = text;
}

setId(id: string) {
  this.id = id;
}
```

There are three setters, and just to be sure, here is the complete code of the model:

```
export class Post {
    private id = '';
    private title;
    private text;
    private author_id = '';
```

© Victor Hugo Garcia 2023
V. H. Garcia, *Getting Started with Angular*, https://doi.org/10.1007/978-1-4842-9206-8_11

```
constructor(title: string, text: string) {
    this.title = title;
    this.text = text;
}

getTitle() {
    return this.title;
}

getText() {
    return this.text;
}

getId() {
    return this.id;
}

setTitle(title: string) {
    this.title = title;
}

setText(text: string) {
    this.text = text;
}

setId(id: string) {
    this.id = id;
}

}
```

The following modification will be in our common.service.ts.

Common Service

Let's add two new properties:

```
public postToEdit_Observable = new Subject();

postToEdit: Post = new Post('', '');
```

First, add a new observable that we will use to notify when one has been selected to be edited. Then, we declare a variable that will serve to contain said post.

Of course, we need the import statement:

```
import { Post } from '../models/post.model';
```

Next, we add two new methods:

```
notifyPostEdit(msg: string) {
    this.postToEdit_Observable.next(msg);
}

setPostToEdit(post: any) {
    this.postToEdit = new Post(post.title, post.text);
    this.postToEdit.setId(post._id);
    this.notifyPostEdit('');
}
```

The first method will issue the notification to which all consumers of the observable can subscribe.

In the second method, we first create a new post based on the user's selection. Remember that in the Post Component the posts that are displayed are *not* post objects. They are simply common objects, but they do not fit the interface of our Post model. That is why we created a new instance of the Post model from the title and text of the post-selected generic object. Then, we use our new setter to assign to the new post the id of the post that the user wishes to edit. Finally, the notification is issued.

Let's clarify this point a little more.

Both in the home and in the dashboard, the posts that are received from the backend have the following format:

```
{
  _id: " 5d05211736b99b35d4f9d458 ",
  title: " Angular ",
  text: " It's great ",
  author_id: " 5ce9c7811b5fc391a55cbcfb "
}
```

And it is that generic object that when selected for editing is used to instantiate an object of type Post with the following structure:

```
{
  id: "5d05211736b99b35d4f9d458",
  author_id: "",
  title: "Angular ",
  text:" It's great "
}
```

Some of you may point out that this is cumbersome, and they are right. It would be much better to have some way of transforming the objects received from the backend to Post-type objects according to our frontend.

Fortunately, such a way exists, and we can implement it in the service that makes the requests. But we will leave this optimization for later.

Post Component

In post.component.html, we will modify the line where the edit icon is shown to respond to the mouse-click event:

```
<i title="Edit" (click)="setPostToEdit(post)"
class="fas fa-edit" aria-hidden="true"
style="cursor: pointer"> </i>
```

Strictly speaking, the only part we have added is:

```
(click)="setPostToEdit(post)"
```

Now add the method in post.component.ts:

```
setPostToEdit(post) {
    this.commonService.setPostToEdit(post);
 }
```

We simply call the Common Service method. As you should know, before we can use it we must add the necessary import:

```
import { CommonService } from '../../services/common.service';
```

And modify the constructor to declare a property:

```
constructor( private commonService: CommonService ) {}
```

With these changes, when the user selects a post for editing, the notification will be issued, but we are not yet reacting to that notification. We are going to change that.

Dashboard Component

First, let's modify the dashboard.component.html to assign an id to the **Add Post** button:

```
<button type="button" #addPost
class="btn btn-sm btn-outline-secondary"
data-toggle="modal" data-target="#exampleModal">Add Post</button>
```

The changes in dashboard.component.ts are more numerous.

First, we will add a property to be able to manipulate the button that we have identified as #addPost:

```
@ViewChild('addPost') addBtn!: ElementRef;
```

Of course, we need to change the import:

```
import { Component, OnInit } from '@angular/core';
```

to

```
import { Component, OnInit, ViewChild, ElementRef } from '@angular/core';
```

Then we rewrite the constructor as follows:

```
builder(
    private postService: PostService,
    private auth: AuthService,
    private router: Router,
    private commonService: CommonService
  ) {
    this.commonService.postToEdit_Observable.subscribe(res => {
      this.addBtn.nativeElement.click();
    });
  }
```

In the constructor, we are subscribing to the notification that will be sent when a post is selected to be edited. In response to that event, the click event of the Add Post button of the child component AddPost will be invoked.

Finally, we must modify the AddPost Component so that the data of the selected post is shown in the modal screen.

First, add the constructor:

```
constructor(
    private formBuilder: FormBuilder,
    private addPostService: AddPostService,
    private commonService: CommonService
  ) {
    this.postForm = this.formBuilder.group({
     title: ['', Validators.required],
     text: ['', Validators.required]
    });
    this.commonService.postToEdit_Observable.subscribe(res => {
      this.post = this.commonService.postToEdit;
      this.postForm = this.FormBuilder.group({
        title: [this.post.getTitle(), Validators.required],
        text: [this.post.getText(), Validators.required]
      });
    });
  }
```

The change from the previous version of the constructor is as follows:

```
this.commonService.postToEdit_Observable.subscribe(res => {
    this.post = this.commonService.postToEdit;
    this.postForm = this.FormBuilder.group({
      title: [this.post.getTitle(), Validators.required],
      text: [this.post.getText(), Validators.required]
    });
  });
```

In the body of the method, we subscribe to the observable that notifies the selection of a post for editing. When the notification is received, the post local variable stores the post to be modified, which is provided by the service. Then, the control group of the form is created, passing the title and the text of the post as values.

The next change is in the onSubmit method. Let's replace the line:

```
this.post = new Post(this.f['title'].value, this.f['text'].value);
```

by

```
this.post.setText(this.f['title'].value);
this.post.setText(this.f['text'].value);
```

We use the Post model setters to change the title and text according to the form values.

At this point, if we select a post for editing, we will see that the form effectively shows the values of the selected post.

However, we have a problem. If we select a post to edit, close the modal window, and then click the Add Post button, we will see that in the form the values of the last selected post are shown. Let's deal with it.

The problem is that we have no way to differentiate when the modal window has been called by clicking the Add Post button of dashboard.component.html and when it has been called by clicking any of the edit buttons of the Post Component instances.

First, let's modify the Common Service as follows. We add a new observable:

```
public postToAdd_Observable = new Subject();
```

a new notification:

```
notifyPostToAdd(msg: string) {
    this.postToAdd_Observable.next(msg);
}
```

and a new method that triggers the notification:

```
setPostToAdd() {
    this.postToEdit = new Post('', '');
    this.postToEdit.setId('');
    this.notifyPostToAdd();
  }
```

Just to be sure, here's the link to the file: https://github.com/Apress/The-Beginning-Angular-by-Victor-Hugo-Garcia/blob/main/Chapter-11/03-common.service.ts.

Now, in dashboard.component.html, add the following button, just below the **Add Post** button:

```
<button type="button" style="display: none" #editPost
class="btn btn-sm btn-outline-secondary"
data-toggle="modal" data-target="#exampleModal">Edit Post</button>
```

In the dashboard.component.ts file, add a reference to the new button:

```
@ViewChild('editPost') editBtn: ElementRef;
```

Now in the constructor, let's change the line:

```
this.addBtn.nativeElement.click();
```

by

```
this.editBtn.nativeElement.click();
```

Also, let's add a new method:

```
resetPost() {
    this.commonService.setPostToAdd();
 }
```

This method calls the setPostToAdd method, which, as we have seen, assigns a new empty Post to the postToEdit variable, and issues the corresponding notification:

```
this.postToEdit = new Post('', '');
this.postToEdit.setId('');
this.notifyPostToAdd();
```

That resetPost method will be summoned by clicking the Add Post button. Modify it as follows:

```
<button type="button" (click)="resetPost()" #addPost
class="btn btn-sm btn-outline-secondary"
data-toggle="modal" data-target="#exampleModal">
Add Post</button>
```

Summing up what we have so far, when the user clicks the **Add Post** button of the Dashboard Component, a Common Service method is invoked that generates a new empty post and issues a notification.

Now, we must change the AddPost Component to respond to the notification.

AddPost Component

Let's replace the constructor as follows:

```
constructor(
    private formBuilder: FormBuilder,
    private addPostService: AddPostService,
    private commonService: CommonService
 ) {
    this.postForm = this.formBuilder.group({
     title: ['', Validators.required],
     text: ['', Validators.required]
   });
    this.commonService.postToEdit_Observable.subscribe(res => {
      this.post = this.commonService.postToEdit;
      this.postForm = this.formBuilder.group({
        title: [this.post.getTitle(), Validators.required],
        text: [this.post.getText(), Validators.required]
      });
    });
    this.commonService.postToAdd_Observable.subscribe(res => {
      this.post = this.commonService.postToEdit;
      this.postForm = this.formBuilder.group({
        title: [this.post.getTitle(), Validators.required],
        text: [this.post.getText(), Validators.required]
      });
    });
  }
```

As you may have noticed, we are subscribing to the new notification issued by the new observable. However, the code that runs on both subscriptions is identical. Let's solve that.

Let's add a new method:

```
setPostToEdit() {
    this.post = this.commonService.postToEdit;
    this.postForm = this.formBuilder.group({
        title: [this.post.getTitle(), Validators.required],
        text: [this.post.getText(), Validators.required]
    });
}
```

with which we can rewrite the constructor in this way:

```
constructor(
    private formBuilder: FormBuilder,
    private addPostService: AddPostService,
    private commonService: CommonService
) {
    this.commonService.postToEdit_Observable.subscribe(res => {
        this.setPostToEdit();
    });
    this.commonService.postToAdd_Observable.subscribe(res => {
        this.setPostToEdit();
    });
}
```

If we now select a post to edit, close the window, and then click the **Add Post** button, we will see that the fields appear blank, which is the expected behavior.

If now we try to add a new post, we can do it without problems, but if we try to edit a specific post, the only thing we will get is a duplicate post.

We must modify in our onSubmit method the post submission. Immediately after the lines:

```
this.post.setTitle(this.f.title.value);
this.post.setText(this.f.text.value);
```

We will now add:

```
if (this.post.getId() === '') {
    this.addPostService.addPost( this.post ).subscribe({
      next: (result: any) => {
        if (result ['status'] === 'success') {
          this.closeBtn.nativeElement.click();
          this.commonService.notifyPostAddition('');
        } else {
          console.log ( 'Error adding post' );
        }
      },
      error: (e: any) => {},
      complete: () => { console.info('complete') }
    });
  } else {
    this.addPostService.updatePost( this.post ).subscribe({
      next: (result: any) => {
        if (result ['status'] === 'success') {
          this.closeBtn.nativeElement.click();
          this.commonService.notifyPostAddition('');
        } else {
          console.log( 'Error updating post' );
        }
      },
      error: (e: any) => {},
      complete: () => { console.info('complete') }
    });
  }
}
```

Here is the complete code of the onSubmit method:

```
onSubmit() {
    this.submitted = true;

    // stop here if form is invalid
    if (this.postForm.invalid) {
        return;
    }

    this.post.setText(this.f['title'].value);
    this.post.setText(this.f['text'].value);

    if (this.post.getId() === '') {
      this.addPostService.addPost( this.post ).subscribe({
        next: (result: any) => {
          if (result ['status'] === 'success') {
            this.closeBtn.nativeElement.click();
            this.commonService.notifyPostAddition('');
          } else {
            console.log ( 'Error adding post' );
          }
        },
        error: (e: any) => {},
        complete: () => { console.info('complete') }
      });
    } else {
      this.addPostService.updatePost( this.post ).subscribe({
        next: (result: any) => {
          if (result ['status'] === 'success') {
            this.closeBtn.nativeElement.click();
            this.commonService.notifyPostAddition('');
          } else {
            console.log( 'Error updating post' );
          }
        },
```

```
    error: (e: any) => {},
    complete: () => { console.info('complete') }
  });
 }
}
```

However, you may have noticed some problems with our new version of the method. For starters, let's analyze the condition that is evaluated:

```
if (this.post.getId() === '')
```

Probably our IDE warns us that the Post class does not have a getId method. Let's add it right now. In post.model.ts, add:

```
getId() {
    return this.id;
}
```

The next problem is that our AddPost Service does not have an updatePost method. Let's add it.

AddPost Service

In add-post.service.ts, add:

```
updatePost(post: Post) {
   console.log(post);
   const user = JSON.parse(localStorage.getItem('currentUser') as string);

   return this.http.post('/api/post/updatePost', {
       id: post.getId(),
       title : post.getTitle(),
       text : post.getText(),
       author_id: user.id
   });
 }
```

Magnificent. Everything is complete in the frontend. Now we must deal with adding the endpoint in our API.

updatePost

In index.js, let's add:

```
app.post('/api/post/updatePost', (req, res) => {
    mongoose.connect(url, { }, function(err) {
        if (err) throw err;
        Post.update(
          { _id: req.body.id },
          { title: req.body.title, text: req.body.text },
            (err, Doc) => {
                if (err) throw err;
                return res.status(200).json({
                    status: 'success',
                    data: Doc
                })
            })
    });
});
```

With our endpoint running, we can edit posts (Figures 11-1 to 11-3).

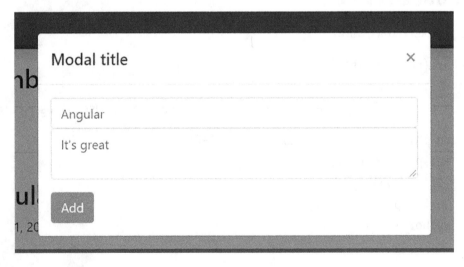

Figure 11-1. *Editing post*

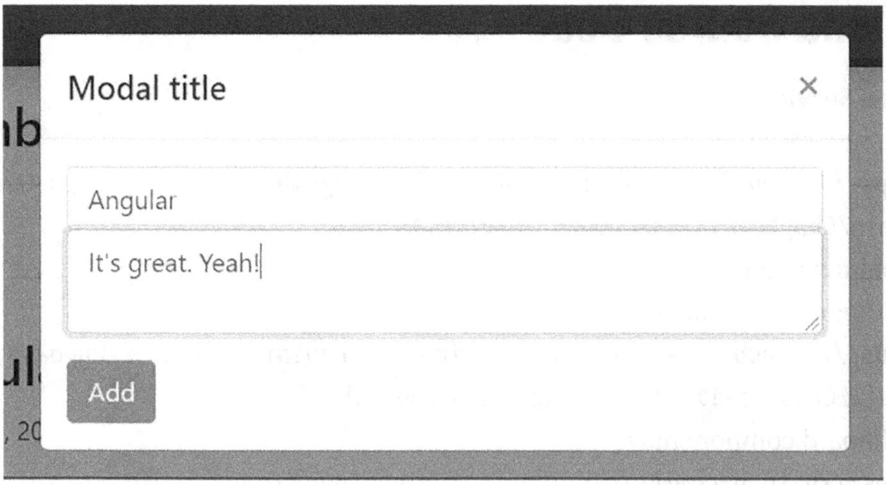
Modal title
Angular
It's great. Yeah!
Add

Figure 11-2. *Editing post*

Angular
January 1, 2014 by Mark
It's great. Yeah!

Figure 11-3. *Editing post*

As always, we close the chapter with links to the code to make sure that everything works correctly.

Backend Source Code

index.js

`https://github.com/Apress/The-Beginning-Angular-by-Victor-Hugo-Garcia/blob/main/Chapter-11/02-index.js`

Frontend Source Code

Common Service

common.service.ts

https://github.com/Apress/The-Beginning-Angular-by-Victor-Hugo-Garcia/
blob/main/Chapter-11/03-common.service.ts

Dashboard Component

dashboard.component.html

https://github.com/Apress/The-Beginning-Angular-by-Victor-Hugo-Garcia/
blob/main/Chapter-11/04-dashboard.component.html

dashboard.component.ts

https://github.com/Apress/The-Beginning-Angular-by-Victor-Hugo-Garcia/
blob/main/Chapter-11/05-dashboard.component.ts

Post Component

post.component.html

https://github.com/Apress/The-Beginning-Angular-by-Victor-Hugo-Garcia/
blob/main/Chapter-11/06-post.component.html

post.component.ts

https://github.com/Apress/The-Beginning-Angular-by-Victor-Hugo-Garcia/
blob/main/Chapter-11/07-post.component.ts

AddPost Component

add-post.component.ts

https://github.com/Apress/The-Beginning-Angular-by-Victor-Hugo-Garcia/
blob/main/Chapter-11/08-add-post.component.ts

AddPost Service

add-post-service.ts

https://github.com/Apress/The-Beginning-Angular-by-Victor-Hugo-Garcia/
blob/main/Chapter-11/09-add-post.service.ts

The functionality of our application is closer to being complete. We only have to take care of post deletion to complete all CRUD operations.

Summary

In this brief chapter, we added the functionality to edit posts, making use again of the observables. The next chapter, where we will deal with the elimination, will be equally brief. Once the basic functionality is complete, we will devote ourselves to polishing details of our application to improve its efficiency and appearance.

CHAPTER 12

Blog App Part 7: Deleting Posts

The logic that we will use to eliminate posts is very similar to the one we use to edit components. From the post component, which is responsible for showing each of the posts that the user has created, an event will trigger when the elimination icon is clicked.

This event will cause that in the class of the component, a method will be executed that will send the selected post to the Common Service. This will perform some operations with said post and issue a notification. In the Dashboard Component, we will subscribe to this notification, to present a modal window where the confirmation of the deletion is requested.

Common Service

We will start defining a new observable:

```
public postToDelete_Observable = new Subject();
```

and a new property of type Post:

```
postToDelete: Post = new Post('', '');
```

Make sure you have the corresponding import:

```
import { Post } from '../../models/post.model';
```

Then we add the notification method:

```
notifyPostDelete(msg: string) {
    this.postToDelete_Observable.next(msg);
}
```

© Victor Hugo Garcia 2023
V. H. Garcia, *Getting Started with Angular*, https://doi.org/10.1007/978-1-4842-9206-8_12

Finally, the method that receives the post to be deleted, operates on it, and sends the notification:

```
setPostToDelete(post: any) {
    this.postToDelete = new Post('', '');
    this.postToDelete.setId(post._id);
    this.notifyPostDelete('');
}
```

That's it on the Common Service side. Nothing that we have not seen previously.

Dashboard Component

Let's start by modifying the dashboard.component.html file. First, add a modal window that will show a confirmation message when we click the delete icon that appears next to the edit icon in each post.

Following the line:

```
<app-add-post> </app-add-post>
```

copy the following:

```
<div class="modal fade" id="deleteModal" tabindex="-1" role="dialog"
aria-labelledby="exampleModalLabel" aria-hidden="true">
        <div class="modal-dialog" role="document">
            <div class="modal-content">
                <div class="modal-header">
                    <h5 class="modal-title" id="exampleModalLabel">
Delete Post</h5>
                    <button type="button" class="close" data-dismiss="modal"
aria-label="Close">
                    <span aria-hidden="true">& times;</span>
                    </button>
                </div>
                <div class="modal-body">
                    Are you sure you want to delete this post?
                </div>
```

```
            <div class="modal-footer">
                <button type="button" class="btn btn-secondary"
data-dismiss="modal">Cancel</button>
                <button type="button" (click)="delete ()"
class="btn btn-primary">Delete</button>
            </div>
        </div>
    </div>
</div>
```

Here is the link to the file with the code snippet: https://github.com/Apress/The-Beginning-Angular-by-Victor-Hugo-Garcia/blob/main/Chapter-12/01-dashboard.component.html.

For this window to be displayed, it is necessary to add a button that will not be displayed but will serve to trigger the event that calls that window.

Next to the following line:

```
<button type="button" style="display: none" #editPost
class="btn btn-sm btn-outline-secondary"
data-toggle="modal" data-target="#exampleModal">
Edit Post</button>
```

add:

```
<button type="button" style="display: none" #deletePost
class="btn btn-sm btn-outline-secondary"
data-toggle="modal" data-target="#deleteModal">
Delete Post</button>
```

We have a button with an id of deletePost. Now, in our dashboard.component.ts file, we should include a property that makes reference to the new button:

```
@ViewChild('deletePost') deleteBtn!: ElementRef;
```

Also, add a property that will contain the post to be deleted:

```
postToDelete: Post = new Post('', '');
```

Where will we assign to that variable the post that has been selected to be deleted?

When we respond to the notification that the Common Service will send, and to which we must subscribe to the constructor, the method remains as follows:

```
builder(
    private postService: PostService,
    private auth: AuthService,
    private router: Router,
    private commonService: CommonService
 ) {
    this.commonService.postToEdit_Observable.subscribe(res => {
      this.editBtn.nativeElement.click();
    });
    this.commonService.postToDelete_Observable.subscribe(res => {
      this.postToDelete = this.commonService.postToDelete;
      this.deleteBtn.nativeElement.click();
    });
 }
```

Notice also that on our **Delete** button of the modal confirmation window, we are defining the following:

```
(click)="delete()"
```

We will be listening to the click event in order to trigger an event **delete**, which for now define as:

```
delete() {
    console.log(this.postToDelete);
 }
```

Post Component

The first change will be made in the post.component.html file. Replace the line showing the deletion icon with the following:

```
<i title="Delete" (click)="setPostToDelete(post)"
class="fas fa-trash-alt" aria-hidden="true" style="cursor: pointer"> </i>
```

Actually, the only thing we are adding is:

```
(click)="setPostToDelete(post)"
```

Logically, the setPostToDelete method does not exist yet. Our next step is to create it in post.component.ts:

```
setPostToDelete(post: any) {
    this.commonService.setPostToDelete(post);
}
```

The method receives the selected post and passes it to a setPostToDelete method of our Common Service, starting the cycle that we commented on at the beginning.

With these changes in position, when clicking the delete icon of a post, we should see something like Figure 12-1.

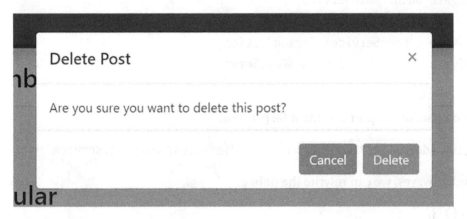

Figure 12-1. *Delete post*

When we click Delete, the console will show us something like Figure 12-2.

```
                                        dashboard.component.ts:56
  ▶ Post {id: "5cf2b74d862746a62ab083ca", author_id: "", tit
    le: "", text: ""}
```

Figure 12-2. *Delete post console*

We have only kept the id of the post to be deleted, which is the only thing we need.

Let's now write the method that will call the API to delete the post, sending as parameter the id of the selected post.

In add-post.service.ts, let's add:

```
deletePost(post: Post) {
  return this.http.post('/api/post/deletePost', {
    id: post.getId()
  });
}
```

It's a super simple method.

Now let's go back to our Dashboard Component and rewrite the delete method. But before that, we must declare a property of type AddPost Service in our constructor:

```
builder(
  private postService: PostService,
  private auth: AuthService,
  private router: Router,
  private commonService: CommonService,
  private addPostService: AddPostService
)
```

Of course, the import line must be present:

```
import { AddPostService } from '../../services/add-post.service';
```

And now, yes, we can rewrite the delete:

```
delete() {
  this.addPostService.deletePost( this.postToDelete ).subscribe(
    (res) => {
      this.getPosts();
    });
}
```

With that, we have finished the frontend part; now it is our turn to take care of our API.

index.js

In the index.js file, we create the following method:

```
app.post('/api/post/deletePost', (req, res) => {
   mongoose.connect(url, { },
function(err) {
      if (err) throw err;
      Post.findByIdAndRemove(req.body.id,
         (err, Doc) => {
            if (err) throw err;
            return res.status(200).json({
               status: 'success',
               data: Doc
            })
         })
   });
});
```

And here's the file with the corresponding code snippet: https://github.com/
Apress/The-Beginning-Angular-by-Victor-Hugo-Garcia/blob/main/Chapter-12/02-
index.js.

With these changes, the removal will work. Let's try it, add a post and try to eliminate
it. It works, but there is a problem. The modal confirmation window continues to be
displayed. Some of you will have already figured out how to solve the problem. That's
right, we'll add an id to our **Cancel** button next to a reference in our Dashboard
Component to be able to summon your click method programmatically.

First, in dashboard.component.html we modified the definition of the button
Cancel:

```
<button type="button" #cancelBtn class="btn btn-secondary"
data-dismiss="modal">Cancel</button>
```

We can now include a property:

```
@ViewChild('cancelBtn') cancelBtn!: ElementRef;
```

and get to our final version of the delete:

```
delete() {
    this.addPostService.deletePost( this.postToDelete ).subscribe(
      (res) => {
        this.getPosts();
        this.cancelBtn.nativeElement.click();
    });
  }
```

We have completed our removal functionality. As always, I will include the code of all the modified files.

Frontend Source Code

Common Service

common.service.ts

https://github.com/Apress/The-Beginning-Angular-by-Victor-Hugo-Garcia/blob/main/Chapter-12/03-common.service.ts

Dashboard Component

dashboard.component.html

https://github.com/Apress/The-Beginning-Angular-by-Victor-Hugo-Garcia/blob/main/Chapter-12/04-dashboard.component.html

dashboard.component.ts

https://github.com/Apress/The-Beginning-Angular-by-Victor-Hugo-Garcia/blob/main/Chapter-12/05-dashboard.component.ts

Post Component

post.component.html

https://github.com/Apress/The-Beginning-Angular-by-Victor-Hugo-Garcia/blob/main/Chapter-12/06-post.component.html

post.component.ts

https://github.com/Apress/The-Beginning-Angular-by-Victor-Hugo-Garcia/blob/main/Chapter-12/07-post.component.ts

AddPost Service

add-post.service.ts

https://github.com/Apress/The-Beginning-Angular-by-Victor-Hugo-Garcia/
blob/main/Chapter-12/08-add-post.component.ts

Backend Source Code

index.js

https://github.com/Apress/The-Beginning-Angular-by-Victor-Hugo-Garcia/
blob/main/Chapter-12/09-index.js

Summary

Throughout these last chapters, we have built a functional application that illustrates concepts such as communication between components and use of services to communicate with an API hosted on a server. Our blog performs the basic CRUD operations on a type of entity, and in that sense, it is very simple, but at the same time with it as a guide, we can build arbitrarily complex applications. There are details to be polished, and we will take care of them as you add material to this book.

CHAPTER 13

Testing

There should be no doubt about how important it is to thoroughly test the applications we develop. I would even say that the word is not "important," but "essential."

And here it is worth making an important clarification. That we test our application does not imply that it will be free of defects. It is practically impossible, except in the most trivial cases, to ship a product with no errors. But this does not mean that testing is useless. On the contrary, testing allows us to

- Find many defects before they become errors (when they have already been detected by the user)

- To a large extent limit the possibility of a change breaking existing code

But if testing is so important, why are we so reluctant to do so? One of the reasons is that building and running tests is a tedious process.

Well, with Angular, this boredom is greatly reduced, which means that we have fewer excuses to test our products.

In this chapter, we will see the tools that Angular offers developers to perform unit tests, and we will build suites with specs to test classes, pipes, and services.

Jasmine

What makes it so simple to write tests with Angular and run them? On the one hand, it is the fact that Angular comes from the beginning with Jasmine (`https://jasmine.github.io/`).

Jasmine is a framework to test JavaScript code. It is not exclusive to Angular; on the contrary, if we work on the backend using NodeJS, we can use it perfectly. It's just that Angular has integrated it so we can use it without extra settings. And to make everything easier, Angular has also incorporated a tool called Karma.

© Victor Hugo Garcia 2023
V. H. Garcia, *Getting Started with Angular*, https://doi.org/10.1007/978-1-4842-9206-8_13

Karma

Karma is a test runner developed by the Angular team, designed to automate tasks related to the execution of the developer tests with Jasmine.

We will create a new project:

```
ng new angular-test
```

After executing the command, we will obtain the new angular-test directory where our project is located. We know we can execute it simply by typing:

```
ng serve -o
```

on the command line. The flag -o is simply used to indicate that we want to use the default browser of our operating system. We will see the familiar screen shown in Figure 13-1.

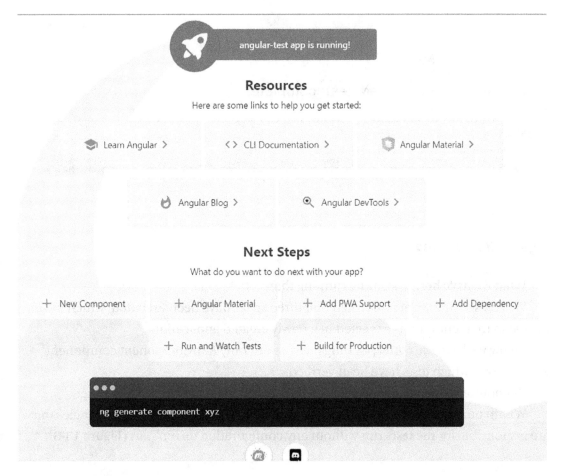

Figure 13-1. *Angular-test*

We have not yet modified a single line of code, and yet we can run the first tests of our application.

Let's stop project execution by pressing Ctrl+C. Always from our angular-test directory, we execute:

```
ng test
```

This will open a new browser window with the output shown in Figure 13-2.

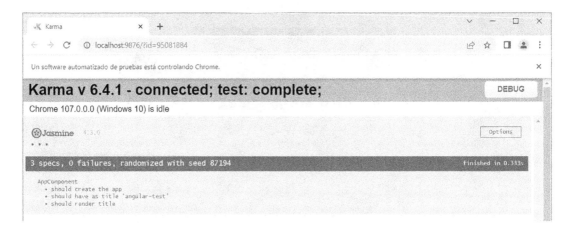

Figure 13-2. *Karma*

What we have here is Jasmine running thanks to Karma.

We can see that we are informed that three specs have been executed, which have passed in their entirety, as expected in a newly created application.

Below we have the corresponding entry to our only AppComponent component, which shows which tests have been verified.

But now let's open our project in the IDE to understand what is happening.

Within our application, in the package.json file, we have a list of dependencies that are responsible for the tests run without any configuration on our part (Figure 13-3).

```
Help                           package.json - angular-test - Visual Studio Code

{} package.json  ✕

{} package.json > ...
   20         @angular/platform-browser-dynamic": "~8.1.2",
   21         "@angular/router": "~8.1.2",
   22         "rxjs": "~6.4.0",
   23         "tslib": "^1.9.0",
   24         "zone.js": "~0.9.1"
   25       },
   26       "devDependencies": {
   27         "@angular-devkit/build-angular": "~0.801.2",
   28         "@angular/cli": "~8.1.2",
   29         "@angular/compiler-cli": "~8.1.2",
   30         "@angular/language-service": "~8.1.2",
   31         "@types/node": "~8.9.4",
   32         "@types/jasmine": "~3.3.8",
   33         "@types/jasminewd2": "~2.0.3",
   34         "codelyzer": "^5.0.0",
   35         "jasmine-core": "~3.4.0",
   36         "jasmine-spec-reporter": "~4.2.1",
   37         "karma": "~4.1.0",
   38         "karma-chrome-launcher": "~2.2.0",
   39         "karma-coverage-istanbul-reporter": "~2.0.1",
   40         "karma-jasmine": "~2.0.1",
   41         "karma-jasmine-html-reporter": "^1.4.0",
   42         "protractor": "~5.4.0",
   43         "ts-node": "~7.0.0",
   44         "tslint": "~5.15.0",
   45         "typescript": "~3.4.3"
   46       }
```

Figure 13-3. *Karma configuration*

We can see there the references to Jasmine and Karma. This configuration, as we said, comes by default, and we should not modify it unless we want to replace Karma with some other test runner, for example, Jest (https://jestjs.io/), or we want to replace Jasmine with another testing framework. However, for the vast majority of cases, the original configuration will allow us to create and run all the tests we need in an organized way.

We will also find in our project a karma.conf.js file (Figure 13-4).

```
K karma.conf.js ✕
K karma.conf.js > ...
  1    // Karma configuration file, see link for more information
  2    // https://karma-runner.github.io/1.0/config/configuration-file.html
  3
  4    module.exports = function (config) {
  5      config.set({
  6        basePath: '',
  7        frameworks: ['jasmine', '@angular-devkit/build-angular'],
  8        plugins: [
  9          require('karma-jasmine'),
 10          require('karma-chrome-launcher'),
 11          require('karma-jasmine-html-reporter'),
 12          require('karma-coverage-istanbul-reporter'),
 13          require('@angular-devkit/build-angular/plugins/karma')
 14        ],
 15        client: {
 16          clearContext: false // leave Jasmine Spec Runner output visible in browser
 17        },
 18        coverageIstanbulReporter: {
 19          dir: require('path').join(__dirname, './coverage/angular-test'),
 20          reports: ['html', 'lcovonly', 'text-summary'],
 21          fixWebpackSourcePaths: true
 22        },
 23        reporters: ['progress', 'kjhtml'],
 24        port: 9876,
 25        colors: true,
 26        logLevel: config.LOG_INFO,
 27        autoWatch: true,
 28        browsers: ['Chrome'],
 29        singleRun: false,
 30        restartOnFileChange: true
 31      });
 32    };
 33
```

Figure 13-4. *package.json*

This is the file that we should modify to run another framework other than Jasmine using Karma. Again, I don't find too many reasons to do so.

Now we can get into what is the code of our application.

Inside the src directory, we have our app.component.ts file where the AppComponent class declaration appears. Accompanying this file, we can see another called app.component.spec.ts. Each time we create a new component, service, or pipe using angular-cli, the corresponding spec file is created unless explicitly stated otherwise. The file will have the following content:

```
import { TestBed } from '@angular/core/testing';
import { AppComponent } from './app.component';

describe('AppComponent', () => {
  beforeEach(async () => {
    await TestBed.configureTestingModule({
      declarations: [
        AppComponent
      ],
    }).compileComponents();
  });

  it('should create the app', () => {
    const fixture = TestBed.createComponent(AppComponent);
    const app = fixture.componentInstance;
    expect(app).toBeTruthy();
  });

  it(`should have as title 'angular-test'`, () => {
    const fixture = TestBed.createComponent(AppComponent);
    const app = fixture.componentInstance;
    expect(app.title).toEqual('angular-test');
  });

  it('should render title', () => {
    const fixture = TestBed.createComponent(AppComponent);
    fixture.detectChanges();
    const compiled = fixture.nativeElement as HTMLElement;
    expect(compiled.querySelector('.content span')?.textContent).
    toContain('angular-test app is running!');
  });
});
```

Let's analyze it.

In Jasmine, a set of tests or specs are included under a **suite**. The simplest form of a test file in Jasmine would be the following:

```
describe ("A suite", function() {
```

```
    it ("contains spec with an expectation", function() {
        expect(true).toBe(true);
    });
});
```

describe is a function whose first parameter is a text string that indicates the name under which the specs will be grouped. In the case of the specs we run for our AppComponent, the name of the suite is precisely AppComponent.

it is a global Jasmine function that is used to define the specs. Its first parameter is the description of what that spec expects to obtain as a result.

Then we have **expect**, which takes a value and performs a check on that value.

Returning to the specs file of our AppComponent, after the declaration of the suite we have the following:

```
beforeEach (async (() => {
    TestBed.configureTestingModule ({
      declarations: [
        AppComponent
      ],
    }). CompileComponents ();
  })) ;
```

beforeEach is a function that will be executed before each of the specs runs. In it we use the TestBed utility, which will allow us to obtain an instance of the module to be tested outside the normal life cycle of the application. The beforeEach function is declared as asynchronous because we must obtain the instance before performing the tests.

Then, we have the specs themselves, which are self-descriptive. For example, let's take the following:

```
it(`should have as title 'angular-test'`, () => {
    const fixture = TestBed.createComponent(AppComponent);
    const app = fixture.componentInstance;
    expect(app.title).toEqual('angular-test');
  });
```

What we are checking is if the title property of AppComponent has the value "angular-test."

If we modify the test as follows:

```
it(`should have as title 'Testing in Angular'`, () => {
    const fixture = TestBed.createComponent(AppComponent);
    const app = fixture.componentInstance;
    expect(app.title).toEqual('Testing in Angular');
});
```

and now we run ng test, we will see a bug (Figure 13-5).

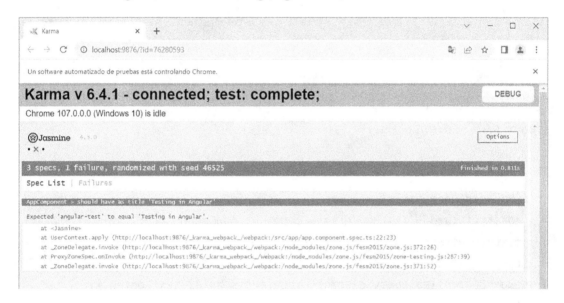

Figure 13-5. *Karma*

And this is to be expected, since we have not modified the value of the title property in our AppComponent. We can make changes, and the window where the test execution results are displayed will automatically refresh.

If we make the modification, that error will disappear, but we will have another (Figure 13-6).

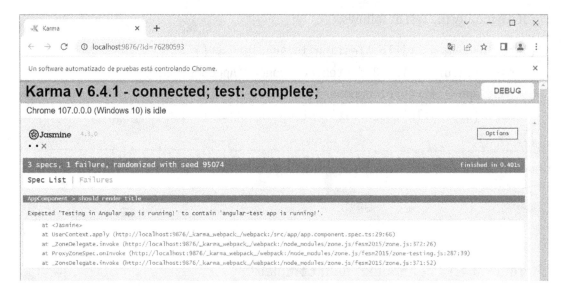

Figure 13-6. *Karma*

That is related to this spec:

```
it('should render title', () => {
    const fixture = TestBed.createComponent(AppComponent);
    fixture.detectChanges();
    const compiled = fixture.nativeElement as HTMLElement;
    expect(compiled.querySelector('.content span')?.textContent).
    toContain('angular-test app is running!');
  });
```

Since we have modified the title, now what we would expect to get is:

```
it('should render title', () => {
    const fixture = TestBed.createComponent(AppComponent);
    fixture.detectChanges();
    const compiled = fixture.nativeElement as HTMLElement;
    expect(compiled.querySelector('.content span')?.textContent).
    toContain('Testing in Angular app is running!');
  });
```

And now the three specs will pass (Figure 13-7).

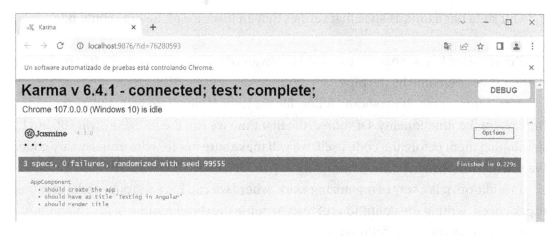

Figure 13-7. *Karma*

As you can see, it is very simple to make checks on the property values of the components and the way they are displayed. Now we will proceed to show how we can perform tests for pipes and services.

Testing a Pipe

We are going to build a pipe that returns a truncated string of characters to a certain limit:

```
ng g p pipes/truncate
```

Two files have been created – one that contains the definition of the pipe and another with the corresponding suite (truncate.pipe.spec.ts):

```
import { TruncatePipe } from './truncate.pipe';

describe('TruncatePipe', () => {
  it('create an instance', () => {
    const pipe = new TruncatePipe();
    expect(pipe).toBeTruthy();
  });
});
```

Our suite has a unique spec that verifies that an instance of the pipe could be created.

But since we know what the expected behavior of our pipe is, we can add a new spec that must be overcome by the pipe.

This is the approach we should follow for the tests. Write them first, and then implement the functionality. Of course, the first time we run the tests they will fail, but by developing them before the code itself, we will make sure not to write unnecessary code. We will only implement what is necessary to pass the test.

In addition, it is a way of organizing work, where we can have a group, perhaps more experienced, writing the definitions of tests to guide the development of functionalities.

Let's modify the file as follows:

```
import { TruncatePipe } from './truncate.pipe';

describe('TruncatePipe', () => {
  it('create an instance', () => {
    const pipe = new TruncatePipe();
    expect(pipe).toBeTruthy();
  });
});

it ('should truncate a string to 10 characters', () => {
  // create instance
  const pipe = new TruncatePipe();
  // pass params
  const ret: any = pipe.transform('abcdefghijklmnopq', 10);
  // assert
  expect (ret.length) .toBe (10);
});
```

Of course, the spec will fail (Figure 13-8).

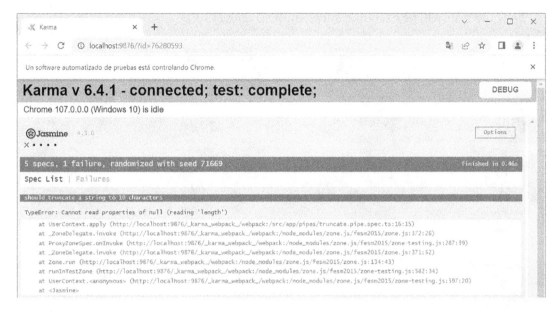

Figure 13-8. Karma

But now we can work on our pipe knowing that there is a test to make sure everything works correctly. Let's rewrite our pipe as follows:

```
import {Pipe, PipeTransform } from '@angular/core';

@Pipe ({
  name: 'truncate'
})
export class TruncatePipe implements PipeTransform {

  transform (value: string, limit: number): any {

    return value.length> limit? value.substr (0, limit): value;

  }

}
```

Now the tests will be executed successfully (Figure 13-9).

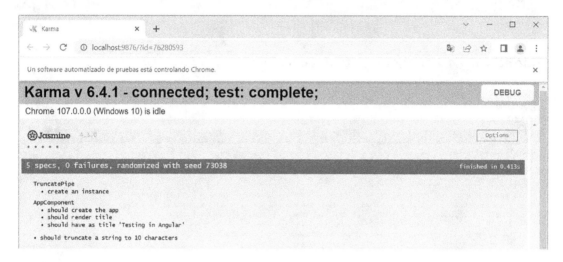

Figure 13-9. *Karma*

Of course, we can make our pipe more complex, for example, declaring the limit parameter as optional and also optionally adding an ellipsis at the end of the sentence. And for each of these modifications, we will act in the same way – creating the specs first, seeing them fail, and then working on the functionality.

Let's add the following spec:

```
it ('should truncate a string to 10 characters plus an ellipsis', () => {
  // create instance
  const pipe = new TruncatePipe();
  // pass params
  const ret: any = pipe.transform ('abcdefghijklmnopq', 10, '...');
  // assert
  expect (ret).toEqual ('abcdefghij...');
});
```

First of all, the IDE will warn us of an error, because we are passing a third parameter when our pipe waits for three. But let's modify it:

```
import {Pipe, PipeTransform } from '@angular/core';

@Pipe ({
  name: 'truncate'
})
export class TruncatePipe implements PipeTransform {

  transform (value: string, limit: number, ellipsis: string = ''): any {

    return value.length> limit? value.substr (0, limit): value;

  }

}
```

Now we will see the test fail (Figure 13-10).

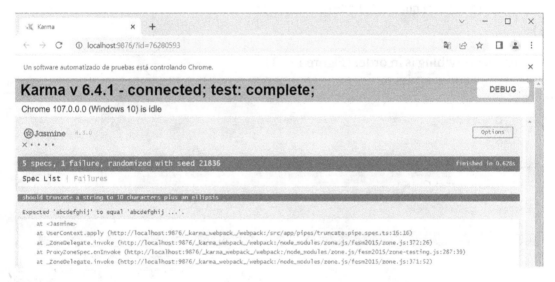

Figure 13-10. *Karma*

That is to be expected, because we are not adding the ellipsis to the return value.

Let's change that:

```
import { TruncatePipe } from './truncate.pipe';

describe('TruncatePipe', () => {
  it('create an instance', () => {
    const pipe = new TruncatePipe();
    expect(pipe).toBeTruthy();
  });
});

it ('should truncate a string to 10 characters plus an ellipsis', () => {
  // create instance
  const pipe = new TruncatePipe();
  // pass params
  const ret: any = pipe.transform ('abcdefghijklmnopq', 10, '...');
  // assert
  expect (ret).toEqual ('abcdefghij...');
});
```

Again, everything is in order (Figure 13-11).

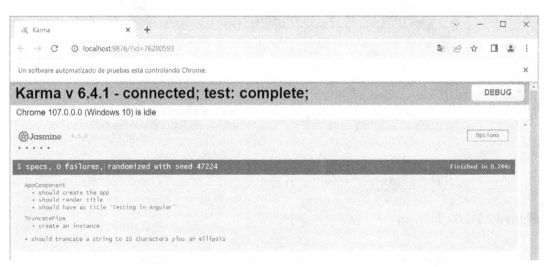

Figure 13-11. *Karma*

With this, we must have a pretty clear idea of how we can test a pipe. Now let's take care of the services.

Testing a Service

First of all, we will create a service to be tested. This service, which we will call auth, will have three methods: login, logout, and isAuthenticated.

The function of the first two is to log in and log out the user, and the third will return true or false depending on whether the user has indicated their credentials or not.

```
ng g s services/auth
```

Let's work a little on our AuthService, simply adding empty methods:

```
import { Injectable } from '@angular/core';

@Injectable({
  providedIn: 'root'
})
export class AuthService {
  constructor() { }

  login() {}

  logout() {}

  isAuthenticated() {}

}
```

In the login method, we should receive a username and password, call an API, etc. But what interests us is the mechanics of the test.

Now let's go to our test file and rewrite it as follows:

```
import { TestBed } from '@angular/core/testing';

import { AuthService } from './auth.service';

describe('AuthService', () => {
  let service: AuthService;

  beforeEach(() => {
    TestBed.configureTestingModule({});
    service = TestBed.inject(AuthService);
  });
```

```
it('should be created', () => {
  expect(service).toBeTruthy();
});

it ('should authenticate the user', () => {
  const service: AuthService = TestBed.get (AuthService);

  localStorage.setItem('currentUser', 'admin');

  expect (service.isAuthenticated()).toBeTruthy();
});
});
```

Of course, the test will fail (Figure 13-12).

Figure 13-12. *Karma*

But if we now modify the isAuthenticated method as follows:

```
isAuthenticated() {
  const currentUser = localStorage.getItem('currentUser');

  if (currentUser) {
    return true;
  }
```

```
    return false;
  }
```

the tests will pass (Figure 13-13).

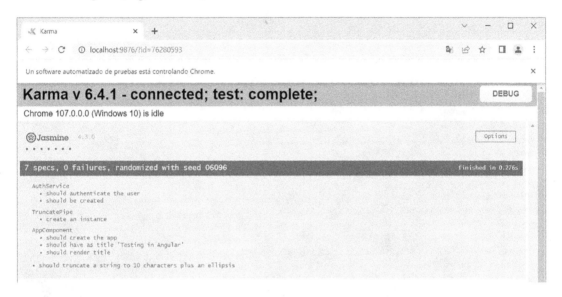

Figure 13-13. *Karma*

Summary

We have seen the tools that Angular offers developers to perform unit tests. We have built suites with specs to test classes, pipes, and services. Of course, this is a minimal part of what we can do, but with these firm foundations, we can continue to explore and expand our skills. When it starts with the issue of testing, it can be tedious, but it has happened to me that Angular has made it not only simple but entertaining, and I trust that the same will happen to you.

Index

A

ActivatedRoute, 113, 114

Adding post
    add-post.component.html, 303, 304
    add-post.component.ts, 301, 302
    dashboard.component.html, 304, 305
    index.js, 307, 308
    login form, 302
    modal errors, 306
    modal window, 305, 306
    models, 308–315
    nodemon, 307
    observables, 315–317
    postForm, 302

add-post.component.html, 303, 304, 313

Advanced Connection Options, 205

Angular, 220
    angular CLI, 4
    Chrome, 3
    errors, 11
    IDE, 5–10
    Ionic, 5
    NodeJS, 3
    Postman, 10
    semantic versioning, 2
    TypeScript, 3, 4
    versions, 1, 2
    website, 1

Angular application, 81

Angular-cli, 77, 123

Angular-cli live server, 148

Angular folder, 75

angular-in-memory-web-api, 99

Angular.json, 128, 148, 163, 164, 239, 292

Angular project, 81, 212, 232

Angular server, 214, 240

Angular 10 Snippets package, 91

AppComponent class, 79, 80, 352

app.component.css, 78

app.component.html, 78, 80, 86, 97

app.component.spec.ts, 78, 352

app.component.ts, 78, 79, 178, 352

App files, 78

Application code, 229

Applications menu, 165

AppModule, 81, 95, 99, 100, 148, 229, 281

app.module.ts, 78, 81, 91, 98, 131, 169,
    173, 217, 218, 223, 227, 229, 281

app.routes, 172

app.routes.ts, 91, 94, 113, 143, 172, 185,
    217, 229, 255, 261, 281, 286, 289

Arrays, 40–44

Arrow functions
    advantages, 36, 39
    anonymous function, 36, 39
    car.accelerate(), 38
    object, 37
    output, 37–39
    parameter, 36
    setTimeout function, 36
    ts file, 36
    variable, 36, 38
    version, 36

© Victor Hugo Garcia 2023
V. H. Garcia, *Getting Started with Angular*, https://doi.org/10.1007/978-1-4842-9206-8

GPSR Compliance
The European Union's (EU) General Product Safety Regulation (GPSR) is a set
of rules that requires consumer products to be safe and our obligations to
ensure this.

If you have any concerns about our products, you can contact us on

ProductSafety@springernature.com

In case Publisher is established outside the EU, the EU authorized
representative is:

Springer Nature Customer Service Center GmbH
Europaplatz 3
69115 Heidelberg, Germany